GENERALS
in International Politics

GENERALS
in International Politics

NATO's Supreme Allied Commander, Europe

ROBERT S. JORDAN, Editor

THE UNIVERSITY PRESS OF KENTUCKY

Frontispiece: Gen. Dwight D. Eisenhower assumes command of SHAPE, 2 April 1951. U.S. Army photo, courtesy of the Eisenhower Library.

Photo of General Eisenhower on page 8 is courtesy of the Eisenhower Library. All other photos appearing on chapter opening pages are courtesy of SHAPE.

Copyright © 1987 by The University Press of Kentucky

Scholarly publisher for the Commonwealth, serving Bellarmine College, Berea College, Centre College of Kentucky, Eastern Kentucky University, The Filson Club, Georgetown College, Kentucky Historical Society, Kentucky State University, Morehead State University, Murray State University, Northern Kentucky University, Transylvania University, University of Kentucky, University of Louisville, and Western Kentucky University.

Editorial and Sales Offices: Lexington, Kentucky 40506-0024

Library of Congress Cataloging-in-Publication Data

Generals in international politics.

    Bibliography: p.
    Includes index.
    1. North Atlantic Treaty Organization—Armed Forces.
2. North Atlantic Treaty Organization—United States.
I. Jordan, Robert S., 1929-   II. Title: Supreme Allied Commander, Europe.
UA646.3.G345   1987   355′.031′091821   87-5921
ISBN 0-8131-1623-6

To Col. Merrill G. Hatch, U.S.A. (Ret.)
and his wife, the late Charlie East Hatch

CONTENTS

Acknowledgments ix

Foreword. Multinational Military Leadership in Today's World xiii
    GEN. BERNARD W. ROGERS

Introduction. The Development of SHAPE: 1950-1953 1
    ANDREW J. GOODPASTER

1. Eisenhower: Rekindling the Spirit of the West 8
    STEPHEN E. AMBROSE with MORRIS HONICK

2. Ridgway: Trying to Make Good on the Promises 31
    GEORGE EUGENE PELLETIER

3. Gruenther: Attempts to Retain NATO Solidarity 53
    ROBERT S. JORDAN

4. Norstad: Can the SACEUR Be Both European and American? 73
    ROBERT S. JORDAN

5. Lemnitzer: Surviving the French Military Withdrawal 93
    LAWRENCE S. KAPLAN and KATHLEEN A. KELLNER

6. Goodpaster: Maintaining Deterrence during Détente 122
    LEWIS SORLEY

7. Haig: The Diplomacy of Allied Command 151
    MORRIS HONICK

Conclusions. What Can We Learn from the NATO Experience in Multinational Military Leadership? 175
    ROBERT S. JORDAN

Notes 197

The Contributors 221

Index 222

Illustrations follow page 136

ACKNOWLEDGMENTS

This book is intended to be a companion to my book on the North Atlantic Treaty Organization (NATO) secretaries-general, *Political Leadership in NATO: A Study in Multinational Diplomacy*. It seems to me that, as with the office of the NATO secretary-general, the office of the Supreme Allied Commander, Europe (SACEUR) is generally underrated in terms of its unique character and its effect on world politics.

This book also can be related to Douglas Kinnard's book *The Secretary of Defense* in that I attempt not to provide a comprehensive overview of the tenures of the various Supreme Allied Commanders, but rather to point up some specific, possibly lasting, attributes of the mix of the office and the man that are worthy of more than passing note. This significant military office, in my opinion, possesses many of the characteristics of traditional military/political leadership; yet it has also created, often incrementally, new attributes that, because of its multinational character, can be regarded as transcending the immediate conditions of the superpower rivalry.

NATO is not a monolithic entity, composed as it is of independent member-states that reserve to themselves, according to their respective conceptions of their national interests and national traditions, the final decision as to whether or not to go to war. The Alliance must be responsive to conditions of time and space—which interact—and to overall global circumstances. These circumstances have changed in several fundamental ways since the signing of the North Atlantic Treaty in April 1949 and the creation of the Supreme Headquarters, Allied Powers Europe (SHAPE) in April 1951.

For instance, the number of Allies has grown, thus altering methods of Alliance governance as well as both the perceived and the legal obligations of at least some of the member-states. Furthermore, the nature of the threat to be met has changed as military technology, both nuclear and nonnuclear, has made its impact on politics, strategy, and tactics. Finally, the nature of the international economic system has undergone a radical transformation, creating new forms of interdependence and rivalries, embracing West-West, East-West, and North-South. International institutions have, as a consequence, undergone both rapid proliferation and diversification in the military and nonmilitary realms alike, and the distinction between the two, in terms of conceptions of national security and national interest as such, is diminishing. The SACEURs, in other words, have had to adapt in their respective leadership roles to larger political, technological, and economic circumstances over which they have had, to a greater or lesser degree, little or no direct control.

These are the major considerations that motivated me to plan this book. Invaluable encouragement along the way has come from Martin M. Teasley, assistant director of the Dwight D. Eisenhower Library; Donald Hendricks, dean of Library Services, University of New Orleans; Professor Heath Twichell of Salve Regina College; Professor (and former Ambassador) Martin Hillenbrand of the Dean Rusk Center at the University of Georgia; the Honorable George Vest of the U.S. Department of State; Captain Robert Watts, U.S.N., Deputy to the president of the Naval War College; and Dr. John B. Hattendorf, Ernest J. King Professor of Maritime History at the Naval War College. Early inspiration came from my former Oxford supervisor, Professor Norman Gibbs of All Souls College when he was the Chichele Professor of the History of War.

I am especially grateful to Dr. Robert S. Wood, dean of the Center for Naval Warfare Studies and the Chester W. Nimitz Professor of Social and Political Philosophy, Naval War College. Dr. Wood is a professional colleague and a personal friend who helped me in both capacities in many different ways during my

Acknowledgments

two years as a Distinguished Visiting Professor at the Naval War College while this book was being completed. Invaluable was the assistance of Toni Williams, of the Department of Political Science, University of New Orleans, in manuscript preparation, and John T. Trotter of Mandeville, Louisiana.

Responsibility for the book rests, of course, with the various contributors and with me rather than with the Naval War College or any component thereof.

Robert S. Jordan

FOREWORD

Multinational Military Leadership in Today's World

GEN. BERNARD W. ROGERS, SACEUR

This book is about the Supreme Allied Commander, Europe (SACEUR), and from its chapters emerges a common theme: the SACEUR has had a unique role to play in the North Atlantic Alliance. To meet the demands of his position, he has had to exercise certain clearly defined skills and abilities.

Each of the previous seven officers who served as SACEUR from 1950 to 1979 encountered markedly different circumstances during his term of service. A comprehensive analysis of their experiences is not appropriate for, nor the prerogative of, a serving SACEUR. Nor is it my intention to pay homage here to the superb service of the officers who were my predecessors, even though tribute and gratitude are fully warranted. Nor would they wish me to portray them as persons whose qualities and characteristics set them apart from most other officers (although such was generally the case).

Rather, it is my purpose to discuss, from the standpoint of the incumbent SACEUR, the unusual features that would seem to distinguish the SACEUR's command and responsibilities from those of other military leaders. The opportunity to indulge in such analysis comes to us serving commanders only rarely. Often, when it does come, we are too overwhelmed with the urgencies of the moment to take the longer-range, more detached view that is necessary. But the benefit of such an effort may be a wider understanding of our great Alliance. Thus, these insights are offered in the hope that, through such an understanding, broader support can be gained for NATO's efforts to meet the challenges it faces today and those that lie ahead.

THE SACEUR's MISSION AND ALLIED COMMAND EUROPE

The responsibilities of any military commander are derived from the mission assigned. The SACEUR's mission has remained essentially unchanged since Gen. Dwight D. Eisenhower assumed the position in December 1950: to contribute to the deterrence of all forms of aggression in the area of Allied Command Europe (ACE) and to take measures within his capability to preserve or restore the integrity and security of that area should deterrence fail.

The mission statement makes clear that ACE has as its most important purpose to deter rather than to wage war. Its forces must be tailored and its strategy designed not only to be successful in combat but also to make unmistakable to any potential aggressor that the costs of an attack would outweigh any conceivable gains. The two purposes—deterrence and defense—are not inherently inconsistent. However, serving both simultaneously requires that at times separate measures be directed toward each end. A force designed to make an aggressor perceive the cost of aggression as incalculably high may not be the best force with which to defend NATO's territories and peoples. To fulfill the requirements of both deterrence and defense, the SACEUR is ultimately responsible for a full range of decisions on such matters as operational doctrine, tactical concepts, force structure, equipment, readiness, and the like. He must also ensure that measures taken on behalf of deterrence on the one hand are not perceived as a signal that ACE's commitment to defense is lessened.

For a military commander, the mission of deterrence can present some complex challenges. Deterrence is an abstract concept that reaches well beyond the military realm. In ACE deterrence depends on several factors: an appropriate military capability, a consensus on the political and military imperatives of collective security, political cohesion among NATO nations,

Foreword

and evidence of the political will to take the steps necessary to carry out Alliance strategy. The SACEUR's efforts to ensure that the military requirements of deterrence are met and that he contributes to the successful attainment of cohesion and will carry him well beyond the scope of more traditional military commands.

The complexity of the SACEUR's mission is compounded by the unusual nature of his command. First, the SACEUR commands virtually no forces in peacetime. Most of the Alliance's military forces (with the exception of the staff of the Supreme Headquarters, Allied Powers Europe [SHAPE], the headquarters of ACE's Major Subordinate Commands, certain air defense forces, and the ACE Mobile Force) fall under national control until times of rising tension or crisis when nations decide that command should be passed to the integrated Allied military organization.

Second, forces that the SACEUR does command in peacetime and would command in wartime are multinational. There are sizable challenges associated with coordinating the efforts of a coalition of forces from thirteen of the sixteen nations which have committed forces to ACE. Organizing, equipping, training, and supporting these forces to prepare them to carry out specific war plans is the SACEUR's responsibility, specifically assigned to him in his Terms of Reference. The prospect of commanding these forces in wartime is a powerful incentive to ensure that these preparations are as thorough as possible.

A third characteristic of the Alliance that adds to the unusual nature of both the SACEUR's mission and his command is the overarching political reality that accounts for NATO's fundamental strength. NATO is a voluntary association of sovereign states. Although the relative security contribution of member-nations varies with the size and resources of each nation, an equality among members is fully respected and practiced. Alliance processes and procedures are a reflection of the basic beliefs and values of the citizens of its member-states: respect for individual freedom and liberties, a preference for democratic political systems, high regard for the rule of law, and other values which distinguish NATO nations in the international community. The concept of collective deterrence/defense was conceived to protect these principles. The conduct of collective deterrence/defense must be organized in conformity with them.

THE SACEUR's ROLE IN THE ALLIANCE

To lead and manage his command in a manner that pulls together its diverse elements in order to accomplish his assigned mission is SACEUR's basic responsibility as a military commander. This role is no more nor less important in ACE than it is in any other command. However, it is made more demanding by the variety of geographic and climatic conditions, economic capabilities, customs, languages, and cultures that characterize the ACE region stretching from northern Norway to eastern Turkey. There are other, less traditional demands placed on the SACEUR. Because of his place within the organization, the Alliance has come to depend on him to play certain roles and to fulfill certain functions that only the SACEUR can perform. These roles and functions are critical to directing the energies of his command and to meeting the larger purposes of the North Atlantic Alliance.

Above all, the SACEUR serves as a symbol of Alliance unity. He is the evidential embodiment of the commitment of the Allied nations to take collective military action prior to the actual need for such action. Being so prepared is a crucial factor in NATO's equation for deterrence. It also allows the Allies to resist another more subtle yet equally dangerous threat—the erosion of the freedoms of Western European nations that would occur should an adversary, wielding overwhelming military superiority, be able to threaten, blackmail, and coerce NATO nations without having to fire a shot.

It is at least in part because of this important role that the SACEUR has always been an American officer. Certainly there have been, and are, exceptionally talented officers of other Allied nations whose qualifications are equal to the demands of the position. But the certainty from the outset of an American commitment to NATO's collective defense is critical to the deterrence of war and the protection of Western freedom. The fact that each serving SACEUR has held simultaneously the responsibilities of commander-in-chief, U.S. European Command (USCINCEUR) has served as a clear demonstration to friend and foe alike of this American commitment.

The SACEUR must also play the role of an unbiased military professional of the Alliance. Based on his military experience and judgment, he must set standards for ACE forces in the areas of manning, equipping, training, sustaining, maintaining, and reinforcing; and he must do his best to ensure that these standards are met. This calls for candid, tough military assessments on his part. The sensitivity of this role is evident. The SACEUR must be free to advise, disagree with, and at times criticize any member nation; but he must do so without being perceived as interfering with sovereign political or military processes. His effectiveness in this role depends in large part upon his credibility as an impartial voice. He must always be perceived as acting in the best military interests of the entire Alliance, never as an extension of the policies of, or on behalf of, any individual member.

Closely associated with the role of an unbiased professional is the function that the SACEUR serves in contributing to the reconciliation of the diverse interests represented in NATO. Parochial nationalism has always tested the Alliance. The resultant strains are the price that must be paid for the strength derived from the volunteer nature of this association of sovereign states. At times when divergent interests produce divisiveness rising to the level of potential crisis, the SACEUR can play a direct role in bridging national differences. To the extent that he is able to maintain his reputation for impeccable impartiality, he is especially suited for this role. He is also well placed to make independent assessments on divisive issues within the Alliance; having made such assessments, he has access to present them to the political and military leaders of Alliance nations. It has always been the SACEUR's task to minimize the effect on his command that diverging national interests might cause and to promote and perpetuate the spirit of cooperation. Fostering and maintaining this habit of cooperation is a key function of the SACEUR, for in the urgency of any future emergency, the nations will function generally as has been their practice in peacetime.

INTO THE FOURTH DECADE: THE CHALLENGES OF TODAY AND TOMORROW

It is beyond the scope of this book to recapitulate and describe the service of NATO's fourth decade of SACEURs. Drawing on my experience since mid-1979 and the accounts contained in the following chapters, I conclude that indeed the past has been, and will be, prologue. None of the major challenges facing the SACEUR today would be totally unfamiliar to my predecessors. They also promise to approximate the challenges that will confront my successors. The reason is that the threat facing the Alliance, though it has increased relatively significantly over the years, has not altered its general nature since the early days of ACE, and the SACEUR has played a generally consistent role in NATO's attempts to meet this menace. Recounting these current challenges and describing them here lends focus to this historical study of the service of previous SACEURs and may shed light on the demands future SACEURs will encounter.

The basic challenge for NATO is to convince our people of the threat to their freedom and to elicit from them the willingness to make the necessary sacrifices to deter it. Several factors affect our efforts to meet this challenge. Complacency, wishful thinking, and a false sense of security lead to underestimating or dismissing the threat. Our efforts to take the measures required to improve our defense often run headlong into the misguided (but often well-intentioned) efforts of those who seek peace and security through such means as freezes or moratoriums on various types of weapons. Movements such as pacifism, neutralism, and unilateralism often have their roots, purely and simply, in people's fear of war and their belief that such movements can ensure the maintenance of peace. Missed—or dismissed—is the historical fact that such movements might well maintain the peace, but at the cost of our nations' freedom of action.

Throughout the history of the Alliance, the perception of the threat has varied. In the early days of the Cold War when Warsaw Pact divisions numbered 175 and NATO could account but for about 12, achieving an awareness of the imminent danger facing Western Europe may have been easier than it was, for example, during the period of détente between East and West in the 1970s. But realizing that the threat exists is only part of meeting the challenge: NATO has consistently found it difficult to attain the support required to maintain forces appropriate to the requirements of deterrence and defense. The reasons for this are numerous, as numerous as are the many and varied other demands for scarce resources against which NATO security needs must compete. We will meet this fundamental challenge successfully only after our people have taken stock of the ever-widening gap between Warsaw Pact and NATO force capabilities, resulting from the unabated Soviet military buildup; after they have decided that adequate and appropriate steps must be taken to address this imbalance; and after they have communicated their desire to our national legislative bodies that they want a reallocation of national resources that favors security needs. The SACEUR's voice must be heard defining the threat to our freedom and seeking our citizens' support in deterring it.

To meet the defined threat, NATO must have an effective strategy. In the 1980s there has been a lively public debate about NATO's strategy of flexible response: its adequacy, its applicability, its need for change. This debate will continue. Although most persons in positions of responsibility within the Alliance agree that flexible response is the proper strategy if adequate forces are provided to ensure its implementation, there are others—mainly academicians—who disagree. These critics offer such alternatives as "defensive defense" and "offensive retaliation." A "defensive defense," consisting of a militia armed only with defensive weapons—air defense and anti-armor—would not deter an aggressor, nor could it eject an aggressor once he gained a foothold in Allied territory. The offensive retaliation theorists would have us react to an aggressor's attack by making our major ground attacks deep into his territory. Should NATO ever reach the point where it had sufficient forces to defend successfully at its General Defensive Position, to protect successfully its rear, and to attack successfully with massive ground forces deep into the enemy's territory in the face of his second strategic echelon, then there should never have been any question in the first place about the effectiveness of our deterrent strategy of flexible response.

Although these two alternative strategies I have mentioned can be dismissed, there is one program under way which might have a future major impact on our strategy of flexible response. That is the Strategic Defense Initiative (SDI) of the United States. If the research on SDI proves that it is feasible and practicable to deploy such a system (i.e., mission- and cost-effective), NATO will need to conduct a very careful and penetrating analysis to determine if its strategy must be changed. In any event, SDI will help fuel the continuing debate about NATO strategy for years to come.

Every SACEUR since Eisenhower's assumption of the first peacetime Allied international command has been compelled to reconcile the military requirements of ACE with the changing nature of the threat, the agreed strategy, and the capabilities made available to him by NATO nations. For some time now, ACE has maintained three types of military forces: strategic nuclear, nonstrategic nuclear, and conventional. The credibility of our strategy depends on our capabilities in all three legs of this NATO triad. Currently, our greatest needs are in the conventional force. If attacked conventionally today, NATO would face fairly quickly the decision of escalating to a nuclear response in order to halt the aggressor's advance. We are in such a posture for several reasons, but primarily because of our inability to sustain our forces adequately with trained manpower, ammunition, and war reserve materiel. The problem is not that our forces will not perform admirably at their defensive positions. On the contrary, we have well-trained,

Foreword

well-equipped, well-led, highly motivated troops; but they would not be able to fight long enough because of a lack of adequate conventional sustainment.

The difficulty of achieving a conventional force that meets Alliance needs is not new. NATO began very early in its history to integrate nuclear weapons into its forces and to take account of those weapons in its strategy. Since that time, there has been a tendency toward overreliance on the deterrent effect of a nuclear response, to the detriment of an adequate conventional posture. This is not to say that nuclear weapons should not play an important role in our strategy. NATO's deterrence must depend on the credibility of the threat of its escalation to nuclear weapons in response to aggression against its territory and people. But the credibility of NATO deterrence is cast into doubt when there exists an overdependence on the quick resort to nuclear options, especially in response to a Warsaw Pact nonnuclear attack. The erosion of the nuclear superiority that NATO once enjoyed by the growth of Soviet nuclear capabilities aggravates this situation.

In short, today we find that we have mortgaged NATO's defense to the nuclear response, and by doing so we are straining the credibility of our deterrence. To correct this situation, we require a conventional capability that would give us a reasonable prospect of frustrating a nonnuclear attack by conventional means. A "reasonable prospect" does not suggest that adequate deterrence requires conventional forces so strong that they virtually eliminate the need for the threat of NATO's first-use of nuclear weapons as a source of deterrence. Such a posture does not fit NATO's deterrence strategy of flexible response. A "reasonable prospect" does, however, entail our having a conventional force of such strength as to permit us, as a minimum, to preserve the integrity of our defense long enough to give us time to make, if necessary, a deliberate, determined decision to escalate to the use of nuclear weapons, as well as permitting us to protect our means of nuclear delivery and our essential command and control structure.

With respect to conventional forces, I am encouraged by

the positive action being taken by NATO nations, by their having adopted in May 1985 the Conventional Defense Improvement initiative of the secretary-general.

Contributing to the efforts to enhance Alliance cohesion has always been another challenge for the SACEUR. The greatest effort must be directed at strengthening transatlantic ties and reducing transatlantic tensions. Occasional differences between the United States and its European Allies are to be expected. They will arise because of differing perspectives on security issues, diverse responsibilities that must be met both within and outside of the Alliance, and diverging opinion on issues outside the direct realm of security, e.g., economic matters. It is necessary to strive constantly to overcome the divisive effects of these differences. These efforts can be successful if Alliance members are patient enough and wise enough to listen to each other and to take account of problems and interests that are peculiar to individual nations.

In the United States the goal must be a greater understanding of the historical and geopolitical realities that affect European public opinion and security policy decisions. Europe is a divided continent, a situation that creates views on issues such as détente, arms control, and trade that may be at odds with official views in the United States. Americans must be aware that Europeans are sensitive to any actions by the United States that might be perceived as a decoupling of U.S. security means from the defense of Western Europe. Such perceived actions will feed long-standing fears that the United States will reduce its commitment to collective, transatlantic security. They also raise the specter of another war—this time most likely a nuclear one—largely confined to European soil. At the same time, the common misperception in the United States that our Western European Allies are not carrying a fair share of the burden of collective defense must be dispelled through a concerted effort to inform the American people about the considerable hidden costs that these nations do shoulder.

In Europe there is also much that can be done to strengthen transatlantic ties. A number of Europeans do not seem to un-

Foreword

derstand the distinct, qualitative difference between the United States and the Soviet Union. The tendency to place the two superpowers on the same moral plane reflects an inadequate appreciation of the distinctions between democracy and totalitarianism, or between the search for stability and the drive of expansionism. There is also a need for Western Europeans to recognize that the United States has accepted global responsibilities, many on behalf of its Alliance partners, and that it needs assistance—at the least, encouragement—in discharging them. We must undergird those Western European leaders who voice support of these American endeavors and speak out against the anti-American outbursts that sometimes occur in Western Europe.

For the SACEURs of the fourth decade and beyond, there is good reason to be confident about NATO's ability to rise to the challenges I have mentioned. The bases for this optimism have existed for some time and will continue into the future.

The first is the strength of the common, fundamental principles upon which the North Atlantic Alliance is based. We are a defensive Alliance dedicated to the preservation of peace and the protection of our freedoms. We seek no territorial gains at the expense of any other nation, pact, or alliance. No NATO nation will ever fire the first shot of a future conflict; ours is a basic policy of "no first-use" of any type of force. Alliance nations are justifiably proud of these principles, and NATO draws strength from them. Our challenge is to build upon these common principles so that we can resist the pressures that could drive us apart.

A second cause for optimism is the soundness of the Alliance process and structure. Collective security works. We have known peace with freedom in Western Europe for over forty years, and NATO has been the major contributing factor. It is the most successful peace movement in history. Judged by procedural standards, NATO has been equally successful. Never before have so many sovereign nations maintained an effective peacetime alliance for so long in close proximity to such a powerful military threat. Despite our occasional differences, we have proven our ability to work together, to grow, and to progress.

Finally, we can be optimistic because our cause is just, and it is readily identifiable as such to anyone who considers it objectively. Ultimately, our efforts as an Alliance are directed to bringing about a more stable world with reduced and balanced levels of forces of all categories. We recognize that such a world is attainable only through negotiated arms reductions. Thus, our decisions, policies, and programs must be formulated with a careful eye to their impact on this process. History has taught us that weakness, indecisiveness, complacency, self-delusion, ignoring the threat—and the movements that stem from these attitudes—will not contribute to successful negotiation of equitable arms reductions. There is ample evidence that the best incentives to serious Soviet negotiation of such reductions are Alliance determination, resolve, political cohesion, unity, solidarity, and, finally, taking the steps that will ensure the military ability to maintain our security.

It is to help move the Alliance toward these ends that all SACEURs have dedicated their efforts. They will continue to do so through NATO's fourth decade and into the decades beyond.

INTRODUCTION

The Development of SHAPE: 1950-1953

ANDREW J. GOODPASTER

My first connection with NATO came on 16 December 1950. It was at a time when the world situation seemed to be deteriorating rapidly. The Chinese had just entered the war in Korea, and the Council of NATO was to meet in Brussels on 18 December to consider urgent action to strengthen and organize defenses against aggression, should it occur in Europe.

Anticipating the action of the North Atlantic Council, the United States government had already begun to assemble in Washington a few officers who would later be involved in ACE. Col. A.D. Starbird had already been transferred on short notice from his Engineer District assignment on the Oahe Dam in South Dakota and sent to France to start work on the location of the headquarters. On 16 December, then serving in Washington, I received a request from Col. R.J. Wood, until then an instructor at the National War College, later to be the Staff Secretary at SHAPE, to leave for Paris at noon the next day. After a flight to the Brussels conference and a train ride to Paris, Col. R.F. Worden of the U.S. Air Force and I found ourselves late on 18 December comprising the initial contingent of what was to become the European headquarters of the NATO Allied forces. Gen. Alfred M. Gruenther, who followed us to Paris after the Brussels meeting, had instructed us to establish an Advanced Planning Group and to develop plans and proposals for the organization and buildup of the headquarters and the command structure of the Allied forces. We were joined in Paris by officers sent from the principal U.S. military commands in Europe.

The organization developed by several distinct stages. The Advanced Planning Group came into full operation with the arrival in early January 1951 of the contingent that had been assembled in Washington. It was ready to serve the Supreme Commander, Gen. Eisenhower, on his arrival on 7 January. The group went ahead with its own organization and expansion at the same time and by mid-January became international, with the arrival of staff officers from the other NATO nations. Meanwhile, Eisenhower had begun his initial survey trip, visiting the NATO capitals in Europe in order to learn what efforts the various countries were prepared to make and what problems they anticipated.

The organization of the Planning Group became the organization headquarters when it was declared operational on 2 April 1951. Among the primary features of the organization, probably the most important was that the headquarters was both international and integrated. The headquarters would not function as a committee made up of a number of national delegations, but rather as a single unified organization in which all officers, regardless of nationality, worked for the common mission assigned to Eisenhower: to develop an integrated, effective force for the defense of Western Europe and to conduct that defense, should hostilities occur. The second feature meant that officers of all services—land, air, and sea—were assigned, not in general to separate army, navy, and air components, but throughout the single organization according to where their particular skills and experience were needed. Unity of thought and action was, therefore, stressed to meet the principle of teamwork that Eisenhower had established as fundamental.

The organizational structure followed relatively conventional lines. Staff divisions for Personnel and Administration, Intelligence, and Logistics were set up. The G-3 function (a staff division) was split into Plans, Policy, and Operations as one division, and Organization and Training as another. Following naval organizational advice, we established Signals as a staff division coordinate with the rest because of the complexity of

INTRODUCTION 3

the signal problem in an area involving so many national states. Each staff division was headed by an assistant chief-of-staff. The officers designated were drawn from four different nations and from all three services. Deputy chiefs-of-staff for Plans and Operations and for Logistics and Administration were appointed. Field Marshal Lord Bernard Montgomery was appointed deputy to SACEUR, and naval and air deputies were also designated. One special feature was the appointment of an executive for National Military Representatives (NMRs), Gen. Anthony Biddle, through whom staff liaison with national representatives was coordinated. National representatives were located at the headquarters to represent national points of view to Eisenhower; staff officers were removed from this responsibility.

With some reorganization in 1953 to expand the air deputy's office and functions, this organization (SHAPE) endured without change. Under the staff direction of Gen. Gruenther, who served as chief-of-staff until his appointment as Supreme Commander in 1953 to succeed Gen. Matthew Ridgway, it was successful in providing harmonious, industrious, and effective staff operation.

The command of which SHAPE was a part was also speedily established. Eisenhower viewed his command areas as a major peninsula bordered by two land-sea complexes. He proceeded to establish joint commands on the two flank areas. In the north this joint command was placed under an admiral of the Royal Navy; later a British army general took the command. In the south the situation was more difficult. A joint command was etablished under Adm. Robert Carney of the United States. Later, following the entry of Greece and Turkey into NATO, the problem of providing for the defense of the Mediterranean line of communications was resolved by readjusting the structure and establishing an additional command under Adm. Lord Louis Mountbatten.

In the center, through which the threat of sudden onslaught by massive forces loomed most strongly, Eisenhower decided to retain for himself the joint operational command with subordinate land, sea, and air commanders at Fontainebleau. By 1953 Allied strength in this area, then under Ridgway, had grown to the point where it was deemed desirable to establish a separate commander-in-chief, to which position Marshal Alphonse Juin was designated.

Further echelons of command, linking the top headquarters with the fighting units in the field and at sea, were gradually built up until an integrated force, responsive to the direction of the Supreme Commander, existed.

Meanwhile, what of the fighting forces themselves? From the outset it was Eisenhower's stated view that the defense of an area could not be provided by Roman walls erected from outside sources alone—that it must come basically from the spirit, the will, and the energy of the people of the area itself. He found in his survey trip that the efforts to which the NATO nations in Europe were pledged gave promise of providing this essential basis. This conclusion he reported to the American Congress on his return to this country at the end of January 1951. Only after Eisenhower's estimate of European intentions had been made could the United States turn to the cooperative effort of building the military forces.

The task was a staggering one. There were at that time less than fourteen divisions available to the Allies. These fourteen divisions faced a possible total strength in being of 175 divisions, not counting satellite forces, with an additional 125 divisions as immediate reserves. While the combat effectiveness of Allied forces varied, it was generally low throughout. Logistic support lines, which had been located primarily for occupational duties, were wrongly placed for the new threat.

Air forces in Europe were, if anything, less advanced. They were in exposed locations and numbered less than a tenth of the adversary's possible strength. Jets were lacking and there was hardly any semblance of strategically located, logistically supported, interrelated airfields.

Navies were in varying states of readiness and repair. They

were critically deficient in minesweepers and antisubmarine vessels. Only very limited joint exercises had been held by the separate national navies involved.

By untiring, persistent effort and leadership, a degree of progress was achieved which Gruenther had rated as "almost fantastic" when measured against the situation that had greeted Eisenhower. Upon the foundation of confidence that followed Eisenhower's survey, forces were increased about fourfold within three years and their effectiveness probably no less. In every field of weakness, effort and emphasis had been concentrated and real progress had been attained.

At the same time, however, no one felt that an adequate level of defense had been reached to meet attack if it should come. In fact, a high-level review of the practicability of providing adequate defense had been necessitated in late 1951 and early 1952 as the impact of the rapid military expansion began to be felt in the economic sphere. Inflation arising out of unbalanced budgets and depletion of currency reserves resulting from adverse balance of payments caused real alarm in some quarters. A special commission, soon dubbed the "Wisemen," was charged with the task of reconciling military needs with so-called politico-economic capabilities. They consulted the military commander throughout their deliberations and carried out a careful analysis of the politico-economic factors. Their work culminated in the so-called Lisbon goals, a program for expansion over the three succeeding years which was accepted as being generally feasible and, at the same time, constituting a buildup of military strength that would substantially promote Western security.

From mid-1952 to mid-1953 under Ridgway, great emphasis was given to bringing the NATO forces to a high state of combat proficiency, to building up reserves of ammunition, which had remained critically low, to constructing airfields, signal networks, pipelines, and storage facilities, as well as to the myriad other activities essential to effective, modern army, air force, and navy forces. A series of land, sea, and air exercises and maneuvers, employing the services separately and in combination, was successfully carried out. Simulated atomic operations—both the defensive and the offensive phases—against enemy aggression were worked into these field exercises. A great deal of careful staff work was required to accomplish this within the letter and intent of U.S. laws.

Plans specifying what every commander would do in case of enemy attack were worked out and placed in effect; in addition, longer-range plans were developed, indicating the operations that the commands should work toward. Provision was made therein for the progressive integration of atomic operations, as the new weapons became more numerous and more diversified.

Through all of this buildup, the provision of U.S. military equipment to assist in the arming of the contingents provided by the other NATO nations remained essentially under the Mutual Defense Assistance Program (MDAP), which had antedated the establishment of SHAPE. Military materiel, both from World War II surplus stocks and from current production, was in fact already being received by these nations when our initial group arrived. As provided by American law, it was administered and continued to be administered by a solely United States structure—the Military Assistance Advisory Groups (MAAGs) in European national capitals.

Eisenhower and his successors at SHAPE looked to this program to provide equipment for the buildup of forces beyond the resources of the recipient countries. Close liaison was established between U.S. officers at SHAPE and the U.S. military aid officers to assure that, insofar as possible, equipment from the United States was channeled to those units having the most critical operational roles. The importance of this equipment, which probably exceeded $10 billion in value by mid-1954, to the creation of the forces in Europe would be difficult to exaggerate. It is fair to say that without it the units built—army divisions, air squadrons, naval units, and their support elements—would not have been of the same military order of magnitude as the threat against them in Western Europe.

INTRODUCTION

The picture that I carried away from Europe when I left in mid-1954 was thus one of great accomplishment under the combined leadership of the Supreme Commanders—Eisenhower, Ridgway, and Gruenther, in turn—plus a truly remarkable team of senior deputies and subordinate commanders at all echelons. In that part of the world, a considerable degree of stability in the military situation had been achieved. But we know from these commanders themselves of the massive and difficult problems, requirements, and deficiencies which, although ameliorated, still faced the command.

1. Eisenhower

Rekindling the Spirit of the West

**STEPHEN E. AMBROSE
with MORRIS HONICK**

Nearly two decades ago, the late Alastair Buchan, an eminent British authority on international relations, reflecting on the durability of alliances, said with some doubt: "Alliances are a means to an end, whether it is primarily to increase the security of a group of sovereign states in the face of a common adversary, or to increase the diplomatic pressure which they can bring upon him, or to share the economic cost and the international system in an environment in which the fears and goals of nation states, whether they be allies or adversaries, do not remain constant; consequently, alliances—especially those embracing large states or a large group of states—have rarely lasted for a long span of time."[1]

Buchan did not specify what he meant by a "long span of time." Nor had there ever existed an alliance of nations comparable to the North Atlantic Alliance. Indeed, Professor Buchan might today have expressed some wonderment at the longevity of the Alliance[2]—an entente of nations from which no signatory has withdrawn since the signing of the Treaty that institutionalized it,[3] but rather to which four nations,[4] in addition to its original twelve adherents, have acceded during its lifetime.

Fifteen years prior to Buchan's observation, Gen. Dwight Eisenhower anticipated the difficulties inherent in the commitments the NATO nations had made. "It is true," he said, that a union among sovereign bodies is a very difficult thing to accomplish. If you take fourteen grains of sand on the seashore and put them in your hand and attempt to make a ball of them, you would not be trying anything more difficult than to get fourteen independent nations working together for a common purpose.

But we do know that we can go to another part of the countryside, get a bit of rock, make some cement from it, and then—out of those fourteen grains of sand—create something that is practically indestructible.[5]

Buchan's "long span of time" remained, of course, a relative concept, beyond definitive measure, much as the Alliance has not been readily comparable to other eras and coalitions. And a study of the history of NATO, of its unprecedented commitment to the unified, regionally planned defense of the territories of its members and of the evolution of methods developed for concerted action, must inevitably invoke a requirement for the application of new yardsticks of measurement in examining alliances in international relations.

But constructive research in such a study also would reveal that among the major instruments and steps toward increased security which the NATO nations have developed for nearly forty years have been the establishment of an unprecedented Allied military command, ACE, and the appointment of a Supreme Allied Commander who, ultimately, would be responsible for implementing NATO's internationally agreed defense plans in Europe through SHAPE. Indeed, these steps constitute the foundation of the unity which the Alliance slowly but progressively has acquired in wider areas in addition to defense matters—even if that unity often appears to be a fractious one.

When nearly a decade of upheaval on the periphery of the NATO area had passed after NATO's creation without a direct encroachment by the Red Army on the Allied nations, Eisenhower, now President Eisenhower, could go further and in 1957 observe that "the heart of the collective security principle is the idea of helping other nations to realize their own potentialities—political, economic and military. The strength of the free world lies not in cementing the free nations into a second monolithic mass to compete with that of the communists. It lies, rather, in the unity that comes of the voluntary association of nations which, however diverse, are developing their own capabilities and asserting their own national destinies in a world of freedom and mutual respect."[6]

Returning to SHAPE a little more than two years later, when the Alliance had completed its first decade of existence, he addressed the staff of his former headquarters and told them that "a member of SHAPE is engaged in far more than a mere mastery of intricate staff practices and procedures.... he is in the pursuit of an ideal that free peoples may, by joining themselves together, make more certain that peace will be for them, their children and their grandchildren, a greater probability. This is a far worthier ambition in itself than merely to witness a battle; for a battle, after all, is destructive. Its chief purpose is to gain or hold what we have. It does not obtain for us more freedom."[7]

In December 1950, however, a mere five and one-half years had passed since the defeat of Nazi Germany, and Europe was once again on the edge of despair. The hopes of 1945 for a newer, better world had given way to a Cold War that had numerous obvious parallels with 1939, chief of which was an aggressive dictatorship that was on the offensive. But there were major differences, too; the United States was committed in advance to the defense of Europe through NATO, and it had provided a leader around whom the Western Allies could rally. In 1939 no one man had been able to inspire confidence throughout Western Europe; but in 1950 when Pres. Harry Truman announced that he had appointed Eisenhower as SACEUR, hope replaced hopelessness, gloom gave way to joy. More than any other individual, save only Churchill, "Ike" was the symbol of the 1945 victory, the man who had shaped, held together, and directed the Grand Alliance. More than a military man, he was a statesman who was on intimate terms with most of Europe's leaders, was trusted, liked, and admired almost to the point of adulation by all of them.

For Eisenhower personally the appointment was ideal. It allowed him to escape the relative boredom of being a university president and, incidentally, proved a perfect platform from which to run for the Republican nomination to the presidency. But most of all, it represented a challenge worthy of his talents; he considered it to be the most important military job in the world.[8] The job, he said, would give him the sense that "I am doing the best I can in what I definitely believe to be a world crisis. I rather look upon this effort as about the last remaining chance for the survival of Western civilization."[9]

The challenges were real; there was a definite possibility of failure. The only firm decision that the NATO Council of Ministers had made was that they wanted Eisenhower as their commander. But of what? A multinational force? Independent national armies, joined together in a loose alliance? How many troops? Where would they come from? Truman had indicated that he was ready to send six American divisions to Europe, but Sen. Robert A. Taft and other Republicans, who had voted against the treaty, were challenging the president's right to ship American troops to Europe in peacetime. And although few dared to say so in public, all the NATO partners knew that NATO would never be able to match the threat from the East without German troops. Eisenhower himself felt that German participation was necessary for the security of Western Europe,[10] but West Germany was not yet sovereign, was not a member of NATO, and in any event, the French, Dutch, Belgians, and others were horrified at the prospect of rearming the Germans only five years after they had been liberated from the Nazis. But the only alternative—to embark on a massive program of rearming themselves—also had no appeal.

To the Europeans NATO meant a guarantee that the United States would not desert them, that they could count on the atomic bomb to deter the Soviet Union. They could see no reason to add a significant military component to NATO, especially when the price would include West German rearmament as well as higher taxes and more sacrifices for their economies at a time when they were just beginning to emerge from the ashes of World War II. Rearmament would merely provoke the Russians, critics said, without creating sufficient strength to repel them—at least without using atomic bombs, which was already assured by American participation in NATO. To succeed as SACEUR, Eisenhower would have to persuade the Europeans that the Germans were their allies, not their enemies, that they could build ground and air forces strong enough to hold back the Russians and their allies, that a genuine military alliance of the NATO partners was, even if unique in history, nevertheless workable.

Eisenhower's January 1951 trip to the capitals of the European NATO countries started in Paris, where he made a Europe-wide radio broadcast in which he asserted his great love for and faith in Europe. He admitted that he had no miraculous plans and that he brought with him no troops or military equipment, but he did bring hope.[11] And his name, the power of which he knew. At an initial NATO planning session, Gen. Lauris Norstad of the U.S. Air Force recalled that everyone bemoaned the weakness of the Western Alliance's military forces.

And I could see General Eisenhower becoming less and less impressed with this very negative approach, and finally he just banged that podium... got red faced.... "I know there are shortages, but I myself make up for part of that shortage—what I can do and what I can put into this—and the rest of it has to be made up by you people. Now get at it!" And he banged the podium again and he walked out.... And believe me there was a great change in the attitude. Right away there was an air of determination—we *will* do it.[12]

One of Eisenhower's major goals on the January trip was to get from the Europeans positive commitments to NATO that he could use back in the United States to counter Senator Taft and the other NATO critics, who were charging that since the

Western Europeans were unwilling to rearm, the United States should not bear the burden and the cost. In Lisbon he told Prime Minister Antonio de Salazar to show some concrete evidence of progress. He told the Danes that unless he could return to Washington and tell Congress that the Europeans were willing "to sacrifice some of the high standard of living and social welfare gains," Congress could not pass the necessary appropriations to support NATO. He told the Dutch that The Hague was not "showing a sense of urgency or a determination to pull its full share of the load." In every capital he urged the leaders to be an example to the others.[13]

Eisenhower gave pep talks to the Europeans. He was at his most dramatic in Paris, where he told Defense Minister René Pleven that the French did not have enough confidence in themselves and that they should try once again to reach their potential as a nation. These words had a profound effect on Pleven who said, "I thank you; you have aroused new confidence in me already." When Eisenhower's chief-of-staff, Gen. Alfred M. Gruenther, told him he had been "superbly eloquent," Eisenhower grunted, "Why is it that when I deliver such a good talk it has to be to an audience of one!"[14]

When talking with the French, Eisenhower avoided the delicate subject of West German rearmament, but he did begin to lay a basis for the creation of a German army by making a trip to the American Rhein Main air base in West Germany, where he held a press conference. He opened by saying that although he had previously felt antagonism toward Germany and a hatred for Nazis, he was ready to put these feelings behind him. He hoped that "some day the great German people [will be] lined up with the rest of the free world."[15]

In late January, Eisenhower flew back to the United States, where he spent four days at the Hotel Thayer at West Point writing a speech for delivery to Congress. He found it one of the most difficult to prepare of his entire career because of the number of themes, some of them contradictory, that he had to expound. He had simultaneously to convince the American politicians that the danger was great and imminent but that it would not cost America an excessive amount of money to meet it; that the Western Europeans were too weak to defend themselves but that they had the spirit and dedication to do so if given American help; that he needed American troops in Europe immediately but that he would not need too many of them nor for too long a period. As he told a friend, "NATO needs an eloquent and inspired Moses as much as it needs planes, tanks, guns and ships," and he intended to be that Moses.[16]

The speech itself was a triumph. He told the Congress that the United States, by itself, would not be responsible for defending Europe, that with forty divisions NATO could mount an effective defense, that only six of those divisions need be American, that the most urgent need was not for American troops but for an immense flow of American-produced military equipment, that he was fully aware of the needs in Korea. He emphasized the moral factor, assuring the congressmen that if they showed the Europeans that the United States was behind them, they would respond with a vigorous rearmament program of their own.

Eisenhower carefully avoided the German question, although in executive session he stressed that all the talk and bickering about West German rearmament had given the Germans the idea that they could blackmail the United States. To such threats, he said, he had told the Germans: "I am not going to come on my hands and knees for anything. If you people don't see your welfare lies with the free West, I am not going to beg you, a conquered nation." But he also admitted that "the Western European situation is really not going to be stable until that day arrives that we have Germany a decent respectable member, contributing its regular part."[17]

It was a convincing performance. Reporters concluded that Eisenhower was far more effective in presenting NATO's case than the Truman administration had been. Even Senator Taft, who had voted against the North Atlantic Treaty on the ground that "it was contrary to the whole theory of the United Nations charter" and because he "felt that it might develop aggressive features more likely to incite Russia to war than to deter it from war," willingly admitted a few weeks later that Eisenhower's trip had met favorable response.[18] He wrote: "General Eisenhower has made progress in persuading the European pact members that their own safety depends on arming themselves adequately in a united defense against possible Russian attack.... Our aim should be to make Europe sufficiently strong so that American troops can be withdrawn from the continent of Europe."[19] Two months later, Congress approved the dispatch of four divisions, plus supporting naval forces and air wings, to Europe. It also voted increased appropriations for MDAP. With these American contributions, NATO by mid-1951 was well under way to creating a genuine military force.

Meanwhile, Gruenther and his planners back in Paris were struggling with the manifold new problems involved in trying to set up an "integrated international staff" as required by the directive of the North Atlantic Council of September 1950. One problem was whether the French, American, or British type of staff organization would be best.

Briefly, the American staff system is based on four major sections known as "Gs" (i.e., general staff divisions), as follows: G-1, Administration; G-2, Intelligence; G-3, Plans and Operations; G-4, Supply, including medical, construction, and communications. The French *état-major* (headquarters) is somewhat similarly organized into the First Bureau, Organization and Personnel; Second Bureau, Intelligence and Topographical Service; Third Bureau, Operations; and, added after 1917 (possibly influenced by American practice in World War I), a Fourth Bureau, Supply. Historically, the United States staff system has retained features of British, French, and Prussian practice, with French characteristics predominating. The British practice breaks down the staff organization into two major categories: "G" for the General Staff and "A/Q" for Administration and Quartermaster service.

The solution at SHAPE was to break down the staff into two major top-level branches, each under a deputy chief-of-staff and each responsible for four subordinate staff divisions. One major branch was Logistics and Administration, under which came the Logistics, Budget and Finance, and Communications divisions, and the adjutant general; the other major branch was Plans and Operations, under which were grouped the Personnel, Intelligence, Organization and Training, and the Plans, Policy, and Operations divisions. It is interesting to note that the problem of solving staff organization through compromise with national or regional custom is not new in American military annals. Lt. Col. J.D. Hittle, United States Marine Corps, upon whose research the above distinctions are outlined, makes this germane observation in the course of discussing American staff organization. "Washington's force was in no sense a national army. Rather, it was little more than a conglomeration of detachments from thirteen separate sovereignties and each sovereignty set its own military system. Some reflected the French influence, some tried to copy Prussian methods and some followed the British."[20]

On the point of staff organization in the early days of SHAPE, Lord Ismay, the first secretary-general, commented:

It was indeed fortunate for the planners at SHAPE that the Western Union command organization had already studied analogous problems and had prepared the plans which served as the foundation for future dispositions. Western Union had created the precedent of an international and inter-service staff.... they had bequeathed to SHAPE... a number of officers of different nationalities with the invaluable experience of working together as an Allied team. ...Thanks to the work of their predecessors and their own unremitting labors, the SHAPE planners were able to settle most of the fundamental problems by the time General Eisenhower got back to Paris.[21]

Other problems encountered at that time were the proportion of staff appointments to be allotted to each nation, the kind of a command structure that would best fit the pattern of defense they intended to establish, and the location of permanent headquarters. Upon its creation, SHAPE absorbed the military functions performed hitherto by the various European Regional Planning Groups which had operated under both

Western Union and NATO. Their economic, social, and political functions were taken over by other agencies of NATO. The new Supreme Headquarters was made responsible to the NATO Council through the Military Committee, composed of the chiefs-of-staff of all NATO signatories, and more directly through the Standing Group, comprised of the chiefs of staff of France, Britain, and the United States, to which the SACEUR reported. Both the Military Committee and the Standing Group had headquarters in Washington, but the supreme commander remained in regular contact with them through a Liaison Office in Paris.

The broad outline of the planning was revealed by Eisenhower in a later report to the Standing Group:

Western Europe, from North Cape to Sicily, had to be surveyed as a whole. There is the main land mass, stretching from the Baltic to the Adriatic—a peninsula, when viewed in perspective, of that greatest of all land masses, which is Europe and Asia combined. On the flanks of this main peninsula we have two main outcrops—apart from the Iberian peninsula and the British Isles. The one is Denmark, almost touching the tip of Scandinavia, whose western half, Norway, is among our brotherhood of nations sworn to defend freedom. The Southern outcrop is Italy, projecting into the Mediterranean, and affording us a strong position for flanking forces with valuable air and seabases. It seemed sound to divide the command of Western Europe into three main sectors: Norway and Denmark as one buttress, Italy and the adjacent waters as the other, and the central mass as the main structure.[22]

The strategic concept envisioned by the SHAPE planners is neither unique nor exclusive. It follows pretty well the pattern of thinking laid down by Gen. H.J. Kruls which postulates that the Soviets will resort to war in Europe "only if they see an opportunity of changing the present unfavorable ratio between their resources and those of their enemies by gaining some quick success in a surprise offensive."[23] The purpose of such an offensive, of course, would be to subdue West Germany and march to the Channel ports in France, Belgium, and Holland. As Kruls pointed out: "Should the rulers of Soviet Russia decide upon open war—perhaps after gaining further successes in the Cold War—then only one road exists by which they may hope to progress toward final victory. That is the road to Western Europe, to the shores of the North Sea and the Atlantic ocean. And if Soviet Russia sets out on this road, she will also have to seize the Middle East."[24]

It was to forestall any such attempt that plans were drawn up for subordinate Allied commands to be established, with equally integrated headquarters, in the three principal geographic areas of Western Europe—North, Center, and South. It was along these lines that the original SHAPE command structure was fashioned. The bulk of the ground and air strength was to be in the center, while smaller land and air forces, with more significant naval support, would defend the northern and southern flanks, both of which were exposed to the sea.

Accordingly, in April 1951 Eisenhower announced the formation of Allied Forces Northern Europe, with British Adm. Sir Patrick Brind as commander-in-chief (CINCNORTH). Maj. Gen. Robert Taylor, U.S. Air Force, was named commander, Allied Air Forces Northern Europe, and the Norwegian and Danish land forces, virtually left under national authority, were under the command respectively of Lt. Gen. Wilhelm Hansteen under the title of commander, Allied Land Forces Norway, and Lt. Gen. Ebbe Gortz, under the title of commander, Allied Land Forces Denmark. Soon after organization of the latter command, Gortz was supplanted by Lt. Gen. Erik Moller.

Eisenhower himself retained overall control of the center and appointed Gen. (later Marshal) Alphonse Pierre Juin of France as commander, Allied Air Forces Central Europe, and Vice Adm. Robert Jaujard of France as flag officer (later commander, Allied Naval Forces), Central Europe. Eisenhower later confessed that at this time in Western Europe there were fewer than fifteen NATO divisions adequately trained and equipped for war. "We had fewer than 1,000 operational aircraft available in all Western Europe and many of these were of obsolescent types."[25]

Gruenther later dramatized this initial weakness by recounting that when Eisenhower first surveyed the scene and asked one of his staff officers what the Russians would need to march to the Channel, the staff officer replied simply, "Shoes, sir."[26] But the condition did not hold for long. By January 1952 Truman was able to report to the American people that there was a fighting force in Europe.[27]

The solution of the problem of the southern, or right, flank was neither so simple nor so prompt. As Adm. Robert Carney's *First Annual Report* written some time afterward pointed out, Eisenhower had trouble organizing his right flank, partly because of "politically and philosophically divergent opinions. Finally, he received concurrence in establishing a Southern Command which partially solved his military needs, although this initial solution left much to be desired."[28]

The political difficulty stemmed from the fact that while the Mediterranean had always been a "British lake" and was regarded as "the supply line of the Empire," virtually the only real modern naval strength was the United States Sixth Fleet. The philosophical difficulties alluded to are not immediately clear unless the controversy involved military doctrine, as most observers are inclined to believe.

Among the competing concepts was, for instance, the American strategic formula of massive retaliation, based on air power and nuclear weapons; and the French concept of a line defense on land, with the rivers forming the principal bulwarks, as against the respective American and British landwarfare concepts of defense of strong points and defense in depth, achieved by letting the enemy through in certain places and then encircling isolated units and destroying them. Nevertheless, on 19 June 1951, more than two months after SHAPE had become operational without a southern flank, Carney was appointed commander-in-chief, Allied Forces Southern Europe and concurrently commander, Allied Naval Forces Southern Europe. Gen. Maurizio L. De Castiglioni, Italian army, was named commander, Allied Land Forces Southern Europe, and Maj. Gen. David M. Schlatter, U.S. Air Force, was designated as commander, Allied Air Forces Southern Europe.

At the time of his appointment, Carney attended a conference of all NATO commanders at SHAPE headquarters in the Astoria Hotel, Paris, and made it plain at a press conference which followed that the only forces he had then were the United States Sixth Fleet, which was in the Mediterranean.[29]

Ismay, writing from another point of view as secretary-general, and four years after the event, gave this description of the situation: "The problem of command in the Southern area was more difficult to resolve, complicated as it was by the special position of the British Naval Force which had for so long wielded control of the Mediterranean. However, in June, 1951, Admiral Carney (USN)—succeeded in 1953 by Admiral [William M.] Fechteler (USN)—was selected to be Commander-in-Chief Allied Forces Southern Europe.... The solution of the Mediterranean Command was to wait for two years."[30] The solution referred to by Ismay was the eventual setting up of a new command, Allied Forces Mediterranean under Adm. Lord Mountbatten, with the British Mediterranean Fleet as the nucleus. The new command (CINCMED) and Carney's (later Fechteler's) command (CINCSOUTH), although independent, were pledged to cooperate whenever necessary.

Eisenhower, in his first *Annual Report*, mentioned no difficulties, but only stated the facts. "The Organizational framework of SHAPE was *virtually* completed in June [1951] when Admiral Robert B. Carney was appointed to command Allied Forces Southern Europe.... Subsequently, two sea-area commands were organized by Admiral Carney, one under Vice Admiral Leon Sala and the other under Vice Admiral Massimo Girosi."[31] (The problem of organizing the Mediterranean is discussed further in the following chapter.)

Carney noted that the staff was organized with a view to force contributions by the different member-states and with due regard for planning and operational responsibilities. American and Italian officers predominated, but France and Britain were also represented.[32]

"Very quickly after the establishment of the command structure," declared Eisenhower in his *Report* to the Standing Group in April 1952, "we began to see definite improvement in the morale and readiness of troops. But first and foremost was the need for more forces. The United States and Great Britain alone possessed previously formed and disposable reserves, and they proceeded to deploy additional strength in Germany—four divisions from America and two from the United Kingdom."[33] Eisenhower added that France already had four divisions in Germany. Although air reinforcement was also needed, it had to wait until crews could be trained and aircraft and airfields could be built.[34]

During this time Eisenhower was also highly conscious of the unique and indeed unprecedented leadership role that he and his staff were assuming, and he wanted to make certain that those around him understood the need for unity. He told them that he wished to make clear that once a man had been accepted on his staff, he no longer would have an official nationality. To Belgian leaders with whom he met, he expressed the sentiment that he himself already felt "$1/12$th Belgian."[35] To some, this signaled an unwarranted move into an unauthorized area of national sovereignty—or withdrawal from another, depending on how it was seen.

But Eisenhower persisted. He held that SHAPE officers could not represent their ministries of defense or anyone else as staff officers. He did plan, however, to have someone at his headquarters representing the national points of view, someone who would be free to come and go to his own national defense establishment and report what was taking place, including developments and plans.[36] Gruenther had affirmed Eisenhower's intentions a few days earlier when he told the first of the then-National Liaison Officers that he was sure they realized that "any officer who becomes a member of the [SHAPE] staff no longer is working for his nation, but is working for the allied cause." "We consider," Gruenther said, "that an officer who comes to the staff doesn't so become overnight. It can be done in time, however; General Eisenhower's headquarters during the war made great progress; and Western Union [WUDO] has done it."[37]

Later Gen. Lyman L. Lemnitzer, when he was SACEUR,

went further in elaborating on the rationale for the international status of the Allied officer. At the SHAPE command exercise, SHAPEX, in 1969, he said:

> I recall that early in my days as SACEUR a prominent newspaper wrote that Supreme Headquarters Allied Powers Europe was an integrated headquarters and that consequently "its members must be responsive to the national military and political requirements of their own countries as to those of the Atlantic organisation". I said then and I say now, that such a statement is completely in error.
> The fact is that staffs at all the NATO Headquarters must look at problems from the viewpoint of the mission assigned to their international command, rather than that which might exist from the view of any particular country. Such missions involve purely professional matters and thus it would be improper for an officer to be only an advocate of his own country's position, for that national position may be dictated by many factors besides those pertaining to the Alliance as a whole. If SHAPE were made up solely of special pleaders for national positions, without regard to Allied Command Europe, as a military entity, it would not be a military headquarters, but a debating society.[38]

Indeed, from the first, queries from official U.S. national agencies for direct access to information concerning the staffing of SHAPE and ACE were referred to data normally supplied to those agencies through releases made via their National Military Representatives. Information sought by national agencies that involved matters of subjective staff judgments and that had not been released to a national agency were to be forwarded to the chief-of-staff prior to any further national contact with the international staff.[39] NATO civilian staff members, on accepting appointments with NATO, were required to sign a declaration undertaking "not to seek or accept instructions in regard to the performance of... duties from any government or from any authority other than the Organization/Headquarters."[40]

Thus, the delicate matter of appearances by NATO officers or staff members before national parliamentary bodies or responses by NATO members to national inquiries was considered a matter for bold but diplomatic handling by the SACEUR from the beginning. When requests have come from European parliaments for the testimony of officers on the SACEUR's international staff—requests often prompted by public and governmental reactions in those parliaments to politically sensitive military matters—Eisenhower and his successors have refused permission. The SACEUR's own situation has been different, however. As commander-in-chief of the U.S. European Command (CINCEUR), all SACEURs have frequently testified before committees of the U.S. Congress. Indeed, they are invited to do so in that capacity and occasionally they have also briefed national parliamentarians in other forums, such as the Assembly of the Western European Union.[41] Every SACEUR has had to deal with these problems.[42]

In the months following the establishment of his headquarters outside Paris, Eisenhower devoted most of his time to building support for NATO, which he called his most important objective.[43] He carried out a brutal schedule to meet it—press conferences and numerous trips to the various capitals, where he was careful to talk not only to government figures but also to opposition party leaders, trade union officials, intellectuals, and molders of public opinion.

In his extensive correspondence with American politicians, businessmen, and publishers, Eisenhower concentrated on selling NATO. Most of the incoming letters were pleas that he run for the presidency; his standard reply was that he had no interest in politics and that in any event the job he held was so important that he had to concentrate his full energy and time on it. Then he would launch into advocacy for NATO, usually ending by urging the recipient to spread the word. The "word" was that "the future of civilization, as we know it, is at stake," that the true defense of the United States was on the Elbe River, that the American way of life was dependent upon raw materials that could only come from Europe and its colonies and on trade and scientific exchanges with Europe, and that only through collective security could the United States and Europe meet the Soviet threat.[44]

In his correspondence Eisenhower dealt directly with two major objections to American support for NATO. The first was that Europeans, led by the Labour party in Britain, were going socialist, which led many of Eisenhower's friends to demand why they should support them. Eisenhower reassured them that Europe was fully committed to a free, democratic way of life, that it was not about to go communist (unless the United States abandoned it), and that "it would be a terrific mistake to demand conformity in all political and economic details. We would soon fall apart!"[45]

The second objection, far more serious, was that the United States was committing itself to an indefinite defense of Europe at a tremendous cost that would continually go higher. Eisenhower admitted the force of the objection. "We cannot be a modern Rome guarding the far frontiers with our legions," he said. He recognized that the economic strength of the United States was the greatest asset the free world had, and he agreed that the expenditures of billions of dollars for defense would, in the long run, bankrupt the United States, thus presenting the Soviets with "their greatest victory." But he insisted that a program of support for NATO was a short-run proposition. American aid for NATO was essential now, in 1951, but it could be phased out rather quickly. He flatly declared, "If in ten years, all American troops stationed in Europe for national defense purposes have not been returned to the United States, then this whole project will have failed."[46]

Within Europe Eisenhower considered morale to be his biggest problem. Less than six years after the most destructive war in history, Europeans just did not want to think about fighting—or building the forces to fight—another war. Further, the figures on ground strength were so stark and discouraging (NATO had less than fourteen divisions, the Russians 175) that it seemed impossible ever to stop the Soviet army without using atomic bombs, and if the Americans were going to use atomic bombs anyway, why bother to build European ground strength, especially when it would be so expensive, would slow or halt economic recovery, and would only provoke the Russians? All SACEURs had to confront this attitude.

In his talks with the European leaders, Eisenhower attempted to build their confidence. Inevitably, he had to ask them to dig deeper and spend more, but he did so within the context of recognizing political realities. As his principal aide, then-Colonel Goodpaster, later explained: "He had a great sense of how the governments of the various countries worked and what the practical constraints were on the political leaders, that you couldn't crowd them too far, you couldn't ask too much of them.... But at the same time he was constantly able to point to the basic scope of resources on which we in the West could draw if we could simply mobilize them and organize them properly."[47]

Eisenhower, therefore, emphasized morale, which cost little or nothing to build. "Civilian leaders talk about the state of morale in a given country as if it were a sort of uncontrollable event or phenomenon, like a thunderstorm or a cold winter," he complained in his diary, while "the soldier leader looks on morale as...the greatest of all his problems, but also as one about which he can and must do something."[48] To Gen. Omar Bradley Eisenhower said that "men in uniform...are the only ones who can educate and inspire our civil leaders."[49] Thus he continued to urge, cajole, encourage. For example, on the seventh anniversary of Overlord, Eisenhower went to Normandy to deliver a Europe-wide radio broadcast that reminded the Western Europeans of what was at stake. He stressed that a "campaign of liberation" must never be fought there again.[50]

West Germany was Eisenhower's most delicate problem, however, as it was for several of his successors. No matter how successful he was in persuading the other nations of Western Europe to increase their defense spending, his goal of forty divisions was simply unattainable without a German army. Eisenhower had extracted from the French a promise of twenty-four divisions for NATO, but in fact the French at the outset of NATO had only three divisions which later became the equivalent of four in West Germany and six in France, with no immediate prospect of making any further contribution. This was because ten French divisions were tied down in Indochina in an apparently endless war.

Whenever Eisenhower asked the French for more support for NATO, they countered with a request for more American support for their effort in Indochina. "I'd favor heavy reinforcement to get the thing over at once," Eisenhower wrote in his diary, "but I'm convinced that no military victory is possible in that kind of theater."[51] In his view, the French had to give Vietnam, Laos, and Cambodia their independence, then let them fight their own war while the French army came home to defend France. But he could not convince any French leader of the wisdom of that course. That meant that the only alternative for NATO was to create a West German army, but the French would not allow that either.

"We are either going to solve this German problem," Eisenhower believed, "or the Soviets will solve it in their favor."[52] Or, as West German Chancellor Konrad Adenauer put it, "The Western Allies, especially France, have to... answer the question of which danger is the greater: the Russian threat or a German contribution to a European defense community."[53] After going through various contortions, including a proposal that the West Germans provide the enlisted men while the French supply the officers, the French finally offered the Pleven Plan. The West Germans would build an army that would have no unit larger than a division as part of an integrated NATO force commanded by Eisenhower; the West German contribution would be limited to 20 percent of the integrated force.

Originally, Eisenhower did not think much of the Pleven Plan; he feared that it would be divisive, as it included "every kind of obstacle, difficulty, and fantastic notion that misguided humans could put together in one package."[54] But after six months as SACEUR, Eisenhower changed his mind because, as he reported to Secretary of Defense George Marshall, NATO needed "some spectacular accomplishment" to keep American public opinion behind the organization and to spur the Europeans to do more toward their own defense. Further, "the plan offers the only immediate hope that I can see of developing, on a basis acceptable to other European countries, the German strength that is vital to us." In addition, he had a larger goal. "I am certain that there is going to be no real progress towards a greater unification of Europe except through the medium of specific programs of this kind."[55] In other words, rather than waiting for the creation of a "United States of Europe" to achieve an all-European army, he felt that by forming the army first, the political unification would naturally follow.

He thought the new super-nation should include all the European NATO members, plus Greece, Sweden, Spain, and Yugoslavia. A United States of Europe, he argued, would "instantly... solve the real and bitter problems of today.... So many advantages would flow from such a union that it is a tragedy for the whole human race that it is not done at once." He brushed aside objections, saying he was tired of hearing about a slow, cautious approach. He saw no reason why "a socialist Sweden could not live alongside a capitalist Germany" so long as there existed a simple bill of rights in the constitution and the elimination of trade barriers and all economic and political restraint on free movement.[56]

In December 1951 he urged Defense Minister Pleven to issue a call to the European members of NATO "to meet in an official constitutional convention to consider ways and means for promoting a closer union." Such a "dramatic and inspiring call to action," he said, would be a great help in getting a European army under way. But although Eisenhower carefully flattered Pleven, the Frenchman did not respond.[57] The French, in short, had still not answered in their own minds Adenauer's question: which do you fear most, the Red Army or a new German army?

As SACEUR, Eisenhower had to insist that both the Western Europeans and the Americans do more to bolster their defense and to take their allies where they could find them (thus, he wanted not only West Germany but also Yugoslavia in NATO). But he was also a Republican candidate for the presidency, although not yet announced, and as such had to advocate a balanced U.S. budget and lower taxes. Such a financial program could be accomplished only through drastic cuts in defense spending, and the most obvious place to cut was MDAP and American forces in Europe. The Korean War was still being fought; the French in Indochina needed more assistance; massive expenditures were crucial to keeping ahead of the Russians in atomic warfare.

Eisenhower's solution was to cut American costs by persuading the Europeans to do more in their own defense, to form an all-European army, and to reduce overall NATO expenditures. Thus, he rejected the U.S. Navy's arguments for supercarriers which were too expensive, argued for trimmer divisions with more fighting men and fewer support systems, and rejected the army's argument for more and heavier tanks. In 1918 he had been one of the army's first proponents of the tank; in 1951 he became one of the first detractors. He believed that developments in recoilless weapons had made "the expensive tank... about as valuable as a piece of warm butter." The tank would soon go the way of the Dreadnoughts; what he wanted was not heavier tanks but lighter, cross-country vehicles of "great speed, reliability, and low silhouette."[58]

On 23 January 1952 Eisenhower wrote Truman, "We are in a critical period in NATO affairs." He was looking forward to a meeting of the North Atlantic Council in Lisbon where basic issues were to be discussed. Eisenhower thought that if the meeting could produce some progress on the all-European army, on European unity, on Greek-Turkish membership in NATO, and adequate force goals, the future would look more encouraging. If it did not, his whole period as SACEUR would be a failure.[59]

The meeting met all his hopes. The Council set the most ambitious force goals of NATO's history—fifty divisions, four thousand aircraft, and 704 combat vessels by 1952; seventy-five divisions and sixty-five hundred aircraft by 1953; ninety-six divisions and nine thousand aircraft by 1954, with thirty-five to forty divisions to be ready for combat at all times. The Council approved the contribution of twelve West German divisions within the framework of the all-European army and formally welcomed Greece and Turkey into NATO. Eisenhower was highly pleased and called the Lisbon conference a landmark.[60] His successor, Gen. Matthew B. Ridgway, might not have been so ebullient, as discussed in the following chapter.

Shortly thereafter, Eisenhower sent in his letters of resignation so that he could return to the United States to campaign for the presidency. One letter went to Secretary of Defense Robert A. Lovett, one to Truman, and one to French Gen. Paul Ely, chairman of the NATO Standing Group. To Lovett he emphasized that he had achieved the goals that had been set for him when he assumed the SACEUR position. "The special organization and initial planning missions that were deemed critical in the late weeks of 1950 have now been accomplished.... The situation has changed from one of exploration and initial negotiation to one of confident planning and development." To Truman he emphasized that "patterns of development have been devised, security plans prepared, organizations set up, logistic and support sources initiated, first candid reexamination made and, from now on, progress will of necessity follow the lines that have already been marked out in more or less distinct fashion." To Ely he stressed that "when I entered upon my duties in December 1950, I was sure that our common task in Europe was a job that had to be done. From later experience, I am convinced that it can be done and that, given full cooperation, it will be done."[61]

Then Eisenhower issued his *Annual Report*. In it he claimed that "the tide has begun to flow our way and the situation of the free world is brighter than it was a year ago.... The national units pledged to this command a year ago were for the most part poorly equipped, inadequately trained and lacking essential support in both supplies and installations.... They could have offered little more than token resistance to attack.... But already our active forces have increased to a point where they could give a vigorous account of themselves, should an attack be launched against us."[62]

All those upbeat conclusions in his letters of resignation represented the kind of self-serving assessment any presidential candidate would make of his own performance in his most recent job. And there were elements of gross exaggeration in his *Annual Report*. Field Marshal Lord Montgomery, his deputy, in commenting on it, told Eisenhower that "it is all right to be a *little* optimistic but this goes so far as to be quite misleading."[63]

Nevertheless, much had been accomplished. Although the numbers of troops in the field and in reserve fell far short of the goals Eisenhower himself had set, the morale situation was incalculably better. Eisenhower's greatest achievement as SACEUR, by far, had been to convince Europeans and Americans that NATO could work, that Western Europe could be defended. Among his myriad duties as SACEUR—organizer, trainer, strategist, diplomat, commander—the one he concentrated on, and the only one in which he achieved almost complete success, was as the promoter of an idea, the idea that free men must and can defend themselves against their adversary. Along the way he had managed, by no means singlehandedly but nevertheless as the individual most responsible, to achieve what seemed unachievable in December 1950—to include West Germany as a military partner in the defense of Western Europe. His one great failure, aside from his inability to achieve the force levels he deemed necessary, was to create an integrated, multinational European army as a part of a genuine United States of Europe, but even here he had managed to goad the Europeans into progress. In May 1952 the Europeans signed a treaty creating the European Defense Community (EDC). It still had to be ratified by the various legislatures (and, of course, the French eventually rejected it), but it made possible Eisenhower's start on West German rearmament.

Thus, even if accomplishments were more of the spirit than in tangible military forces, it was still true that Eisenhower had helped lay the groundwork for what has proven to be the most enduring peacetime alliance in the history of mankind.

2. Ridgway
Trying to Make Good on the Promises

GEORGE EUGENE PELLETIER

As pointed out in the previous chapter, General Eisenhower at the time of his departure had claimed that "already our active forces have increased to a point where they could give us a vigorous account of themselves, should an attack be launched against us."[1] There were also major deficiencies, but the supreme commander's *First Annual Report* did not list them in detail, as his successor, Gen. Matthew Ridgway, was to do a year later. Eisenhower put greater emphasis on the promised fifty divisions by the end of 1952, the prospective German contribution through EDC, and the building of priority reserve divisions.[2]

Eisenhower was also heartened by the growing flow of material under the MDAP, and he had emphasized that the future strengthening of the defense capabilities of the Western powers would depend greatly upon increased training and greater production of equipment. He was to remain as SACEUR for two months beyond the April 1952 *Report*. During this period a new set of references established by the NATO Council gradually altered the role of SACEUR. In the beginning the SACEUR had of necessity to be concerned with political, economic, social, and other factors of the developing Alliance; from now on, his concern was to be primarily and almost exclusively military. The Council, along with the secretary-general, would concern itself more and more with political and economic matters among the partners. It would be the

SACEUR's job to coordinate the activities of the various military forces assigned or earmarked for him and, above all, to propose measures for their effective training and for balanced and flexible logistical support.

Eisenhower himself concluded that the actions taken at the Lisbon Conference in February 1952 would materialize during his successor's regime. "The tide," he asserted, "has begun to flow our way and the situation of the free world is brighter than it was a year ago.... At Lisbon, our member nations.... agreed to the concept of a European Defense Community and a close relationship with the German Federal Republic. They approved a program to establish this year a force of fifty standing and reserve divisions and 4,000 aircraft.... Now our governments must convert the Lisbon program into actuality."[3]

These were the problems that would confront Ridgway. The promises had been made handsomely to Eisenhower and, among NATO nations, to one another. For instance, at the dedication of the newly built SHAPE headquarters buildings at Rocquencourt on 23 July 1951, Pres. Vincent Auriol of France, in the presence of Defense Minister René Pleven, told Eisenhower, his staff officers, and a public audience gathered there for the ceremony, "It is a moving symbol to see that collective security now rests on her [France's] soil, twice invaded, twice ravaged and pillaged, as she recalls how greatly she suffered from being alone at the beginning of those two wars."[4]

President Auriol added that "by the end of the year, France, keeping her pledged word, would place at your disposal the 10 divisions promised for December 1951—namely five divisions on a war footing and five divisions on a three-day mobilization order. In the spirit which is yours, we wish to establish collective security on a firm foundation. We wish to contribute to the constitution of a Europe united politically, economically and militarily."[5] These were brave words, and they echoed the similar assurances that Eisenhower had heard in Rome, Brussels, The Hague, and other capitals. It was to be Ridgway's job to try to get the NATO nations to implement the promises with men and equipment.

There were also other things to be done. The command

structure was well in hand, but it would need elaboration to take in Greece and Turkey, alteration to include the control of America's nuclear power, and delicate adjustment to satisfy British prestige in the Mediterranean area and French aspirations as a land power in a renascent Europe. These were the footnotes, the small print in the Eisenhower legacy which stated: "This is a great task—a noble charge.... It can be done, given the will to do it.... Then the Atlantic Community will have proved worthy of its history and its God-given endowments. We shall have proved our union the world's most potent influence toward peace among men—the final security goal of humanity."[6]

It was to this unfinished task that Ridgway was to devote the fourteen months during which he was SACEUR. A man of deep religious feeling, he made it clear when he assumed his new duties that he was dedicating himself and his staff to something more than the building up of a military organization. To the group assembled just outside Supreme Headquarters just before noon on 30 May 1952, he said: "There is here no aggressive intent, no effort to tear down, no effort to destroy. There is but a single purpose—to protect, to safeguard, to preserve, to enlarge man's dignity and liberty: his freedom to think, to work, to worship, to raise his family within decent standards of living, according to the dictates of no human despot, but according to the laws of a power higher than any on earth."[7] He drew comfort from the new association which would bring him again in contact with comrades of former days—Field Marshal Lord Montgomery, Marshal Alphonse Juin, and others. He was particularly cordial to Montgomery, whom he respected greatly.[8]

He threw back his shoulders as he uttered his *envoi* to the man who had brought SHAPE to its present status and who was returning home in hope of becoming president of the United States. "To you and Mrs. Eisenhower," he said, "Godspeed and His richest blessings."[9]

As mentioned earlier, the character of the North Atlantic Council was changed somewhat at the Ninth session, held

20-25 February 1952 at Lisbon. Until that time the Council had been composed exclusively of ministers and had met two or three times annually. But the Lisbon meeting "took action to adapt the Treaty Organization to the needs arising from the development of its [the Council's] activities from the *planning* to the *operational* stage."[10] Consequently, it was decided that the Council, "while continuing to hold periodic Ministerial Meetings, will henceforth function in permanent session through the appointment of Permanent Representatives."[11] The new permanent representatives were to have the title and status of ambassadors and would reside in Paris, meeting two or three times a week to carry on regular business.[12] Thus, it happened that the permanent representatives at their first meeting in Paris on 28 April 1952 announced the appointment of Ridgway to succeed Eisenhower as SACEUR.

Ridgway's appointment brought a rather enthusiastic response in American quarters, but Europeans were more restrained. The latter, largely because they knew him better and longer, would have preferred Eisenhower's popular chief-of-staff, Gen. Alfred Gruenther. Indeed, an Associated Press poll taken at this time showed Gruenther to be the wide favorite of Europeans who were asked their preferences.[13] However, since it was announced simultaneously that Gruenther would continue as chief-of-staff under Ridgway, there was general agreement with President Truman's prediction that "they will make an outstanding team for our common defense."[14] In announcing Ridgway's appointment in Washington (simultaneously with the NATO Council's action), Truman said, "General Ridgway brings exceptional knowledge of present-day combat and modern training needs and training methods to the common task of preparing our collective forces for the defense of Europe."[15]

While there was press agreement on Ridgway's experience as a soldier, some doubts were expressed as to whether his diplomatic and political assets would prove as effective as Eisenhower's had been. Some quarters emphasized, however, that the political phases of the organization of the defense of

Western Europe were now completed and that the emphasis would be toward building effective military forces, active and reserve, base and port facilities, and air power. These developments had been foreshadowed in Eisenhower's *First Annual Report*. A prominent analyst of Franco-American affairs and roving correspondent for the *Reader's Digest* reflected this last view when he wrote in a syndicated column: "Eisenhower's job in Europe has been at least fifty per cent political.... General Ridgway will primarily face a strictly military assignment for which he is perfectly fitted. He proved that in Korea."[16] The *Cleveland Plain Dealer* editorialized that "General Ridgway's appointment serves notice to the world that the European defense plans will be brought to realization."[17] The *Atlanta Constitution* took note that "some Americans, as well as Europeans insisted that the command go to... General Gruenther. We are now convinced of the latter's ability as a diplomat and as an administrator. However, he has not earned the prestige which goes with command of troops in battle."[18]

There can be little doubt that Ridgway was somewhat handicapped, in comparison with either Eisenhower or Gruenther, as a political negotiator in Europe. He had done well in the Far East, but he was a newcomer across the Atlantic. In personality he was more restrained than the publicly ever-smiling "Ike" and the ebullient, dynamic Gruenther. Both the latter men had considerably wider experience in dealing with the civilian authorities of NATO. To Ridgway also fell the principal burden of convincing a hostile French public to support EDC (which, in effect, called for rearming the West Germans). Performing such a task did not make a man popular and effective at the same time. Drew Middleton, the *New York Times'* chief correspondent in Germany, called America's "premature declaration" in favor of German rearmament "one of the major diplomatic mistakes into which our immaturity has led us."[19]

The principal actors themselves recognized the differences in the tasks that the first SACEUR had been expected to perform and those that his successor should best concern himself with. Eisenhower had said that many of the problems he had faced had been economic, political, and psychological, rather than military.[20] Ridgway explained his position in this way. "The search for solutions to the major problems... gives rise to serious political, economic, financial and social difficulties.... the estimates which follow constitute *a military estimate*.... Appraisal [of some of the problems] goes far beyond the military field.... *All but the military aspects are beyond both my competence and responsibility.*" (Emphasis added.)[21]

The *Milwaukee Journal* expressed the general view that Ridgway was qualified for the new command both as a soldier and as a statesman, saying he had shown ability as a field commander both in Europe during World War II and more recently in Korea, and that "he has, moreover, earned trust and esteem for diplomacy, tact, patience and all around expertness."[22] The *Minneapolis Tribune* was disturbed by a report that neither the White House nor the Pentagon had consulted France or the other NATO governments before announcing the choice of Ridgway. "It is disturbing," the *Tribune* editorialized, "to be told by... William H. Stoneman that the White House did not consult France and at least 10 other NATO governments before fixing upon Ridgway as Eisenhower's successor.... It puts Ridgway off to a less favorable start than Eisenhower had at the outset."[23]

Stoneman was a competent and experienced European correspondent for the conservative *Chicago Daily News* Foreign Service, and there may have been something to what he wrote. However, consultation of a kind at least is implied in Secretary-General Lord Ismay's account of Ridgway's selection. "General Eisenhower had asked [on 2 April] to be released from his command in order to interest himself actively in United States politics. *The Council decided* that the Supreme Command in Europe should continue to be held by an officer of the United States Armed Forces: and on the nomination of President Truman, *they appointed* Matthew B. Ridgway to this vital position. *General Gruenther remained as Chief of Staff.*" (Emphasis added.)[24] The brevity of this statement by the secretary-general indicated that the Council acted favorably on

Truman's nomination of Ridgway. The italicized phrases imply that the Council decision that the supreme commander remain American was unanimous. There can be little doubt that there was consultation of some sort between 2 April, when Eisenhower asked to be relieved, and 28 April, when the appointment was formally made.

In fact, when Ismay learned of Eisenhower's desire to retire from SHAPE, he held several talks with the U.S. permanent representative, William H. Draper, as it was evident to him that the next SACEUR would also be an American general necessarily nominated by the president. Ismay followed up these discussions with a series of informal talks with each of the other thirteen Allied representatives to ensure that their governments would agree to ask the United States to appoint a new commander and that there would be no objection to the individual selected. Ismay maintained continuous contact with Draper and the other permanent representatives, so that when Truman nominated Ridgway he was smoothly and unanimously approved.[25]

Thus, with the final appointing power under the Treaty resting with the North Atlantic Council, the normal process by which a supreme commander is chosen had been followed— that is, the Council had asked the president of the United States to recommend, Ridgway had been recommended, and the Council had acted favorably.[26] It is true, however, that in the case of Eisenhower, the NATO Council (then comprised of ministers) had asked for the nomination by the United States of the wartime supreme commander by name.[27] In the case of Ridgway, the initiative in obtaining a relief had been taken by Eisenhower and the final action had been taken by the newly organized Council of Permanent Representatives (served by a secretary-general who had himself only been in office at the time for four weeks).[28] Therefore, by the very method of appointment, the prestige of the position, probably inevitably, had declined somewhat.

As to the appointment of Gruenther as chief-of-staff, Ismay's quoted statement that "General Gruenther remained as

Chief-of-Staff" seems to bear out, by implication, that Gruenther's selection had been made by the Council instead of by the prospective supreme commander, who was thousands of miles away in Asia, and that Gruenther's retention as chief-of-staff may well have been a condition to the Council's speedy ratification of Truman's nominee for SACEUR, which, as noted, did not meet with overwhelming enthusiasm, at least initially, throughout the Alliance.

But James Michener, writing in *Life Magazine*, emphasized that Ridgway's truly triumphant military performance in Korea was the key to his selection over the combat-inexperienced Gruenther. "It was this combat experience and skill," Michener said, "which... made him the choice over the brilliant General Gruenther (who has had no combat commands) to head NATO forces in Europe."[29] One of the imponderables of the situation was Truman's evaluation of Soviet intentions in Europe, based upon secret intelligence reports available to him at that time.

Some light, however, so far as daily journalism is enlightening, was thrown on the subject by the *Washington Star*'s regular Pentagon representative, John Giles. He wrote that the choice was made as the result of a contest in which two five-star generals backed two four-star generals. Giles said the chairman of the Joint Chiefs of Staff, Gen. Omar Bradley, Ridgway's wartime boss in Europe, was for Ridgway; Eisenhower was for Gruenther. According to Giles, "President Truman backed Bradley."[30] At that time the 1952 presidential campaign was getting under way, and GOP spokesmen were critical of Bradley and ammunition shortages in Korea. Eisenhower was virtually in the presidential race. How much these factors affected the choice is a matter of speculation.

Giles noted that an informal Associated Press poll of representatives of NATO countries who had contact with or close knowledge of Gruenther during his service as chief-of-staff at SHAPE strongly preferred General Gruenther. His article added that "just before the Presidential announcement [of Ridgway's appointment] word came out of Paris that NATO would accept General Ridgway on condition that General Gruenther remain as Chief of Staff."[31]

In summary, there is no doubt that Ridgway had not the same freedom of choice with respect to his chief-of-staff that Eisenhower had had originally, or that Gruenther exercised in July 1953 when he personally selected. Gen. Courtlandt van R. Schuyler as his chief-of-staff.[32]

These various factors—the difficulty of succeeding so popular a wartime and postwar hero as Eisenhower, the apparent contest between Bradley (whose influence with Truman was rising) and Eisenhower to select the new supreme commander, the lack of free choice in the matter of chief-of-staff, and the fact that the selection of Ridgway seemed to many Europeans to indicate the imminence of war—gave point to the comment already quoted that Ridgway was "off to a less favorable start than Eisenhower had at the outset."[33]

Another factor, largely psychological, which may have had some effect was the picture of Ridgway in paratrooper's uniform and steel helmet with two hand grenades hooked to the harness of his parachute. While probably intended to remind Frenchmen and others that this was the man who had personally dropped into Ste. Mere Eglise with the first waves of liberation in 1944 as commanding general of the Eighty-second Airborne Division, the photograph was used widely by the Communists to support their propaganda that Ridgway was a "warmaker."[34] The American public had been regaled a few months previously by the anonymous author of the "After Hours" department in *Harper's Magazine*, who wrote: "General Ridgway's grenade is, of course, his trade-mark. It is a remarkably effective one, since no one has ever thought of it before."[35]

Perhaps the Frenchman who talked with David Schoenbrun, Columbia Broadcasting System correspondent in Paris, best expressed the French feeling at the time. "The fighting paratrooper who wears hand grenades is the sort of man we want to lead our troops to victory. But we're not thinking about victory right now. We in Europe are thinking about peace."[36] The Frenchman's reference was obviously to the paratrooper photograph of Ridgway, grenade and all, which had been given worldwide circulation. This photograph, enlarged and framed, hung in a number of offices at SHAPE, and a color version also hung in the office of the SHAPE Liaison Office in the Pentagon. There can be little doubt that it was the general's preferred likeness.

But whatever the divergencies of opinion as to the validity of the choice of Ridgway that may have existed between American and Western European leaders, there is no doubt that his arrival in Paris was to be the signal for a Communist propaganda effort of major proportions. They were ready to pin on him the label of "*germ assassine*," "American monster," and to paint on the retaining walls of the Seine or blank walls elsewhere the slogans "U.S. Go Home" and "Ridgway—*A La Porte!*"[37]

He seems to have anticipated that such charges would be leveled at him, because before leaving the United States he told a joint session of Congress: "I am constrained... to refer again to the officially propagated allegations of Communist leaders that the United Nations Command in Korea has employed both germ and gas warfare. I wish to reiterate what I have repeatedly stated publicly, that these allegations are false in their entirety.... In the whole black record of false propaganda, these charges would stand out as a monumental warning to the American people and the free world."[38]

Ridgway arrived in Paris on 27 May 1952. On the day before his arrival, the Contractual Agreement ending the occupation of the Federal Republic of Germany had been signed at Bonn by the United States, Britain, and France.[39] Despite police vigilance, there were street riots in Paris and in other French communities the next day. Hundreds of Communists were taken into custody, including the redoubtable Jacques Duclos, acting secretary of the French Communist party and member of the French National Assembly. Guns were found in his car, but because he had taken the precaution to carry also two dead pigeons in the back of his automobile, he was able to explain that he had been hunting.[40]

The anti-Ridgway demonstration was labeled a blunder by

the late acute American observer of European affairs, Theodore H. White, who had spent five years (1948-53) as a correspondent on the European scene for *Time* and *The Reporter* magazines. "The most remarkable demonstration of political stupidity by French Communists," he wrote, "was the mechanically successful riot to protest the arrival of General Ridgway.... The stupidity of the Communists, from a political-insurrectionary point of view lay in the choice and timing of their issues. On the very day of the riots the EDC treaties were signed at the Quai d'Orsay.... Given the remembered cruelty of yesterday's [German] occupation, uncountable numbers of Frenchmen would have backed the Communists in bloody protest... but the discipline of international Communism deprived French Communists of this explosive opportunity" by making Ridgway the focus of their protests instead.[41]

Ridgway himself had been well aware all along of the type of greeting he would get from the Communists. In San Francisco two weeks earlier, *en route* to his new assignment, he told a reporter that "the same forces awaited him in Europe as those he had met in Korea," and said, "It is all a struggle against the same vicious forces."[42]

Generally, however, the French press and public took a wait-and-see attitude toward the new supreme commander. That the Communist outburst mortified many patriotic Frenchmen who saw in Ridgway an able and proper successor to Eisenhower was shown symbolically several months later when two French craftsmen, Messrs. Roger and Sire, designed and presented to Ridgway a medal "in protest to the Communist insults against him." One side of the medal was a seal of the city of Paris; on the obverse was the eagle insignia of an army officer's cap with a large "R" for Ridgway surmounting it and the smaller initials "R" and "S" for the donors, with the notation "9-10-52," the date on which the presentation was made, 9 October 1952. At that time the artisans explained that they felt they represented the feelings of many Frenchmen that only through Allied unity could their country be made safe. Both were veterans of both world wars.

Thus it was that the antagonism which had been on a military basis between the general and the Communists in Korea asserted itself early on a propaganda basis in France and later in Italy and Britain.

The "Yankees—Go Home" campaign, which had made little headway during the Eisenhower era, thus had a violent rebirth. Various incidents were reported. In one instance, two death's-head stickers with the slogan "Americans—Go Home" were stuck to an American's automobile windshield while his car was parked outside his home overnight. Other American servicemen reported their tires deflated or slashed, presumably by Communists or Communist sympathizers. One foggy morning, all highway signs on the Autoroute de l'Ouest indicating the direction to SHAPE were blotted out with red paint. Not only the Communists but the neutralists as well feared that the very presence in France of Ridgway, fresh from a combat command, implied the imminence of war. Col. Bruce Bidwell, U. S. Army, who was at that time military attaché at The Hague, related that such fears were expressed to him by Dutch officials at the time of Ridgway's first visit to The Hague in mid-summer 1952.[43]

Extra police were assigned to places likely to be visited by Ridgway in Paris, exceptional vigilance was exerted at SHAPE and at his official residence at nearby Marnes la Coquette. At the latter, which was an old chateau placed at the supreme commander's disposal by the French government, members of the French Sûreté Nationale, American GI's, and American plainclothes counterintelligence personnel kept watch night and day. While crank letters were received occasionally at headquarters, some of them couched in threatening language, no untoward actions were ever reported.[44]

These were the circumstances and this was the atmosphere in which the new SACEUR assumed his task. There was still another factor, which a Kansas City editorialist put succinctly: in replacing Eisenhower as supreme commander, Ridgway would find that the main organizational problems involved in Western European defense had been worked out already. It was thus a case of getting the Allies to deliver what they had pledged in the way of trained divisions and of obtaining the armaments needed for the defensive forces. Furthermore, "Seeing that a contribution by Germany is transferred from idea to fact will be a major task for General Ridgway."[45]

In the words of one of Ridgway's close personal aides: "The honeymoon was over. His job was to collect on the promises that had been made to Ike."[46] More formally, the same idea was expressed by Don Cook of the Paris office of the *New York Herald Tribune*. Cook wrote in retrospect: "When General Eisenhower came here in the fear-ridden uncertain days of early 1951, the main problem was one of faith and spirit.... spirit was more important than divisions because there were no divisions to speak of.... From this base General Ridgway took over—a soldier determined to do a soldier's job."[47]

The eyes of Europe, as well as of his staff, thus were upon Ridgway as he assumed his new command. They felt the same as James Michener, who wrote in his magazine analysis of the new supreme commander's career, "It remains to be seen how well the general will adjust to an atmosphere in which the grenade clasped to the right breast will be of little efficacy in allaying national jealousies in Western Europe or in winning points from tough-minded Prime Ministers."[48]

Ridgway's first official tasks were a combination of getting acclimated by means of staff conferences and making appropriate visits to the authorities of France, Italy, and Britain to lay the groundwork for completing the NATO command structure. Virtually the first five weeks after his arrival were devoted to these purposes. The significance of his talks with chiefs of state and defense ministers was that Paris, Rome, and London held the keys to the three major command problems still unsolved. They were the problems of the Central Command, which had been makeshift from the beginning; of the Southern Command, which would have to be expanded to cover Greece and Turkish forces newly added to the Alliance; and of the Mediterranean Command, which would have to be established because of historic British naval predominance in the area.

In the Central Area, which included France, Benelux, and

Western Germany, the very heart of the European defense line, Marshal Juin, the seven-star French Marshal who outranked Ridgway, was at that time commander, Allied Land Forces Central Europe, with headquarters at Fontainebleau. He often voiced close to anti-American sentiments, and, as recounted in the following chapter, in 1954 some of his strictures against EDC resulted in his being stripped of certain command functions of a purely national nature by the French government. In October 1952, when a question arose in the United Nations as to the rights of sovereignty of the Arabs of Tunisia and Morocco and it looked for a time as though the United States would back the Arabs, Juin said: "There was nothing to get excited about so long as our opponents were the Arab bloc... and the U.S.S.R.... but today we are seriously threatened with the possibility of seeing the United States join this group.... This fact is very grave for it wounds us sentimentally and strikes at our idea of what should be the international solidarity to which we have already made such heavy contributions."[49]

Juin virtually refused to be served by an American public relations officer, Lt. Col. Alexander Smith, U.S. Army, who had been assigned to that duty. Lt. Col. Smith commented that "the old man [Marshal Juin] will have nothing to do with me; he does not believe in public relations as we understand it." At the unified headquarters at Fontainebleau, the Marshal operated as the coequal of Gen. Lauris Norstad, U.S. Air Force, commander, Allied Forces Central Europe, and of Vice Adm. Robert Jaujard, French navy, who held the title of flag officer, Central Europe, and whose command consisted largely of small gunboats on the Rhine and port facilities in France, the Netherlands, and Belgium. From the beginning of the Eisenhower era and until the problem was finally resolved just before Ridgway left SHAPE in July 1953, Juin desired to be commander-in-chief over all land, naval, and air forces in Central Europe. This position would have placed him on the same command echelon as British Adm. Sir Patrick Brind, commander-in-chief, Allied Forces Northern Europe, and American Adm. Robert Carney, commander-in-chief, Allied Forces Southern Europe. Earlier, Juin had been placated by Eisenhower, who had insisted throughout his tenure on retaining overall command of the Central Area himself.[50]

Juin's ambition had the backing of French officials and the French public generally because of France's past historic role as a military power on the continent. The solution of the problem is stated by Lord Ismay in the following terms:

> In July 1953... it was decided that the Central Command should have its own Commander-in-Chief, as was the case in the North and in the South. Marshal Juin assumed the title and responsibilities of Commander-in-Chief Allied Forces Central Europe, and a French Land Forces Commander was appointed to be directly subordinate to him. His Command includes the Northern Army Group, consisting of Belgian, Canadian, Netherlands and United Kingdom Forces, and the Central Army Group, consisting of French and United States Forces.... Vice Admiral Jaujard remained as Commander Allied Naval Forces Central Europe.... General Norstad moved to SHAPE as Air Deputy... and was himself replaced by Air Chief Marshal Sir Basil Embry, RAF, as Commander Allied Air Forces Central Europe.[51]

The reshuffling of this command resulted, as will be seen later, in new emphasis on air power. Norstad was brought to SHAPE as air deputy (where he replaced Air Chief Marshal Sir Harold Saunders, RAF) largely because it was necessary to have in this vital top staff position an American who was privy to American atomic developments and who had authority to request, through the supreme commander, the employment of the U.S. Strategic Air Command.

The problem in Italy involved the Southern Command and centered on the rather illogical situation of having Greek and Turkish forces, nearly a thousand miles away in Macedonia and Thrace, under command of an Italian general with headquarters in northern Italy, who in turn reported to an American admiral (Carney) in the latter's capacity as commander-in-chief, Allied Forces Southern Europe. This situation had resulted from the integration of Greece and Turkey into NATO. The problem and its solution were as follows:

> In February 1952, Greece and Turkey became signatories to the North Atlantic Treaty, thus extending the southern defense area of NATO some 1500 miles and necessitating the combining of the SHAPE forces in Italy with those of Greece and Turkey under the over-all command of the Commander-in-chief Allied Forces Southern Europe.... They added to the forces of SACEUR more than 25 army divisions backed by relatively small but efficient air and sea forces. The addition of these forces necessitated the setting up of a new subcommand, Allied Land Forces Southeastern Europe, under Lieutenant General Willard G. Wyman, U.S. Army at Izmir, Turkey.[52]

A subordinate command post was later established at Salonika, Greece. In the course of setting up this subordinate command and of integrating the Greek and Turkish forces into the SHAPE command, Ridgway made several trips to Greece and Turkey, as well as to Rome. On one of these trips, he brought together Greek and Turkish military leaders at a border town between the two countries. They shook hands "for the first time in history as old enmities and grudges were forgotten,"[53] and henceforth came to be regarded as the southeastern anchor of the European defense line, more of which will be said in the chapters which follow.

The problem that had to be discussed in London and solved months later also involved the Southern Area, but more specifically, the distribution of Allied naval forces in the sector. Just as the prestige of France was involved in the problem of the Central Command, cited earlier, so that of Britain, long "mistress of the seas," was involved in the Mediterranean, where up to now Carney and the powerful United States Sixth Fleet had been virtually the only existing naval strength. The British felt that because the Mediterranean was the "lifeline of the Empire," one of their nationals should head a command (taking in the whole Middle East area) coequal with SHAPE and with the Supreme Allied Command Atlantic (SACLANT), which had been created earlier in 1952 with Adm. Lynde D. McCormick,

U.S. Navy, in command, with headquarters at Norfolk, Virginia.[54]

It was intended to incorporate into the proposed new command all Mediterranean units of other Allied navies, excepting American. The solution to this problem, probably the most thorny with which Ridgway and high-level American and British diplomats had to deal, came in December 1952 at a meeting of the foreign and defense ministers of all the NATO nations, the ministerial meeting of the North Atlantic Council in Paris. The announcement stated simply, "The council approved proposals from the Military Committee for the establishment of a Mediterranean Command, so completing the European command structure for the defense of the North Atlantic area. Admiral Lord Mountbatten has been appointed."[55]

The command structure and responsibilities were more fully described by Ismay in these words:

At the end of 1952, it was decided that a further subordinate command should be set up under SACEUR with the title "Allied Forces Mediterranean" and with headquarters at Malta. The first Commander-in-Chief was Admiral the Earl Mountbatten of Burma (UK), and his headquarters came into being in March 1953. Later that year the various national forces under his control were organized into six separate areas, each commanded by an Admiral: one French, one Greek, one Turkish, one Italian and two British. In time of war, Admiral Mountbatten would be responsible for the security of the line of communications through the Mediterranean.[56]

These simple declarations gave no inkling of the amount of talk and compromise which had brought about the new arrangement. It had been the subject of conferences between President Truman and Prime Minister Churchill; between the then-American chief of naval operations, Adm. William M. Fechteler, and Ridgway; between Britain's defense minister, Lord Alexander, and the United States secretary of defense, Robert A. Lovett. Mountbatten and Carney had discussed it between themselves, and when both of them appeared before a press conference at the Palais de Chaillot after the December announcement, they agreed to cooperate.[57]

Later, joint exercises were held between naval forces of the Southern and Mediterranean commands, and as disappointments on both sides wore away there was evidence of genuine teamwork. This became especially noticeable after the original principals had been replaced—Carney by Fechteler in July 1953 and Mountbatten by Adm. Sir Guy Grantham in 1954.

The compromise reached involved British acceptance of the necessity of making the new command subordinate to, not coequal with, SHAPE and American willingness to share naval responsibilities in an area where existing naval power was overwhelmingly an American contribution (both by way of the Sixth Fleet and through naval vessels loaned or given to France, Italy, Greece, and Turkey). The British, who had themselves also experienced hostilities in the Mediterranean during World War II, could not be brought to place the same confidence in carrier task forces as the Americans had done as the result of successful experience during the same war in both the Atlantic and the Pacific.[58]

Since the French situation, with respect to both the Central Command and the outbreak of anti-American sentiment, was nearest at hand and in need of the most immediate attention, Ridgway paid his formal respects to President Auriol at the Elysée Palace on 4 June 1952 and, as mentioned earlier, two days later went to the celebration of the liberation landings of Ste. Mere Eglise, a half-mile from the spot where he had parachuted into France eight years before. He was publicized as "the first American general to touch the soil of France in the invasion."[59] There, he made a stirring speech in the rain, in which he said: "Let no one underestimate our resolve to live as free men.... Above all let no one mistake our patience, our tolerance, our constant quest for peaceful solutions as evidence of fear."[60] He was roundly cheered and applauded, and the town's mayor, M. Philippe, told him, "You are, and always will be, our friend. We wish you God's fortune in your great task as successor to Eisenhower, and above all, we pray for the peace of the world."[61]

He also called on Defense Minister René Pleven, who had recently been to the United States and who was an enthusiastic supporter of NATO, of the new EDC proposal, and of the part the United States was playing in the buildup of Western European strength, both military and economic. Pleven spoke English well, which Auriol did not. To Ridgway, who never made a pretense of learning French, this was a boon. The general and the French defense minister got along famously.[62]

The supreme commander's relations with Field Marshal Montgomery, his deputy, while outwardly pleasant, never became the plainly intimate association that Eisenhower had enjoyed with the testy Briton. During World War II Montgomery had served under Eisenhower; and Ridgway, for a time, had served under Montgomery. Furthermore, Montgomery was the commander of the Western Union military organization under the Brussels Pact which preceded NATO, and he never hesitated to outline his independent views on strategy.[63] In speeches he proposed a radical reorganization of the entire NATO structure.[64] He conducted command exercises (SHAPEX) in dramatic fashion, once appearing in the uniform of a Russian marshal (a gift made to him by a Soviet marshal at the close of World War II), so that he could better illustrate the enemy's thinking in a critique of military problems under study. He sometimes gave the staff a fatherly scolding. On one occasion he told the assembled officers that too many papers were being submitted to top-level officers, thus leaving them no time to think, while subordinate officers, who should have had plenty of time for thinking, spent most of it in writing.[65]

Montgomery's ideas, however, were so fundamental that they drew wide attention. For instance, a speech he made before the National Press Club in Washington in the spring of 1951 so impressed then-Secretary of the Navy Francis P. Matthews that he ordered copies mimeographed for distribution to ranking admirals. The subject was discipline, and the secretary had recently been involved in what was then termed the "Admirals' Revolt," a series of incidents connected with the rival claims of the navy's carrier air arm and the air force on air power. On another occasion, in 1954, a speech made by the field marshal drew a heated retort from Assistant Secretary of the Navy for Air James H. Smith, Jr.[66] But firebrand that he was on occasion, Montgomery was regarded by his SHAPE comrades as an able and loyal soldier. He was proud of the development which he had witnessed from SHAPE's earliest days and publicly proclaimed his readiness to play a humble part as long as he could. In May 1953 he told a large London audience: "Very great progress has been made since the early days of 1951 and our efficiency is increasing steadily. I myself am proud to serve under General Ridgway and to help him in his task as best I can."[67]

There was another, and final, command relationship that was settled during Ridgway's regime. This involved the American army, navy, and air force units and the military personnel of other American agencies in Europe. Before settlement of this problem, the U.S. Army, Navy, and Air Force had each had its own headquarters at Heidelberg, Germany; London, England; and Wiesbaden, Germany, respectively. In addition to this, U.S. forces in Austria and in Trieste maintained separate headquarters. Sometime late in 1951, Secretary of Defense Lovett sought a solution to this problem of integration and asked that Eisenhower become commander-in-chief, U.S. European Command (CINCEUR).

Eisenhower, because of the international character of his position as SACEUR, appointed an ad hoc committee in February 1952 to study the feasibility of establishing the unified American command. This committee was composed of army, navy, and air force representatives. It did not report until after Eisenhower had returned to the United States, and thus it was that Ridgway was the first to be both an international and an American commander at the same time. Before accepting the appointment as CINCEUR, Ridgway discussed the matter with Gen. Thomas T. Handy, who was at that time commanding United States Army forces in Europe. He subsequently appointed Handy as deputy commander, United States Forces Europe, and assigned to him most of the responsibility for administering the new unified American command. On 1 August 1952 headquarters, United States European Command, was established in Frankfurt, Germany. Subordinate to it were army, navy, and air force units in Europe, including Austria and Trieste, as well as military personnel assigned to the United States Military Representative for Military Assistance, the Joint Military Advisory Group Europe, and the Joint United States Construction Agency.[68]

Surveying the situation with satisfaction when it came time for him to make his report to the Standing Group of the Military Representatives Committee, Ridgway was able to say, "There now exists a command structure to control our initial forces along a 4000-mile front extending from Northern Norway to the Caucasus."[69] He added: "Now, in May 1953, the NATO nations, which were almost defenseless in 1950 can be justifiably proud in looking at their increased strength. They can be buoyed up by their accomplishment, not weighed down by their fears. The result should be an improvement in the morale of their peoples."[70]

In a different political context, Ridgway's sponsor for the position of SACEUR, General Bradley, had by mid-1953 and the advent of Eisenhower to the presidency, come to have second thoughts.

Who then would replace Collins as Army Chief of Staff (a matter dear to both Ike and me)? We had many outstanding possibilities, high among them Ridgway. Ridgway was not proving to be the ideal choice for NATO. Matt was a field commander without peer but not a diplomat. Since taking over SHAPE, he had been putting relentless pressure on our allies to do their part with more alacrity and enthusiasm. Some of this pressure was needed—indeed had been endorsed by the NATO Council—but in his zeal, Ridgway had antagonized many politicians among our allies.

Ike, all along, had wanted Al Gruenther to succeed him at SHAPE. Now the opportunity arose to kill three birds with one stone. With his prestige, background and energy, Ridgway would be an inspiring Army Chief of Staff. If he got overzealous, as he tended to, Ike would be right there to restrain him. It would remove a burr from SHAPE and make room for Gruenther. So it was decided.[71]

Obviously, although NATO had acquired a political arm composed of civilians working under the guidance of a secretary-general and of a Council in Permanent Session composed of permanent representatives, the chief military office in the Alliance could not be considered nonpolitical. Questions of national and multinational strategy, national and multinational force levels, national and multinational budget-making were essentially political and not military issues. In sum, a planner who had not necessarily been a combat commander was deemed as well suited if not better suited for the position.

3. Gruenther

Attempts to Retain NATO Solidarity

ROBERT S. JORDAN

Gen. Alfred M. Gruenther's succession to Gen. Ridgway as SACEUR was not unexpected. As discussed in chapter 2, strong indications were already evident that Eisenhower had really favored Gruenther over Ridgway when the latter was appointed. With Eisenhower in the presidency, the appointment of Gruenther seemed a foregone conclusion.

In fact, the personal friendship between the two men transcended the professional relationship, which gave Gruenther, as SACEUR, access to the White House on a more-or-less constant basis that Ridgway could never have achieved even if he had wanted it. A common, strong interest in contract bridge was one basis for the continuing friendship, although Gruenther not only had served Eisenhower as his chief-of-staff at SHAPE, but also earlier had been instrumental in planning some of the major campaigns of World War II.

As Eisenhower's chief-of-staff while Eisenhower was mobilizing enthusiasm and confidence throughout Western Europe, Grunther led the team that was created to put together a credible military structure. Col. Robert J. Wood, secretary of the SHAPE staff, pointed out that "The initial tasks faced by SHAPE were to organize itself while concurrently working out the nature and the organization of the command as a whole. To arrange for the transition of the previous planning groups into command headquarters and also to grasp and push forward certain operational problems of urgent importance, of which the development of 'infrastructure,'... is perhaps the foremost example."[1]

Although Ridgway was nominated in response to a perceived requirement that Eisenhower's successor be a general with field command experience, it was specified at the time that Gruenther would remain as chief-of-staff.[2] Then, with his own appointment as SACEUR, speculation arose that thereafter Gruenther would go on to succeed Ridgway as army chief-of-staff or even become chairman of the Joint Chiefs of Staff. As will be shown later in this chapter, neither event was to transpire. But his very close association with Eisenhower, which could not be duplicated by Ridgway, persisted.

For example, in June 1952 after leaving NATO, Eisenhower wrote a personal letter of appreciation and encouragement to Gruenther.

> I thought some of sending an official letter to the Department of the Army in order that there might be an official record of the brilliant way that you served the country during the past one and one half years. I still may do this—for the benefit of coming generations—but so far as the present is concerned, such action would smack a little bit of effrontry. Your reputation is too well established both in and out of Army circles for any opinion of mine to be affecting it materially. My sense of obligation to you will never diminish.... I suppose that I have taken up a lot of time to tell you the one real message I have for you—I miss you both [he includes Gruenther's wife, Grace].... Take care of yourself and keep your boss working on the idea of European unification.[3]

Interestingly, in this letter Eisenhower also offered some gratuitous comments on his own successor, which appeared to register less than complete confidence. "I do hope that [Ridgway] quickly establishes such relations with all the Governments as will enable him to visit with any of the Ministers freely and frequently. No matter what the particular subject of discussion, he will, I hope, never forget that every sentence, every thought should be directed toward the one great and ultimate purpose of producing political and economic unification of

Europe. I know that you personally will devote yourself to the ideal and your standing with all the NATO countries is such that your influence will be tremendous. But he must help.[4]"

Later, when appointed SACEUR, in a personal, handwritten letter to Eisenhower Gruenther registered his appreciation: "You are always sticking your neck out when it comes to the Gruenther Guy, and your latest gamble is your most risky one. I sincerely pray that it will not turn out to be one of your mistakes. Naturally I am deeply touched over your faith in me and most grateful for giving me the chance."[5]

Maj. Gen. Howard Snyder, who was Eisenhower's physician at the White House, once observed, "They are what a doctor would call 'symbiotic,' like sight and hearing, or taste and smell—they operate better together than they do separately."[6]

When Gruenther was given the SACEUR assignment, he was the youngest four-star general in the army, truly a distinction given the fact that, as pointed out, he had never held a major command in his career, having served either as chief-of-staff or as deputy to famous and successful commanders. He was known as an officer who could assimilate and organize masses of information, converting the whole into coherent operational plans. He had done this for Eisenhower for Operation Torch in World War II and for Gen. Mark Clark for the Italian invasion. He had served as director of the Joint Staff of the Joint Chiefs of Staff and then as deputy chief-of-staff of the army for Plans and Combat Operations—the number three position in the hierarchy.

In this capacity he had briefed Eisenhower regularly when Eisenhower was president of Columbia University. In 1949, when he returned to the Pentagon on special duty, Eisenhower found that "everybody was turning to Al, and he would give the place, time and figures out of his head. It was almost a case of working a good horse to death."[7]

A capsule description of Gruenther's activities when he and Eisenhower were together at SHAPE was provided in an article about Gruenther that appeared in *U.S. News and World Re-*

port: "At SHAPE headquarters, outside Paris, the two generals occupy adjoining offices, with the door usually open. Their living quarters are also adjacent and there is much dropping in of an evening, often for bridge.... [He] lives a regular and abstemious, if hard-working life. He is fussy about his health, makes sure of regular exercise each morning, eats sparingly, does not smoke, seldom touches a cocktail. He enjoys tennis, but his working hours are such that there is little time for that."[8]

In the opinion of close observers at SHAPE, including George Pelletier, author of the Ridgway chapter in this book, Gruenther was seen as the personification of the "joiner-greeter" American type on a high level. Dynamic, ubiquitous, a small jumping jack of a man, he took pride in his Nebraska origins. The sense of informality—he could talk easily for five minutes or two hours as the occasion required—which Gruenther inspired in the staff was in large measure responsible for the unusual harmony with which SHAPE officers carried on their tasks. He had what one observer described as a quality of "authoritative easiness" which made him especially effective in dealing with groups of all kinds. Gruenther was easily SHAPE's favorite among the "big brass" of his time.

He was famous for sending little notes, called "Grunnions," that dealt with details to be looked into. He was also known on occasion to "Gruentherize," which meant to query someone intensely in order to refine a question or situation to its essence, or to send "Gruenther-grams"—similar to Grunnions.[9] As an illustration of the pervasiveness of these messages, even persons no longer under Gruenther's control continued to refer to them, as did, for example, Gen. J. Lawton Collins in a letter to Gruenther written from Saigon. "Your good letter... was much appreciated. I had begun to wonder whether I was on your black list since I'd received no Gruenther-grams in the preceding six weeks."[10]

This careful attention to detail in order to understand the problem to be addressed and then to provide through careful planning the means to achieve the operational solution was what was needed in founding SHAPE. By 1953 it was considered to be sufficiently in place that Gruenther could now go on to perform the more diplomatic, public relations–oriented activities that are such an important part of a multinational commander's responsibilities. One of his most important and most political continuing responsibilities was to maintain the agreed-upon national force levels.

After the first Soviet atomic explosion in August 1949, President Truman set up a high-level interdepartmental committee to undertake a broad reassessment of American military policy. The ensuing document, NSC-68, recommended a major expansion of both general-war and limited-war capabilities and the strengthening of America's allies in Europe. The anticipated date for a major Soviet attack was put as most probable by 1954, and although this document was never officially adopted, after the Korean crisis in June 1950 it became the policy basis for American rearmament and indirectly for the creation of SHAPE and the buildup of American military strength in Europe. Finally, and most important, all of this provided the impetus for American pressure to proceed immediately with West German rearmament.[11]

In fact, as previously mentioned, from the very beginning of NATO, it was assumed in American military planning circles that a German contribution would be needed for the defense of Europe.[12] NATO supported this view officially when, at the Council meeting of foreign ministers of 26 September 1950, they declared that "Germany should be enabled to contribute to the buildup of the defense of Western Europe." The United States had the nuclear capacity to provide the "sword" if needed, in the form of "massive retaliation": what was needed was the "shield" in order that the retaliation would be a last resort.

Thus, by the time Eisenhower had become SACEUR, it was already policy that there should be a rapid buildup of conventional forces in Europe, to include those of West Germany as well as the United States. But as stated in chapter 1, he maintained both privately and publicly that the American forces were to be there only until the European members of NATO were able to provide for their own conventional defense, when American forces could then be reduced.[13]

After becoming president, however, Eisenhower backed away somewhat from a categorical commitment for the eventual withdrawal of U.S. troops. In a long letter to Gruenther in October 1953, reacting to press reports that the administration was contemplating sharp troop reductions in Europe, Eisenhower said:

> From the very beginning, some of our troop dispositions were visualized as temporary or emergency measures. I think none of us has ever believed for an instant that the United States could, over the long term (several decades), build a sort of Roman Wall with its own troops and so protect the world.... Our people would become restive under any idea that we would have to keep our own troops stationed abroad indefinitely.... in all honesty, we cannot allow anyone to get up and protest that we are going to keep troops in Europe *forever*. [His emphasis].[14]

One reason he was making this point to Gruenther was that within the administration itself suggestions had been made that the purpose of the Eisenhower administration's so-called New Look was indeed to make possible reductions in conventional forces, saving both money and political capital at home and with the Allies. Eisenhower told Gruenther explicitly that "the considerations I have outlined are not dependent upon the advent or effectiveness of " 'new' weapons."[15]

Following Eisenhower's earlier lead, Gruenther specifically linked the anticipated West German contribution of conventional forces with the use of atomic weapons as the dual cornerstones of NATO's credible deterrent in Europe. For example, in a statement given in March 1955 to the Senate Foreign Relations Committee, he said: "We state then that we will be able to defend Europe when we have two conditions, an effective German contribution and the ability to use atomic weapons.... Last September we presented a study concerning this question to the North Atlantic Council through the Standing Group. The NATO nations met in Paris and took a very momentous decision. *They said that we should make plans on the basis that atomic weapons would be used."* (Emphasis added.)[16]

But the problem for Gruenther, when he became SACEUR in 1953, was that in both Europe and the United States there was domestic political resistance to the buildup of conventional forces; instead, the tendency was to rely on atomic weapons—a major emphasis or "new look"—to compensate for the weakness on the ground. And the delay in bringing about West German rearmament for NATO purposes only exacerbated the issue for Gruenther.

Consequently, the early strategic imbalance between deterrence and defense, discussed by Gen. Rogers in his foreword to this book, had to be gradually redressed by an increasingly defensive emphasis. Gruenther openly appealed for European support when he estimated that the shield, consisting of "highly trained covering land forces," should provide a "cushion of time" following the failure of deterrence, to allow the mobilization of reserves that would be "brought into action immediately after the outbreak of hostilities." "Hard-hitting air forces" would provide tactical support and Allied long-range air forces would conduct powerful retaliatory attacks deep into enemy territory against industrial and other vital targets.[17]

In a speech to the English-Speaking Union in London in June 1954, Gruenther summed it up thus, thereby also extending the period of maximum danger to NATO from the Soviet Union from 1954 to 1957:

We are working on a philosophy to have a force in being that is the smallest possible, and to depend on reserve forces. That shield must be able to hold long enough for those reserves to mobilize. We feel it will not hold that long unless we have atomic power to support it.

In our thinking, [if war should take place three years from now] we visualize the use of atomic bombs in the support of our ground troops. We also visualize the use of atomic bombs on targets in enemy territory.[18]

In fact, beginning in 1954 a series of plans appeared which substantially cut Allied conventional force requirements and provided instead for tactical nuclear weapons. Under NATO force planning document MC-48, although the requirement for standing forces in NATO remained approximately the same as had been committed under the Lisbon force goals, the reserves and back-up forces were greatly reduced. This was in keeping with the NATO ministerial meeting of December 1953, which had favored a "long haul" in meeting the Lisbon goals, thus disregarding the earlier target year of 1954. The tactical use of atomic weapons as a supplement was implied in the Council's declaration that "special attention should be given to the continuing provision of modern weapons of the latest types to support the NATO defense system."[19] Thus, the reduced reserves were to be replaced by low-yield battlefield atomic weapons under American peacetime custody and control. The final actions in this regard, during Gruenther's tenure, came in December 1955 when the Council decided to equip NATO forces with atomic weapons and then in 1956 when the Council directed him to reappraise the forces needed for the defense of the NATO area.

In summary, during his tenure Gruenther had to preside over the sharp reappraisal and consequent rearrangement of Eisenhower's initial priorities concerning both the duration of the American buildup of forces in Western Europe and the nature of the arms needed to block a Soviet invasion, if such were to occur. In this respect, although he operated with considerably more grace and finesse than did his predecessor, Ridgway, Gruenther had no better luck in stirring up the Allies to greater efforts at defending themselves conventionally. At the same time, he had to witness and be constructively responsive to the contorted negotiations over EDC that delayed the introduction of West German forces. He had, of course, a loyal and effective colleague in Lord Ismay, the NATO secretary-general who, for his part, had to contend with the political disruptions in the Alliance caused by the Hungarian and Suez crises of 1956, as well as the demise of EDC.[20]

As to the prospects for French approval of the EDC Treaty, Gruenther remained optimistic until the very end. He wrote to Eisenhower in December 1953, after a contentious Dulles press conference: "In spite of the first flare ups of the Dulles press conference I believe that the effect has given our side a definite plus. Of course the problem is a difficult one. No one in a responsible position has ever said that it is easy. But the alternatives are much more impossible than EDC.... I am absolutely certain that EDC can be sold to the people—and with relative ease."[21] He went on to observe that two classes, parliamentarians and retired generals, were the most difficult. "The parliamentarians are a very tough nut to crack—and they form a critically important group. They are badly divided."[22]

The dilemma faced by the SACEUR during this period of NATO's history was that the area which was presumed to be the main battlefield in the event deterrence failed was the least defensible. An eastern or forward strategy left no room for a defense-in-depth strategy that relied on reinforcement and recapture of territories as the official doctrine. Instead, the positioning of forces at the inter-German border, which would be the consequence of the effort to integrate West German forces into the NATO command structure, through either EDC or some other arrangement, would leave the SACEUR with little room to maneuver, either politically or militarily. Thus, deterrence—the effort to dissuade the Soviet Union from going to war in the first place in Central Europe—was a policy of necessity as well as of choice. It followed that since the circumstances on the ground were largely predetermined, reliance on America's atomic capacity to strike at the Soviet heartland, using bases in Western Europe (qualifying as strategic) as well as in the continental United States, almost inevitably became the official NATO doctrine by the end of Gruenther's tenure.

Therefore, Gruenther, in fulfilling his responsibilities, was literally forced to plead with his European Allies to increase *their* spending for conventional forces, extending *their* conscription periods, upgrading *their* reserves, reequipping and resupplying *their* existing forces, etc., in the face of a reluctance on the part of the Alliance's major partner to do the same. Gruenther admitted candidly in 1954, "We feel that as of now we still do not have enough to meet an all-out act of Soviet aggression successfully, and that is why we have asked our political superiors, the North Atlantic Council, to furnish more troops."[23] His chances of obtaining these troops without a West German contribution were, however, slim indeed. Gruenther realized this, which is why he considered that without the German contribution NATO's capacity to deter or to counter successfully an act of aggression was doubtful. He also recognized that during his tenure achievement of a truly effective ground and air tactical defense was unlikely. As he put it at the time of the French debate over EDC:

It will take, from the time of decision, approximately 2 years until we have German ground forces, and approximately 3 years until we have German tactical air forces. So we are actually moving our planning cycle ahead for a period about 3 years hence. And we say that, as of that time, if we do have that German contribution and if we are able to use atomic bombs against an act of aggression, if it should take place, we will have a reasonably good chance of defending Europe successfully against an all-out act of Soviet aggression. *Those two conditions, however, must be met.* [Emphasis added.][24]

Without a doubt, Gruenther must have been frustrated because bringing German troops in to supplement the defense of Western Europe had already been under consideration for seven years and, as already noted, he had been intimately involved during most of the period either in Washington or at SHAPE in military force planning activities. This point is underscored with Gruenther's admission that even with German troops," we are not going to be able to match the Soviets in the field of conventional troops and conventional armament."[25]

It is interesting, however, to compare Gruenther's statements in 1954 with those he had made a year earlier, when apparently the prospects of a German contribution were greater, and perhaps the propaganda of the Soviet Union against atomic weapons was not so intense. Earlier, he had assured an audience "that today, October 8, 1953, the NATO forces of Allied Command, Europe are of such a strength that the Soviets today probably do not have sufficient power in

Occupied Europe to launch an attack with any reasonable certainty of success."[26] He based his view on the assumption that the need for the Soviet Union to bring in additional air and ground forces from the Soviet Union itself would provide NATO with enough warning of a coming attack.[27] Reserves would, of course, be required for NATO, and he did emphasize that an allout Soviet attack would be virtually impossible to defeat without recourse to atomic weapons. In other words, Gruenther was making a fine but perhaps artificial distinction between a warning time or pause before hostilities began—defined as a period of buildup of Soviet forces in Central Europe—and the capacity of the Soviet Union to mount a surprise attack using forces already in place but which it was hoped would be insufficient to bring about a rapid Soviet victory.

For NATO, victory would need to be achieved within thirty days, because that was the Alliance's maximum readiness capacity at that time. From this it would be easy to infer that the Soviet Union would be better positioned to prolong an attack beyond this initial period of hostilities precisely because of the weakness of NATO to resupply and to reinforce. This is why emphasis in NATO on air defense was so strong. As Gruenther said, "In 3 years [1951-53] the number of NATO airfields has increased from 20 to 120—a truly remarkable achievement."[28] The construction of the infrastructure for these airfields— roads, pipelines, etc.—was given a very high priority.[29] Obviously, air defense was crucial to compensate for the weaker ground forces that NATO could put up against the Soviet divisions opposing them. And to reduce any Soviet temptation to launch a surprise attack using an estimated twenty thousand operational planes, many of them jets, he asserted that "our air forces must be increased and their effectiveness must be such as to be ready to fight on an instant's notice. We at SHAPE have given first priority to the development of our air forces."[30]

In taking the more optimistic view of NATO in 1953, Gruenther was also comparing that time with the conditions that had existed at SHAPE's creation. From this perspective, a great deal had indeed been accomplished, but it still was not enough, and the Alliance was finding it extremely difficult to sustain its momentum not only because of the delay in achieving agreement over EDC and West German rearmament, but also because of tensions among the larger NATO powers—the United States, Britain, and France—over extra-NATO (or what is now termed "out of area") military situations.

During the period of the debate over EDC, France, and therefore Gruenther, was preoccupied with the war in Indochina, which was going badly and having a very disruptive effect on domestic French politics. As was mentioned earlier, one of the issues was the question of American support for that war, inasmuch as Americans were insisting that the French support West German rearmament. For example, Gruenther wrote to Eisenhower in April 1954:

What I want to see is the French to plan their next move if DBP [Dien-Bien-Phu] goes, but with the disunity that exists in the cabinet that is difficult. Arthur Radford came to see me at 10:30 last night to tell me of Ely's urgent appeal for U.S. intervention. I would not recommend U.S. *unilateral* intervention and I told him so. Of course Ely stressed the need for this intervention—not that it will save DBP but that it will possibly save Indo China—and surely save Europe and NATO. That is a powerful argument, but I dont [sic] think it is valid. I think we can save NATO anyhow in spite of the setback we shall receive from an Indo China reverse. And the disadvantages of unilateral intervention are very great. [His emphasis.][31]

The French claim that lack of support for Indochina could result in a weakening of NATO was resented by both Gruenther and Eisenhower. In responding, for example, to a report from Gruenther that French Defense Minister René Pleven had said that "it (the loss of the Delta) would start a wave of anti-allied outbursts in France with great bitterness because the Allies let us down," Eisenhower recapitulated to Gruenther the attempts by the United States to convince France to internationalize the war in order to achieve a political settlement that would lead to independence. He went on to point out to Gruenther: "As the conflict has dragged on, the United States has more than once offered help of a kind that would tend to keep our participation in the background, but could nevertheless be very effective. I refer to our efforts to get a good guerrilla organization started in the region, our offer to take over a great part of the burden of training native troops, and numerous offers of help in the logistics field."[32] Obviously warming to his subject, Eisenhower then commented, "If Pleven is worrying what the French attitude toward America is going to be, he might take into consideration also what is going to be the American attitude toward France."[33]

This raises the question of the appropriate role for NATO—as a Eurocentric organization, primarily concerned with stemming a Soviet invasion on the Continent, or as a focal point for a global union of states concerned about the survival of the so-called West. At various times both propositions have been advocated. In the pre-SHAPE period, the record of intention was unclear. As one authority put it: "What would then be the scope and nature of the political questions which could appropriately be discussed and even settled within NATO? We get little indication of the answer to this question by looking back on the previous activities of the Council. Only a few questions of a fairly limited nature have been brought up for general discussion."[34]

During the period from Eisenhower's tenure through Gruenther's, the most interest generated among the participating member-states had to do with matters that could be called more strictly military. This would include the organization and staffing of commands, the arrangements for the stationing of forces, the creation of a strategic doctrine, the development of budgetary methods that would sustain proposed force levels, and so forth. As a non-American expert summarized, perhaps too enthusiastically:

> In past wars it has usually taken allies about two years to get properly together, to work out their command system and their political leadership—two years in which errors and weakness in organisation and lack of preparedness have cost thousands of lives and untold

amounts of treasure. Nato's great achievement is that this period of trial and error will not be necessary if another war should come. The details of allied co-operation have been worked out, a complete command system is established, the commanders and staffs are in their headquarters, and the forces themselves are already working together with common Nato signal books and standardised tactics. If the balloon should go up tomorrow morning, troops could be moved, orders sent to shipping, and air formations brought to the alert for defence and counter-attack.[35]

Nonetheless, with the more military aspects being energetically looked after, speculation began as to whether NATO could be seen in a larger political context. Put another way, did loyalty as allies in Europe require loyalty as allies elsewhere, regardless of differing conceptions of either short-term or long-term national interests? For Lord Ismay, as the first secretary-general, there was no firm tradition or habit of consultation on political subjects among the Alliance members to build upon. The general rule was that questions concerning geographical areas not included within the confines of the Treaty could be discussed only insofar as they referred to one of the member-states. But, speaking of the creation of NAT, Ismay said: "I am convinced that the present solution is only a partial one, aimed at guarding the heart. It must grow until the whole free world gets under one umbrella."[36] On another occasion, in February 1953, he reiterated, "We cannot do our business except on a global basis."[37]

Two possible methods of establishing this global basis were postulated by Ismay. The first was to expand the mandate of the Standing Group, which was composed of senior military representatives of the United States, Britain, and France. The second was to create a similar agency that would perform a function wider in scope than planning purely NATO military policy. In both proposals Ismay undoubtedly had in mind some sort of extension of the Anglo-American Combined Chiefs-of-Staff operation of World War II. The problem with this was and is that the smaller powers in NATO have not favored classes of membership; neither, at various times, have France and West

Germany, as later chapters will attest. The SACEUR, in his realm of responsibility, also must take care not to be too much preoccupied with American policy concerns to the detriment of the European members of the Alliance. For example, Gruenther had to persist in his support for West German rearmament, which the United States strongly favored, while ensuring that France not become alienated; as noted earlier, this became very difficult when French interests outside of Europe were brought into play.[38]

As far back as 1950, the smaller member-states had insisted on the creation of the Committee of Military Representatives of their chiefs-of-staff "in order to ensure, on the one hand, that all member nations not represented on the Standing Group are kept in touch with its work and, on the other hand, that the Standing Group is kept informed of the points of view of those other nations."[39]

In any event, the ambiguity concerning the place of the SACEUR in all of this was underscored by an observation of Gen. Omar Bradley, the chairman of the Joint Chiefs of Staff during Eisenhower's and Ridgway's tenures, in describing the creation of SHAPE. "On paper, as chairman of the NATO standing group, I was now Ike's military boss."[40] He could infer this because the North Atlantic Council had provided that NATO's

force will be under a Supreme Commander who will have sufficient delegated authority to ensure that national units allocated to his command are organized and trained into an effective integrated force in time of peace as well as in the event of war.

The Supreme Commander will be supported by an international staff representing all nations contributing to the force.

The Standing Group of the Military Committee... will be responsible for higher strategic direction of the integrated force.[41]

Gruenther was always careful to maintain the distinction between his international and national hats. That was not always easy because the men who were at the pinnacle of the United States military establishment were part of the same group of American officers who were involved with NATO. Their careers, reaching back in many instances to well before World War II, were intimately intertwined. An example of how easy it was to confuse roles was offered late in Gruenther's tenure when his former boss Ridgway, who was just retiring as army chief-of-staff, virtually ordered Gruenther to attend a meeting at Quantico, Virginia, of senior American officers. Gruenther sent to Ridgway's successor, Gen. Maxwell Taylor, a handwritten note to demur.

The message (DA 984093), which I received from Matt just before I left for Norway early on June 30, has distressed me deeply. The statement that my presence at Quantico is of the "utmost importance"... "from a national defense point of view" is indeed strong medicine. Certainly it has caused me to ponder seriously my usefulness as one of the U.S. Commanders. If I lose the confidence of you and of the Army Staff I have serious doubts as to the contribution I can make here....

You are aware, I am sure, that my prime mission here is that of a NATO commander. In fact, when I was appointed SACEUR in 1953 there was considerable discussion in the Pentagon whether or not I should be given the U.S. Hat. The final solution contained a suggestion that I delegate as much authority as practicable to my Deputy. This I have tried to do.[42]

This episode apparently caused Gruenther considerable anguish, as it appeared that he was starting off on the wrong foot with the new chief-of-staff by having to turn down this initial request. In fact, Gruenther went on to say something that may have surprised and even distressed Taylor: "I hope you feel that you have my undivided loyalty. If at any time I become a serious embarrassment to you please have no hesitation in letting me know of that situation. It happens that I could easily make other arrangements which would remove me from the active list with rather substantial financial advantages. I am not asking to retire—of course not—but you are entirely the Boss and I dont [sic] want to be a handicap to you."[43] Taylor replied categorically, "There is no doubt in my mind as to the primacy of your NATO job and the secondary character of your US hat."

After some more comments on the Quantico meeting, Taylor concluded reassuringly, "Now get to your tennis and dismiss any further concern over DA 984093."[44]

By the end of 1955, however, Gruenther's thoughts had definitely turned to retirement. One apparent reason was that Taylor had been named chief-of-staff, thus closing off this career avenue to Gruenther. In March 1955 Secretary of the Army Robert Stevens had written to Gruenther informing him of his intention to name Taylor. Tactfully, having in mind the close relationship between Gruenther and Eisenhower, Stevens went on to say, after having already pointed out that both the president and the secretary of defense had been consulted about this decision: "Naturally, I desired to take into account your outstanding qualifications and record in this connection. The President, however, has declined to consider the possibility of your leaving your present post at this time. In my judgment, no higher compliment can come to an officer than to have achieved such stature in his assignment that the Commander-in-Chief feels it inadvisable to consider him currently as Chief of Staff of the United States Army. Surely that is the way I regard the President's view with respect to your essentiality in your present post."[45]

As early as August 1953, Gruenther's attention was directed at alternative careers. He wrote on 2 August to Eisenhower for advice in view of the very attractive possibility that he would be named president of the National Broadcasting Company at a salary of $100,000 plus a share of the profits, and that thereafter Gruenther could anticipate succeeding David Sarnoff as president of the Radio Corporation of America (RCA). He concluded, "Please understand, I am not asking for a release. I am not at all sure that I am interested in the job at *any* salary. I am just horribly confused, and I need your wise counsel."[46]

Eisenhower categorically replied to Gruenther's request for advice.

As of now, I do not believe that NATO could stand the shock of your leaving; particularly, it could not stand the shock of your leaving for your own purposes. There is no one in sight who can command the respect and confidence that you command in Europe. Without this indispensable foundation on which to stand, nobody in the world could bring about the successful development of the NATO Organization.

After you have, in your turn, found an individual that you can train and equip to take your place in that difficult post, you should of course be relatively free to do as you please. I do not, for example, feel that you are *required* to serve as Army Chief of Staff in the event that post were offered you after you complete your NATO tour....

Considering the time that it would take for you to select and build up some junior—and I mean building him up in the esteem and confidence of all the allies as well as in his own capacity—I do not see how we could contemplate your retirement in less than something like three years. [His emphasis.][47]

After offering some comments on alternative career possibilities, Eisenhower went on to clinch things by saying: "Of course, the matter largely comes back to my utter conviction that you cannot possibly leave at this time without inflicting a sad blow amounting to near destruction to NATO. Knowing your sense of duty, I realize that this expression is by itself sufficient to cause you to drop the subject."[48]

Gruenther replied with evident relief: "You have taken a great load from my mind, and I thank you.... I concluded that if I should decide to pull out now I would be looked upon very much in the same light as if John the Baptist had given up his crusading in order to take over a slot machine concession in Jersey City. I agree with your analysis, and it will not bother me in the slightest to decline the invitation."[49]

It was not until December 1955—not so far away from three years—that Gruenther finally decided it was time to retire. He apparently really meant it this time because he offered a formal and impersonal rationale, as well as confiding in Eisenhower as a personal friend and counselor.

Would you be terribly disappointed in me if I should tell you now that I should like to retire a few months from now? I sincerely hope not. ... Of course, if you tell me "go sit in a corner" I'll do just that. However I am certain Norstad or Schuyler can do a better job than I have done, although I admit I have fooled a good many people who should know better. But I think I should go fairly soon.[50]

Gruenther's reasoning was that his successor should develop the new NATO strategic study that was being undertaken for the 1960-62 period because he felt the commander should believe in it strongly. He based this point on the fact that the present concept had been developed during Gruenther's period as SACEUR, and "if a new commander had come along he might not have bought it at all. For example, General Ridgway or Admiral Carney would have yelled bloody murder if they had inherited such a concept." Finally, he suggested April 1956 as the time and went on to recommend that Gen. Lauris Norstad succeed him. He also mentioned Gen. Cortlandt van R. Schuyler as an alternative, but indicated he preferred Schuyler to remain as chief-of-staff to the SACEUR.[51]

Eisenhower apparently sensed the finality of Gruenther's decision, for, without committing himself either to Norstad or to Schuyler, he said: "I do not quarrel with your right to make a personal decision to retire. But I do have some misgivings as to what will happen to NATO." He went on to explain: "The question that instantly flashes through my mind is, 'Would your retirement from the scene indicate either a sense of defeatism on your part, or of indifference on ours?' A corollary of course is, 'What would be the acceptance among the European nations of any man we might name?'"[52]

In the event, the announcement of Gruenther's retirement was made in April 1956, following the procedure of consultation, now laid down as an established precedent, that the president would be asked by the North Atlantic Council to nominate a successor. Eisenhower named Norstad. Gruenther had officially transmitted his intentions to the chairman of the Standing Group, Gen. Jean E. Valluy, on 9 April 1956. He justified his request in the following way. "The reasons for my decision are purely personal. However, even if those reasons had not developed, I would have considered it desirable and proper to request that I be permitted to relinquish my post within the next several months. In July of this year I shall complete three years as Supreme Allied Commander Europe. I believe that three years is about the maximum time for one individual to hold this position if the organization is to continue to thrive under the impulse of new and imaginative ideas."[53] Gruenther's wish was deferred, however, until November 1956 when he retired from the army and subsequently became president of the American National Red Cross. From this prestigious position, located just a block away from the White House, Gruenther continued his close personal relationship with Eisenhower.

4. Norstad

Can the SACEUR Be Both European and American?

ROBERT S. JORDAN

The eminent historian and diplomat George F. Kennan, in discussing the establishment of diplomatic relations between the United States and the Soviet Union, observed that "most of the difficulties we encountered were of the endemic variety. They were products of what you might call the permanent environmental factors of the Soviet-American relationship—such things as conflicting ideological commitments; different geographic situations; different traditions and customs; different ways of looking at things; differences in the ways the two peoples saw themselves and each other; and the unrealistic expectations each had of the other. We soon became aware of these factors, even if we probably underrated their long-term importance."[1] A similar comment concerning the United States' relations with its NATO Allies could be made by any of the SACEURs, but especially so during the early years culminating with Gen. Lauris Norstad's tenure.

In order to place the role of the SACEUR during this pre-Norstad period in proper context, it is necessary to take account once again of the decisions taken at the Lisbon meeting of the NATO Council of Ministers in February 1952. It was at this meeting, which Eisenhower had viewed as of great importance to his success as SACEUR, that the "O" was put into NATO.[2] The creation of a permanent international staff was authorized, to be headed by a secretary-general who was charged with looking after the political aspects of the Alliance—thus juxtaposed against the already-functioning SACEUR, who had been charged with looking after the military aspects.[3] This dichotomy has never been easy either to achieve or to maintain. In the case of Norstad's immediate predecessor, primary responsibility for the public advocacy role, which included free and open access to the highest political leaders of the governments of the member-states and appeals to domestic audiences as well, fell to the first secretary-general, Lord Ismay of the United Kingdom. His success in this role was noted as his term of office drew to a close. "Ismay has emerged, even more than General Gruenther, as the real successor to General Eisenhower as supreme figurehead and symbol of the Western Alliance."[4] How was it possible, then, we must ask, that with the accession of Norstad as SACEUR, the public, expostulatory function swung back in the direction of the SACEUR?

One important reason, in addition to the fact that Ismay's tenure was ending when Norstad was appointed, was that Ismay chose not to play a leading role in the sensitive question of troop withdrawals from NATO. This left it to Norstad to step into this thorny policy thicket.[5]

As we know, NATO's defense strategy had always been to hold the enemy as far east as possible, and West German entry into the Alliance required that the forward defense line be firmly established along the East German border. The concept remained essentially the same: maintain as large an armed force as far to the east as possible, in order to meet and hold in check a possible invasion by a numerically superior Soviet-led army. Ismay, who along with the NATO military commanders had played a leading role in World War II, was comfortable with this idea. Thus, a buildup of NATO forces proceeded, albeit at a pace that fluctuated in response to the international political environment of the 1950s: in 1949 twelve divisions and four hundred aircraft; in 1954 ninety divisions and upwards of four thousand aircraft.

The place of atomic and hydrogen weapons was given careful study by SHAPE and by national civilian and military officials. Yet no estimate of the effect of nuclear weapons on the military strategy of the Alliance was included in force planning until 1954. Then, following rejection of the EDC Treaty, and as part of the terms adopted in admitting West Germany into NATO, a reevaluation of troop requirements was undertaken. Two additional factors were included in NATO calculations: the contribution of the *Bundeswehr* and the introduction of tactical nuclear weapons. This latter, in turn, reflected the Eisenhower administration's desire to cut defense costs by getting "more bang for the buck" and the absence of a Soviet deployed counterforce, as discussed in chapter 3. Instead of the proposed ninety divisions, an "adequate minimum" of thirty was accepted. As part of the Paris agreement, the United States and Britain undertook to provide and maintain as long as necessary—with certain stipulated reservations in case of emergency, or financial difficulties in the case of Britain—a certain number of their forces on the European continent as their contribution to the shield.

But as often happens in international politics, unforeseen circumstances led the governments party to the agreement to alter their commitments. Upon the outbreak of fighting in Algeria, the French reassigned five divisions from SHAPE to North Africa. The Adenauer government in West Germany decided to postpone conscription in response to domestic opposition, with the result that the twelve German divisions did not materialize on schedule. And in late 1956 the British presented a plan to withdraw about one-third of their Army of the Rhine (BAOR) from the Continent. This last move was opposed by the new SACEUR, whose appointment had been announced in November 1956.

Since the SACEUR's advice was crucial for releasing Britain from its Treaty obligation, Norstad took a leading role in the discussions among the Allies. He cited military justifications for retaining the British divisions. "The defensive forces deployed on the eastern frontiers were an essential part of the deterrent."[5] He also brought in political considerations. "The presence on European soil of British troops...is a symbol. To Europe, it signifies that Britain is with them right from the start."[7]

In speeches on both sides of the Atlantic, in press releases, in his invitation to the permanent representatives to attend a major military exercise of SHAPE, and in his formal report to the Council of the Western European Union (WEU), Norstad sought to forestall the British move. All the while Norstad was making headlines and trying to influence the policy of a major NATO power, Ismay's voice was scarcely heard in public. Taking a position directly opposed to the declared national policy of a member of the Alliance, especially his own country, was not his style. Furthermore, by the time the troop cuts were announced, Ismay had already let it be known that he would resign his post in the spring of 1957. As his successor had already been picked, Ismay no longer commanded the full authority of his position. He did, however, express one strong opinion: if economic reasons underlay the British decision to retrench, those reasons and no others should be advanced. If Britain were to try to soften the blow by raising the possibility of supplanting troops with an equal amount of fire power, then the signal might well be given for other NATO members to employ the same argument, in which case the ground troops composing the NATO shield would melt away.[8]

A compromise was eventually reached under which some withdrawals would occur, others would be postponed for further study, and some forces stationed in England would be earmarked for service on the Continent, if needed. Just as he had not been a central figure in the efforts to forestall the British decision to cut its forces, Ismay was not directly involved, as was the SACEUR, in the bargaining that brought about the compromise because this took place primarily within the Council of WEU. Rather, most of the credit for that accomplishment must go to Paul-Henri Spaak, then Belgian foreign minister and soon to succeed Ismay at NATO.

Spaak had assumed the post expecting to become the chief voice of the Alliance. In this attempt, as with Ismay, he had to share responsibility with both the chief political organ, the North Atlantic Council, and the most visible of the military commanders, Norstad. As Spaak said: "The relationship between civilian officials and the military has always seemed to me to present a difficult problem. I found this to be the case during the war and, in different circumstances, in NATO."[9] Spaak came into office at a time of reinterpretation of the functions of the Alliance. In December 1956, as an aftermath of the Suez crisis that had split the United States off from its chief European allies, France and Britain, the North Atlantic Council had adopted the report of the "Three Wise Men" that, in part, spelled out provisions to strengthen the political-consultative aspect of the Alliance. As it declared, "The transformation of the Atlantic Community into a vital and vigorous political reality is as important as any purely national purpose."[10]

The report provided for an expansion of the secretary-general's authority to enable him to carry out his responsibilities more effectively. The secretary-general was given the right and duty to bring to the attention of the Council any matter that, in his opinion, may threaten the solidarity and effectiveness of the Alliance. He was also empowered to offer his good offices at any time to the parties to a dispute and with their consent, to initiate or facilitate procedures of inquiry, mediation, conciliation, or arbitration. Finally, the secretary-general was made chairman of the North Atlantic Council, meeting in permanent session, which gave him a greater capacity to organize and direct the work of the Council. Thus, Spaak came into office with more of a political mandate than did his predecessor, and this inevitably meant some adjustment between him and Norstad. As Spaak commented: "Norstad was fascinated by politics—perhaps more so than I am by the art of war. However, I gladly turned a blind eye to his interference in matters I considered to be within my own sphere of competence rather than his."[11] Then more charitably, he went on to say: "I readily acknowledge the integrity of his intentions and it was with pleasure that I noted the success he had with some of his efforts.... His was one of the stages in its history—I am referring to the period of 1956 to 1961—when NATO played an important part. I am vain enough to think that both the Secretary-General and the Supreme Commander were not altogether unconnected with this happy state of affairs."[12]

The nub of Spaak's dissatisfaction was not so much with

Norstad as with the reluctance of the member-states to give to the Alliance—and by inference to the secretary-general—the kind of all-embracing, global outlook that Spaak believed was essential for the unity and defense of the West. Time after time he felt he had been rebuffed in expanding the political and economic horizons of the Alliance, both by the larger powers (the United States, France, and Britain) and by the smaller powers as well. His constant advocacy for political consultation on a global scale, and also, together with Norstad, for a NATO nuclear force that would discourage proliferation and would encourage France to remain firmly allied in nuclear affairs with the United States and Britain, created in some of the political and diplomtic persons in NATO more a sense of irritation with him than a sense of willing collaboration. During both Norstad's and Spaak's tenures, it simply was not possible for common global political and economic policies to be forged through the machinery of Alliance consultation. But in Spaak's opinion, "The more NATO is treated as a purely military organization, the weaker it will be—at least in Europe."[13]

Spaak's successor in 1961, Dirk U. Stikker of the Netherlands, had had a heart attack in 1959 and experienced more ill health, including cancer of the colon, during his tenure. This, in itself, gave more scope to the SACEUR and especially to one who had already been in his post for five years and who was accustomed to power and the international attention that came to him as a consequence. Norstad was careful to establish a close personal relationship with Stikker, however, thus avoiding the tensions that otherwise could have cropped up. Furthermore, the two men were sensitive to the need to act in harmony in order to encourage member-states to do likewise.[14] Spaak's aggressiveness had perhaps helped to encourage the opposite. Stikker agreed with his predecessor that the Council should take seriously its supervisory functions of the military side of NATO, and so he encouraged the civilian international staff to request reports from SHAPE.[15] But he did not go as far as Spaak in attempting to restrict the public statements of military officials in order to reinforce his role as NATO's chief political spokesman. Most Council members, as well as those of SHAPE, had opposed the effort, and Norstad had simply ignored it.[16]

The role of NATO and that of the SACEUR in particular, in what has come to be called public diplomacy, also caused other kinds of tensions. For example, Spaak recalled in his memoirs how touchy President de Gaulle of France would become when leading political figures would visit either the civilian headquarters in Paris or the military headquarters just outside of Paris, without observing the formalities of calling upon the head of state of the host country. This was especially the case when Chancellor Adenauer's chief ministers, such as Defense Minister Franz-Joseph Strauss, would visit Norstad.[17] Obviously, with the SACEUR responsible for formulating military strategy for the Alliance and the supporting budgets, there had to be unofficial discussions between the SACEUR and the leading NATO national politicians. Norstad, in fact, encouraged this because he saw himself as being very effective in interpersonal relations. In this respect, he was not unlike Eisenhower. In fact, one political journalist made the following comparison. "Like the American president, Norstad has to be many men: an expert soldier, a diplomat, a backstage politician, a perfect host, a considerate guest, a tireless traveler, a careful reader, a budget student and a complete chamber of commerce in at least half a dozen languages."[18]

Norstad also dealt with the issue of American nuclear policy. From the start, NATO's SACEUR had been concerned that the United States provide nuclear information to its Allies. Eisenhower had chafed under American legal restrictions. "The matter of nuclear strength and possible deployment was troublesome from the beginning," he said. The McMahon Act of 1946 controlling the production of fissionable materials, the manufacture and storage of nuclear weapons, and the transfer of such weapons to other nations "prevented us from making any workable agreements with our partners in NATO respecting nuclear weapons—indeed it was difficult and embarrassing, because of the restriction imposed upon us, even to discuss the matter intelligently and thoroughly." In spite of these hindrances, discussion took place at SHAPE during Eisenhower's tenure concerning the implications of battlefield nuclear weapons for European defense; and Eisenhower noted that "the effect of the nuclear deterrent was taken in account in all our joint planning."[19]

Subsequently, Norstad praised the advance of the Atomic Energy Act of 1954, "which permitted the use on an allied basis of more atomic information than had been allowed previously." At the same time, he noted that "the restrictions imposed by that act still prevent NATO forces from training on a fully realistic basis or developing the operational capability and readiness status required, particularly in view of the many types of modern atomic-weapons systems which are now becoming available." To further improve the situation, he endorsed changes in the Act which would "provide greater latitude for the dissemination of essential information within this Allied Command."[20]

Norstad had also shown a growing concern for an adequately stocked NATO nuclear armory. Both he and Gruenther had lobbied in Washington during the mid-1950s for the creation of a "NATO atomic stockpile" through which the United States would retain control of atomic warheads but would distribute to its Allies nuclear-capable delivery vehicles, train Allied military personnel in the use of these vehicles, and help to develop a supply system for them. These efforts had been relatively successful. Norstad advocated publicly that "mid-range ballistic missiles, land and sea based, and with great mobility, should be made available to NATO as a part of the weapons modernization program, to meet the presently assigned functions of this command."[21]

On 6 December 1959, in a speech at the University of Southern California, he proposed making NATO the "fourth nuclear power" through the creation of a multinational atomic authority. He developed this idea further on 2 March 1960 at a press conference at SHAPE; on 12 October in Coventry, England; and on 21 November to the NATO Parliamentarians'

Conference. To the parliamentarians Norstad said that "consideration should be given to guaranteeing to the Alliance the availability of a basic pool of atomic weapons, those essential to the direct defense of Europe, and to giving all nations of the Alliance an essentially equal voice in the control of these particular weapons." Later, he made public the proposal that a NATO Executive Committee might include the United States, Britain, France, West Germany, and perhaps one or two additional participants.[22]

He was speaking of tactical and not strategic weapons, making the point in various forums that, although there had been built up a nuclear weapons stockpile, still lacking was "a satisfactory procedure in terms of the alliance exercising its authority, and this is something which the United States does not dictate." To augment NATO's authority, he believed that machinery should be established which could authorize the use of American nuclear weapons even though custody of bombs or warheads might remain under American control. "Let's keep our own custody," he said, "but let's let them collectively participate in the decision by which a limited number of weapons would be used in the NATO context, and, if possible, when they should be used." The decision-making procedure should be such that there would "be a certain minimum number of weapons which will be available even if the United States, which is most unlikely, would positively dissent from the decision and not commit its own forces."[23]

The primary decision-making body, the Executive Committee, would consist of heads of government who would establish a permanent subordinate group of "people who would live with the subject, actually live with the subject, in whom the Prime Minister or President or Chancellor had great confidence and to whom he had direct access." Norstad asserted that the creation of this group would only formalize existing custom. "This proposal for a Heads of State group was not pulled out of the air," he said. "This is confirming practice, at least practice during my time. These are the people with whom I maintained the contact. These are the people whom, when I got into difficulty, I called on the telephone or I went to see, or they called me on the telephone."[24]

Secretary-General Spaak summed up the appeal, both specific and general, which the so-called Norstad Plan(s) might have. The possibility that NATO might become "the fourth atomic Power in the world," said Spaak, would be "a new milestone for the Alliance.... It constitutes a valid and lasting answer to the problem of the atomic armament of Germany. It is also an answer to the queries and the anxieties of France. It may put an end to the dangerous controversies now developing in the United Kingdom. It constitutes for the Alliance as a whole, and more particularly for Europe, a tremendous increase in its power."[25]

Nevertheless, the idea ultimately ran into American opposition. Even though during the 1950s the United States had cooperated by liberalizing its nuclear security policy, as pointed out earlier, to allow the dissemination of certain types of information and later the deployment of tactical nuclear delivery systems with the forces of its Allies, there was a limit. This policy had been capped by the announcement in the communiqué of the NATO heads-of-government summit of December 1957 that NATO has decided to establish stocks of nuclear warheads, which will be readily available for the defense of the Alliance in case of need" and that "intermediate range ballistic missiles will have to be put at the disposal of the Supreme Allied Commander Europe."[26]

With the change of administration from Eisenhower to Kennedy, a direct clash occurred between Norstad and Washington, which Norstad was bound to lose. The Kennedy administration felt that its policy of nonproliferation and centralized control ruled out a NATO nuclear force that was not ultimately subject to American veto.[27] To Norstad this was almost a vote of nonconfidence in the SACEUR, whose wings, in effect, were being clipped. Thus the era of what might be called the "proconsular" period in the history of NATO's SACEURs was drawing to a close. The Kennedy administration's reluctance to make NATO a nuclear power according to Norstad's vision was clearly stated by Secretary of Defense Robert McNamara, who said he "would not favor" Norstad's plan. "I think it would be unwise," he said, "to divide the nuclear force of NATO into two categories without a proper linkage between them, granting to one group of nations authority to use one category and... another group of nations or a single nation authority to use the other category. Nuclear war is indivisible." He continued: "I know of no single member of NATO who would recommend that the authority to utilize nuclear weapons be granted to three to five other nations of NATO.... Nor do I know of any member of NATO that would wish to see the United States delegate its veto power to any other member of NATO or to any grouping of NATO nations."[28]

Even though Gruenther, during his tenure, witnessed the beginnings of NATO nuclear proliferation when the French decided to embark on building a *force de frappe*, the issue was joined during Norstad's tenure with the question of whether there should be a nuclear role for the Federal Republic of Germany.

The West Germans, after their integration into NATO, felt they should have a strong voice in the discussion of NATO nuclear doctrine. The 1954 concept that massive retaliation by the United States against the Soviet Union would be the response to any Soviet invasion of Western Europe had become suspect as the Soviet capacity to strike directly against the continental United States became more evident. Somehow, there had to be some breathing space between capitulation on the ground in Europe and mutual nuclear destruction by the superpowers. This is where tactical nuclear weapons came in. According to Norstad, they could provide the condition of "pause" that would enable the Soviet Union to refrain from actual invasion, or, if hostilities had broken out on the ground, the defending NATO forces would have time to consider the intent and scale of the conflict in order to determine whether going to full-scale nuclear war was justified by battlefield circumstances.

Thus, on 12 April 1957 it was announced that the United

States would make available advanced weapons, including Honest John, Matador, and Nike, to certain Allies. These tactical nuclear weapons, which Norstad advocated should be made available to the new West German forces, would serve as something of a *quid pro quo* in return for the stationing in Europe of tactical intermediate-range ballistic missiles (IRBMs), something the United States felt was necessary to counter the Soviet Union's development of strategic intercontinental ballistic missiles (ICBMs).[29] In a television interview Norstad gave in West Germany in February 1958, he put it thus:

Q: Many people believe that the atomic arming of the German forces would increase the tension between East and West. The American forces in Germany have tactical nuclear weapons. Do the German troops also require them, in your opinion?

NORSTAD: So long as the over-all situation does not change, defensive atomic weapons are absolutely indispensable for the strengthening of the defensive power of the Bundeswehr—for the protection of the Federal Republic and all NATO nations; that is the purely military standpoint.

Now, however, for the German standpoint: a comprehensive defense contribution by the Federal Republic is coming into being. It is wholly unthinkable that these forces should be condemned to a second-class function, in which they would be practically useless for defense.

We cannot give the German forces inadequate arms; the German nation cannot allow its soldiers to be armed with weapons long since obsolete.[30]

Thus, at this particular juncture of his career as SACEUR, Norstad was in general consonance with both United States and West German thinking in regard to NATO nuclear policy (although falling out later with the United States). He was not in step with the French viewpoint, but this did not necessarily diminish his political effectiveness because no other senior NATO official was having any success with the French.

In fact, as discussed earlier, Norstad had become a foremost advocate of a strong, united European dimension to implement and reinforce the Atlantic dimension of the Alliance. This "dumbbell" approach was consistent with his advocacy of a Western European military structure. Just as Eisenhower, after some reluctance, came to embrace the notion of EDC as a means to bring about rapid West German rearmament during the Korean War,[31] so Norstad came to agree with the West German position that integrating West German forces into a larger multinational entity was essential for European stability. Further, these forces should not be inferior in their equipment to that of their presumed opponent.[32]

Obviously, Norstad's proposals for a NATO nuclear force could forestall the development of a West German drive to attain an independent nuclear capability by presenting an indirect road on which the Germans might keep pace with nuclear developments. Norstad and Adenauer had discussed the issue as early as 1957; Norstad recalled that:

> The Chancellor was the first to raise with me, in 1957, two questions which he said had been raised in the Federal Republic as well as in other countries in Europe. One was: If all these countries organized their defense on a foundation of nuclear weapons, was it not reasonable for the European countries to ask that a certain number of weapons be firmly committed, on the basis that they would not be withdrawn by unilateral decision of the United States? The other was: should not NATO have some degree of influence, perhaps even control, over the conditions under which the weapons would be used. No one said at the time that they wanted control, they just said due influence....
>
> I sought to provide a specific answer to the questions. My proposal was that we establish an Executive Committee within NATO consisting of the United States, Great Britain, and France. The Secretary General could be chairman and Germany would have a special relationship to this group which would have some control over any nuclear weapons deployed in Europe.[33]

After his retirement, however, in a pamphlet published by the Critical Issues Council of the Republican Citizens Committee of the United States and prepared by a task force under the chairmanship of Norstad, he appeared to back away from his earlier position. The pamphlet stated: "It can no longer be taken for granted that what is good for the narrow circle of countries seeking a powerful political merger will necessarily serve the purposes of those other allies with whom they are aligned in the crucial task of collective Atlantic defense.... We must now reappraise our view of European unity... in terms of America's own interest."[34] By 1964, in other words, partly because of the difficulties in resolving the need for a coherent NATO military doctrine that could reassure the West Germans and at the same time take account of the ever-changing technology of warfare brought on by nuclear rivalry, even Norstad was willing to draw back from a strong European military dimension standing somewhat apart from the American nuclear contributions, both strategic and tactical.

Even though nuclear weapons played no formal part in the early planning of NATO, for reasons discussed above, Norstad, as commander, Allied Air Forces Europe, had emphasized to Eisenhower that NATO could not just ignore them. Norstad's attitude was quite consistent: some way must be found to give the European Allies a sense of sharing in the formulation of the doctrine for their employment and possible use if deterrence were to fail. As we have seen, his attempts did not bear much fruit, and in the process at times he ran afoul of the French.

On the question of how to share in the command and control of nuclear weapons, Norstad had some sympathy with the Gaullist view that the American nuclear deterrent had by 1958 and Sputnik lost some of its credibility. In a system of Soviet-American mutual deterrence, it could be fairly questioned whether the United States would be willing to destroy itself in order to protect Western Europe.

In particular, the French argued that although they found no fault with American intentions to defend Europe, they were not convinced that the Americans could be expected to live up to their commitments in all possible crisis situations. This was not a uniquely American weakness, they pointed out; it was a fact of international life that no state would likely invite its own destruction in order to defend others. In this kind of nuclear stalemate, the "others" must be armed with nuclear weapons so that if the nuclear umbrella failed to operate, the smaller Allies would still have an independent means of deterring possible moves against their vital interests. It would be, in other words, in order to cover the 5 percent of hypothetical cases when the United States might *not* retaliate that Europe should have its own nuclear weapons.[35] From Norstad's perspective, this 5 percent needed to be taken seriously and plans made to demonstrate how to meet this concern, which was shared by others in Europe besides the French.[36] For Norstad there was a practical reason why he—or any other SACEUR—would be greatly concerned. As one scholar put it, "An alliance in which each nation is independently drafting plans to fight *its* political objectives is an alliance bound to lack coordination and common purpose."[37]

Good intentions by Norstad notwithstanding, by the fall of 1958, after de Gaulle had proposed his famous notion of a three-power "Directorate" to supplant what he saw as the Anglo-American "special relationship"[38] and to which he felt President Eisenhower had given an inadequate reply, relations between the United States and France had deteriorated badly. For example, France vetoed the American plan for meeting the costs of new missile sites in Europe for IRBMs through the collective NATO infrastructure budget. Then in the spring of 1959, the French escalated their protest another dramatic step with the abrupt removal of one-third of their Mediterranean fleet from NATO command.

Norstad, in turn, immediately protested this move to de Gaulle; he had what he felt was a compelling argument, because although the ships flew the French flag, they were in fact legally owned by the United States. They had been made available to France for NATO purposes and under the law that provided this, the SACEUR must certify to the United States that equipment of that size and cost was necessary for NATO use. Norstad told de Gaulle that he was prepared to "decertify"—an example of the power of the SACEUR. Norstad was advised by his American colleagues, however, that although legally he could do it, decertifying would cause more political trouble than it would be worth, probably even resulting in French withdrawal from NATO, so he did not carry out his threat.[39]

In June de Gaulle refused to allow the United States to stockpile nuclear warheads on French soil unless France could participate fully in the decision to use them. This created a serious situation that "forbade any precaution being overlooked."[40] Without the nuclear warheads being retained under American control, the problem of a possible West German desire to possess them might also arise, thus complicating the desire of the United States to restrict the decision-making authority where nuclear weapons were concerned. And by 1959, for the first time, West Germany was making a larger contribution to NATO than was France.[41]

Finally, in December 1959 the French derailed the scheme for the integration of tactical fighter forces under the SACEUR because they insisted they could not be armed with nuclear weapons unless the weapons were under French control. Given the fact that Norstad, prior to becoming SACEUR, had been the air deputy to his predecessor, he had a special commitment to the notion of strengthening NATO's tactical air defense capability, which included tactical nuclear weapons. The French action could have crippled the air defenses of Western Europe, and so Norstad ordered the withdrawal of some eight squadrons of fighter-bombers from France and repositioned them in West Germany. He had tried to avoid this confrontation with de Gaulle, even going so far as to say: "I've been around here (NATO) a long time. I know that in NATO, in a national position, one has no authority as a consequence of a body of laws or precedent. You make your own authority and you make it by succeeding not by failing, so I don't force a major confrontation unless I know damn well I can do this."[42] In contrast to his earlier threat, Norstad was indeed capable of carrying through on this threat partly, of course, because the United States agreed with him that there were no circumstances in which, under American law, France could have control of those nuclear warheads.

In Europe by the late 1950s, the role of the NATO forces was changing; it was conceived more and more in terms of limited military operations and no longer, as earlier, as defense against massive, calculated invasion. General war seemed unthinkable and totally self-defeating. Instead of being perceived as conducting a holding operation while the sword of the U.S. Strategic Air Command was wielded in massive retaliation, the NATO ground force shield was now thought to have the more modest task of preventing limited aggression by ruling out the possibility of early gains. As mentioned earlier, Norstad, to support this thesis, had advanced the concept of the "pause." In the event of large-scale fighting in Central Europe, which he envisaged would come about as the product of miscalculation or "momentary rashness," the NATO ground forces, both nuclear and nonnuclear, would "enforce a pause" in the hope that diplomacy could avert the recourse to strategic air attack.[43]

Experts identified with the incoming Kennedy administration, however, believed that if the role of the NATO ground forces was conceived in these terms, the policy of immediate tactical nuclear response was inappropriate because it would tend to expand, or escalate, the conflict, which was the opposite of the outcome being sought.[44] Going beyond Norstad, these persons, led by the new chairman of the Joint Chiefs of Staff, Gen. Maxwell Taylor, who replaced (some might say displaced) Gen. Lyman L. Lemnitzer, took the position that a doctrine of flexible response was required to forestall, by the use of conventional forces for as long as possible, the recourse to nuclear weapons.

Also, in December 1960 the North Atlantic Council approved the notion of creating a multilateral strategic nuclear force (MLF), to which Norstad was not favorably inclined, in response to some of the European members' wish for a greater voice in the use of nuclear weapons. As pointed out earlier, it was also intended to serve as a riposte to a revived West Germany's sense of exclusion from the nuclear club, which is why Norstad in the late 1950s had advocated a land-based tactical MRBM. But the Eisenhower administration, under Secretary of State Christian Herter (the Herter Plan), had recommended instead a two-part program whereby Polaris missile submarines would be assigned to the SACEUR, to be manned then by a multinational crew from at least three NATO member-states.[45] While formal custody would remain in American hands, warheads would be released under prearranged procedures that would provide some European involvement in strategic nuclear defense, thus furthering the principle of integration.

In both plans—the Norstad Plan and the Herter Plan—the underlying issue was how to involve the Germans without putting their "finger on the trigger." By 1961 Germany was the only European state that had increased substantially its conventional military capability; by doing so, thereby making the Kennedy administration's desire to move toward flexible response more plausible, the Germans had generated more leverage in support of their desire to be more involved in the formulation of overall NATO military doctrine, which for them meant more, rather than less, integration. MLF, incidentally, was also bitterly opposed by the Soviet Union on the grounds that it would in effect make West Germany a nuclear power, thus violating international agreements against proliferation in general and West German national acquisition of nuclear arms in particular.

Norstad, through these two fundamental issues of NATO military doctrine, had placed himself in a position not entirely consonant first with the post–Dulles Eisenhower administration and then in open disagreement with the Kennedy administration. It also did him little good that he was a protégé of Eisenhower and was seen as having been very close politically to the Republicans. Hence the change of command at NATO in 1962, which Norstad accepted reluctantly. For his successor the MLF issue assumed crisis proportions, not just because the French had barely concealed their contempt for the MLF from its beginnings, intent as they were on preserving their own independent nuclear force, but also because of the Skybolt fiasco, which broke in December 1962.

At a strained meeting in Nassau, the Bahamas, the Anglo-

American agreement whereby the United States would supply Skybolt missiles to the British when they became operational in return for bases for American nuclear submarines, was scrapped by President Kennedy without appropriate warnings to Prime Minister Harold Macmillan or to the British public. Even the substitution of the more satisfactory Polaris missiles was badly handled, and while in fact the British emerged with a cheaper and more effective weapons system for their long-range nuclear armory, the impression left in France and elsewhere was that United States promises were not to be trusted and that Britain occupied a special but subordinate role in American military planning.[46] One consequence of Skybolt was immediate: de Gaulle's veto of British membership in the European Economic Community in January 1963.

Such were the atmospherics in Europe in the months between the announcement of Lemnitzer's appointment in July 1962 and his actual taking command of SHAPE on 1 January 1963. The original date of 1 November had been postponed for two months because of the Cuban missile crisis in October, but Lemnitzer was in France during most of this period in his other capacity as CINCEUR at his Camp les Loges headquarters outside Paris. Small wonder then that Lemnitzer spoke soberly at the change-of-command ceremonies on 2 January 1963 of "the great responsibilities that accompany this important assignment." He made a point of pledging to "accept my obligations to *all* of the nations of this great Alliance with humility, solemn purpose and the determination to be worthy of the confidence and trust that have been placed in me."[47]

In conclusion, we must return to George Kennan's point about "difficulties... of the endemic variety." The SACEUR, along with the secretary-general, must speak for and on behalf of all the Alliance, while not alienating himself from the Alliance's largest and most powerful member, the United States. If the SACEUR finds himself caught in the middle, then in the final analysis he must be prepared to suffer the consequences, as was Norstad's fate. Unfortunately, the following observation by a distinguished Dutch political scientist is only too appropriate. "With respect to the need to maintain allied cohesion, national governments have failed in at least two areas. They have failed in many instances in their task to inform their electorates adequately about the reality of the international situation and the dilemmas of allied security. They have equally failed in their understanding of the psychology of mutual confidence in allied relations."[48] Without a doubt, Norstad attempted to make up for these two failures, which made him one of the most influential as well as one of the most controversial of the distinguished occupants of this vitally important—and unique—position.

Overall European sentiment toward Norstad was probably expressed by Adm. Lord Louis Mountbatten, who is reported to have said that he had doubted when "this young airman" was appointed SACEUR that Norstad was right for the job, but he later saw that he was mistaken. Although Mountbatten thought that Norstad was misguided on tactical nuclear weapons, he believed that, in general, Norstad did an almost impossible job with exemplary skill.[49]

Even de Gaulle paid him a sincere compliment at the time of Norstad's retirement.

When I say that you are detaching yourself, I am of course referring only as regards the duties which were yours here. For, insofar as your work is concerned, it exists and will remain. No doubt, as the strategist you are, you have sometimes seen your plans, in turn, somewhat complicated by the soldier. The fact remains that, in six years, you have done everything that could and should be done on behalf of the Atlantic Alliance. I wish to render you my very sincere recognition of this.[50]

5. Lemnitzer

Surviving the French Military Withdrawal

LAWRENCE S. KAPLAN AND KATHLEEN A. KELLNER

No SACEUR, except Eisenhower, had a more intimate association with NATO than Gen. Lyman L. Lemnitzer. Not even Eisenhower had as many links to the Alliance and organization because Lemnitzer was literally present at its creation as Secretary of Defense James Forrestal's delegate to the Military Committee of the Brussels Treaty Organization (i.e., WUDO) in the summer of 1948. In January 1949 as the negotiations over the North Atlantic Treaty came to a conclusion, he was appointed the Defense Department representative on the Foreign Assistance Correlation Committee, whose function was to coordinate the planning of a military assistance program for the future members of the Alliance. When both the Treaty was ratified and the military assistance program passed in the fall of 1949, Lemnitzer was placed in charge of the new Office of Military Assistance, where he served as liaison between the Defense Department and the State Department's directors of the program and advised the Joint Chiefs of Staff on broad military criteria for the MDAP (see chapter 1, above).

While service in Korea and on the Joint Chiefs of Staff in the 1950s diverted him temporarily from absorption in NATO concerns, his appointment as SACEUR was built on a career that made his six-year tenure at SHAPE fittingly longer than any of his predecessors to date.

The impressive credentials Lemnitzer had compiled prior to his assumption of command in January 1963 extended from combat in Italy in World War II to command of the Seventh Infantry Division in Korea, to army chief-of-staff in 1960, and ultimately to chairman of the Joint Chiefs of Staff (JCS), 1960-62. Given this record, Lemnitzer should have been welcomed with unreserved enthusiasm in all quarters of the Alliance when Pres. John Kennedy nominated him to succeed the ailing Lauris Norstad in July 1962. It would be his last assignment, at an age close to retirement. Only the position of SACEUR could match the distinction of his post as chairman of the JCS.

Instead, a barrage of denigrating rumors emanating from a variety of sources and causes coalesced around the announcement, to diminish at least temporarily what should have been the culmination of a distinguished career. The first such negative sign came from the apparent sluggishness with which the NATO Allies approved Lemnitzer's appointment. President de Gaulle used this occasion as another opportunity to express his disenchantment with the organizational structure of NATO, with American dominance, and with France's exclusion from the nuclear partnership of the United States and Britain. Indeed, as recounted in the preceding chapter, Lemnitzer's actual assumption of command, postponed because of the Cuban missile crisis in the fall of 1962, followed closely on Britain's embarrassment over the failed Skybolt missile program and the almost concurrent French veto of Britain's membership in the European Economic Community. But while Kennedy turned aside criticism of his choice, his comment that Lemnitzer was "very adequately equipped" and the "best officer for that position at this time" could be construed as less than enthusiastic.[1] It took yet another day before the president mustered the appropriate words for the occasion. "We are confident that the General will carry on in the traditions of his illustrious predecessors in this assignment most vital to the security of the free world."[2] The five-day pause that followed before NATO Council agreement, in deference to de Gaulle, ended with unanimous acceptance by the Council.[3] In brief, it is reasonable to assume that de Gaulle's animus was directed not at the new leader but at the appearance of Council action being nothing more than a rubber stamp of an American decision.

Still, the *arrière-pensées* were not wholly removed. The *Times of London* devoted most of its space to praise for Norstad's accomplishments as SACEUR (July 21), reflecting the "sense of shock" Secretary-General Dirk Stikker expressed when he noted on behalf of the Council the "great loss" NATO would suffer from Norstad's departure. *Le Monde* bluntly touched on points not particularly flattering to Lemnitzer. One was labeling him as having a marked military bearing but lacking personality; another was observing that since he was of retirement age the appointment seemed to suggest a transition or a temporary solution until some better candidate was found.[4]

Le Monde was not alone in its apparent doubts both about the general's personal qualities and about Kennedy's attitude toward him. One member of the Kennedy circle used such a patronizing term as "amiable"; another observer praised him as one of a species of military men with good war records but who were "bland, passive men in Washington." Still another claimed that, while he was highly regarded by Eisenhower, he had not developed much rapport with Kennedy or Secretary of Defense Robert McNamara.[5]

At the heart of the problem was the usually unstated role Lemnitzer had played in the Bay of Pigs fiasco shortly after Kennedy took office. As chairman of the Joint Chiefs of Staff, his imprimatur was a prerequisite for the ill-fated presidential decision to support a clandestine invasion of Fidel Castro's Cuba by American-trained Cuban exiles. Even though the president accepted responsibility for its failure, inevitably the military and intelligence chiefs would feel the anger and resentment of the new administration. These feelings were not assuaged when, after Lemnitzer's testimony before a closed hearing of the Latin American Subcommittees of the Senate Foreign Relations Committee on 18 May 1961, the Senate demanded the ouster of the Joint Chiefs.[6] It took more than a week for the administration to break its silence after this front-page attack and to assert that the members of the JCS would serve out their terms. Lemnitzer had begun his two-year term the previous September.[7]

While this incident was elliptically identified elsewhere in Europe, open reference appeared in the 1 August 1961 issue of *Der Spiegel*, subtitled "Out of the Bay of Pigs." This article dredged up Kennedy's rejection of Lemnitzer and his anger over Lemnitzer's apparently erroneous judgment. Quoting an anonymous Pentagon official, *Time* magazine also noted: "The President finds Lemnitzer simply too inflexible. He is just not the strong, dynamic and convincing personality, which the situation demands." The spate of aspersions was to prepare the reader for the major message of the article: that Kennedy's selection of a "pensionable" sixty-seven-year-old general in place of Norstad, age fifty-five, indicated a decision to downgrade the value of NATO for America. The officer best qualified to be SACEUR would have been Maxwell Taylor, according to *Der Spiegel*, who instead was to be Lemnitzer's successor as chairman of the JCS. Furthermore, the Lemnitzer appointment reflected a rebuke to Norstad and his concept of a European nuclear partnership. Norstad's departure would not only keep nuclear power exclusively American but would also symbolize a resigned acceptance of French nuclear independence.

The new SACEUR certainly did not fit into the mold of Camelot, as the members of the Kennedy administration would identify their new frontier in Washington. Lemnitzer was indeed of the wrong age, a friend of the wrong president (Eisenhower), and a man of the wrong temperament (a soldier with strong personal discipline rather than articulate bursts of initiative). He had little of the charisma of the bold, new visions identified with Taylor. Taylor indeed was the favorite military man of the Kennedy administration, brought in first to investigate paramilitary operations after the Bay of Pigs and then to promote flexible response in place of the more rigid and noncredible massive retaliation of the Dulles years. When the equally dynamic new secretary of defense, Robert McNamara, claimed that "the public manager must be either a judge or leader," he made clear his own preference for an active leadership for himself and his associates.[8] Taylor seemed to fit this model (and it would not preclude the new secretary of defense's supporting Taylor for the JCS chairmanship in order to get him out of the White House, where he was military adviser to Kennedy, and back to the Pentagon where he would be under closer control).

This image of Lemnitzer was not in fact correct. For example, when McNamara designated the air force as the primary agency for military space projects in order to stop interservice duplication, Lemnitzer criticized McNamara both for the terms of the designation and for what in Lemnitzer's view was an excessively fast decision. The implication that was leaked to the press (presumably by the navy) was that the general had argued against the final version of the decision rather than against a preliminary draft, and Lemnitzer protested that he was being treated unfairly.[9] He also did not hesitate to oppose Taylor's plans for changing the organizational arrangements of the JCS, creating a single military chairman and separating the service chiefs from supervising overall plans and operations as a group. This opposition was expressed civilly but clearly in a speech before the National Security Industrial Association on 27 September 1962, three days before Taylor was to assume the chairmanship of the JCS.[10]

Granted that Lemnitzer's style may not have been Kennedy's, but his views were not so divergent as his manner may have suggested. As early as May 1960 Maj. Gen. Charles T. Bonesteel, then-secretary to army Chief-of-Staff Lemnitzer, noted his chief's awareness of the limitations of massive retaliation. Recognizing the stakes involved, Lemnitzer pressed for strengthening conventional defense without sacrificing the nuclear option for strategic defense. In this respect he shared most of the assumptions of McNamara's new strategic conceptualizatons.[11]

Furthermore, as his record as SACEUR came to reveal, he undoubtedly possessed diplomatic talents. The *Times of London* perhaps understated the case when it noted that Lemnitzer's "recognized diplomatic skills will...be valuable to SHAPE". As the president's letter to Stikker pointed out, Kennedy was "confident that under General Lemnitzer's leadership the highest ranking officer in the United States armed forces" would continue the work of his predecessors.[12]

Lemnitzer's briefing notes for the secretary of defense when he became SACEUR show that he was under no illusion about the magnitude of his task. To bolster confidence in him, he planned a tour of all the member-nations to make clear in Paris and elsewhere that rumors of great changes of strategy or policy were false.[13] If any changes were to be made, they would not come from SHAPE but from the North Atlantic Council. Even though he had practical, immediate problems to deal with, such as land acquisitions for facilities, improvements in lines of communication, and costs of stronger covering forces, Lemnitzer first had to allay the uneasiness that his appointment had created in Europe generally and in France in particular. He did so by affirming in his tour the integrity of national forces (leaving out any specific references to the MLF) and soft-pedaling plans for implementing a doctrine of flexible response.

On MLF, Lemnitzer was very conscious of the problems it had created for Norstad on both sides of the Atlantic. When questioned by a British journalist late in 1963 about his responsibility for implementing the force if it were set up, Lemnitzer made an effort to link it to other forces, such as the British V-bomber force, that would be under his command. He deftly expressed military deference to political authority on the use of nuclear weapons while denying that that process would be dangerously cumbersome "on the military side because our communications are very rapid. On the political question, I don't think any man alive can answer. But if there was an all-out nuclear attack on Allied Command Europe I don't think there would be much difficulty in getting an immediate decision to retaliate in kind."

When asked about the possibility of delay until the NATO Council had thrashed out a unanimous decision, he responded:

"There is no alternative. I have no authority to use nuclear weapons. I must wait for political authority. But this sort of situation doesn't occur like a snap of the fingers. It takes days for a conventional attack to develop.... It is not as though they would have a request for authority come out of the blue."[14]

Inevitably, the new SACEUR's attention turned away from the older doctrine of massive retaliation that had dominated the middle years of the 1950s. As pointed out in the preceding chapter, the doctrine was increasingly lacking in credibility partly because of the Soviet acquisition of a weapons delivery system that could threaten the United States directly and partly because of Western Europe's demand for a response to something less than a massive Societ nuclear attack on the West. Studies in the Eisenhower period, such as the Gaither Report, which had been leaked to the press, and Henry Kissinger's widely applauded Rockefeller-supported study of tactical nuclear weapons, *Nuclear Weapons and Foreign Policy*, pointed the way to doctrinal change.

Within SHAPE itself Col. Richard G. Stilwell, director of the strategic studies group under the Plans and Policy Division, produced a study paper in 1957 that recognized the erosion of NATO's strategic doctrine. The alternative suggested in the paper would be a forward defense concept involving use of conventional forces combined with tactical nuclear weapons in an escalated response to attack. Although the Stilwell study had received the active support of Norstad, it had been shelved at the Pentagon by Secretary of Defense Charles Wilson.[15]

In contrast, under the Kennedy administration the flexible response advocated by Norstad was made official American policy. The older shield concept had been only superficially related to conventional defense, since the function of ground forces under the NATO force planning document MC-70 was to hold just long enough for the weight of massive retaliation to be brought to bear. Bolstered conventional defense, which had not been stressed since the Lisbon conference in the early 1950s, was at the heart of a strategy of flexible response, and if conventional forces failed to check aggression, then options for nuclear weapons, tactical and strategic, would then be available. The threat of escalation was to be the new deterrent.[16] The consequences of this new strategy had immediate implications for the new SACEUR. One of them was political pressure to reorganize the SHAPE staff into two sections—one nuclear and one conventional. He resisted this on the grounds that the two elements were inseparable even though he welcomed the NATO Council decision taken in Athens in 1963 to have the SACEUR appoint a nuclear deputy to the SHAPE staff. The intention was to allow broader participation of all the member-nations in nuclear matters. A more difficult problem for Lemnitzer was how to project a credible forward defense, which meant, as he put it, that "we intend to defend all allied territory in Europe. No area will remain uncovered."

But the price to be paid for this new strategy was greater defense spending on the part of the Allies to secure "greater firepower and cross-country mobility." To achieve this result, Lemnitzer advocated more personnel carriers, self-propelled artillery, and fast-moving light and medium tanks. In short, NATO had to be modernized, a task that held important political, economic, and military implications.[17]

For example, Chancellor Konrad Adenauer expressed anxiety over the possibility that emphasis on conventional forces signaled an American movement away from its nuclear pledge to NATO. Even though this particular problem dissipated, nuclear uncertainties on the part of the Allies played a role in the Kennedy administration's continuing tinkering with the notion of MLF. Whatever skepticism may have pervaded American planning circles, it would have been swept away if the Allies could have accepted the multilateral forces as an earnest of both American intentions and Western European involvement. The MLF never really passed muster, however, and had become essentially irrelevant as a device to strengthen the Alliance long before Pres. Lyndon Johnson buried it in 1964.

Because of the political void left in NATO by the demise of MLF, a special committee of NATO defense ministers was convened in June 1965 to deal with the problem of adequate interallied nuclear consultation. In November after some hesitation in West Germany over the Gaullist negative reaction, this Special Committee of Defense Ministers was established formally. Then a year later, this committee was further institutionalized as the Nuclear Defense Affairs Committee (NDAC), membership of which was open to all the Allies, and the Nuclear Planning Group (NPC), which was composed of the United States, Britain, West Germany, and Italy, with three other members of the NDAC represented in rotation. The many complications of NATO nuclear defense policy were relegated to these bodies, from problems of target selection and warhead allocation to the coordination of command. In their deliberations the American preference for strengthened conventional capabilities was expressed by both McNamara and Lemnitzer. The Allies' resistance was not because they were unaware of the destructiveness of tactical nuclear weapons—simulations of a prolonged tactical nuclear campaign in Europe had projected a death toll in Europe in the millions. The difficulty, as British Defense Minister Denis Healey expressed it, was in the high cost of conventional weaponry at a time when the British, for example, were hard-pressed to keep up the current level of the British Army of the Rhine (BAOR).[18] For others, particularly the West Germans, conventional defenses conveyed the unwelcome prospect of a prolonged conventional war on the ground and a replication in part of the traumas of World Wars I and II.[19]

Despite these and other reservations, progress was made. As early as March 1965, Lemnitzer was able to call a press conference at SHAPE, the first on-the-record news conference in over five years, to talk about the new ACE Mobile Force as a deterrent against attack on the northern and eastern flanks of the Alliance. This force of some five thousand men, one brigade group, would have a nuclear capacity and was intended to become the model of expansion in the future. Its purpose would be to deploy in any area threatened by invasion a balanced ground force of brigade group strength, augmented by six air force squadrons, especially in those territories in northern Norway and northeastern Turkey bordering the Soviet Union.[20]

As important as the new force's mobility and fire power were, Lemnitzer additionally wished to impress upon the NATO publics the integrated character of the mobile brigades. He called this feature "the governing principle" of NATO. The force's commander, Maj. Gen. Michael Fitzalan-Howard, was British, and six NATO members—the United States, Britain, Canada, West Germany, Belgium, and Italy—were recorded as having nominated battle and service groups for the ACE Mobile Force. While the Canadian group would be stationed in Canada, the other five would be scattered throughout SHAPE and would be available "at very short notice" to form the brigade group.[21]

This advance in NATO integration took place at the very time that President de Gaulle was challenging integration on every level. France had rejected MLF, had not participated in the Special Committee on nuclear consultation, and would not contribute to the ACE Mobile Force. De Gaulle's challenge to the principle of integrated forces, to American predominance in the Alliance, and to a common nuclear policy was a prelude to a dramatic and traumatic departure from SHAPE itself in 1966. There was little, however, that was actually new in de Gaulle's behavior during Lemnitzer's tenure as SACEUR beyond the break itself. His disaffection with his Allies may have had its roots in the inferior position he occupied vis-à-vis the Anglo-Saxons in World War II. Even so, occasionally he had spoken of NATO's utility. For example, in 1949 he had agreed that the Treaty "must be ratified, but it is indispensable to secure from the Americans the firm and final commitment that they will maintain their troops and their bases in France. The Americans have always intervened too late. This time they must be in a position to act without delay."[22] The lack of trust inherent in this grudging acceptance of NATO burst forth periodically during his years out of office. In 1954 he was convinced that in an economic crisis "America would become paralyzed. I say this again, America is like Carthage. Americans have money, they have the sea, just as Carthage did. They do not dominate, they corrupt."[23] And in the wake of American opposition to the French intervention in Suez two years later, he would have scrapped the pact itself. "We should have told the Americans this is what we want to do and if you do not accept it, the Atlantic pact is no more. They would have gone along. Today we are threatened with a stoppage of gasoline supplies. Well, I would say: 'As of midnight tonight, American troops can no longer travel on French highways and there are no longer any American bases in France.'"[24] This was written ten years before he actually put the order into effect.

But more than pronouncements, public or private, heralded the crisis. Upon assuming power in 1958, as discussed in the preceding chapter, de Gaulle asked for a reorganization of NATO that would give France parity with the United States and Britain in the form of a tripartite directorate. When this was refused, as it had been in other forms ever since the Alliance was established, de Gaulle planned his dual-tracked moves to detach France from the Organization and at the same time to assert French leadership of Western Europe in place of American. His pronouncements often had a casual air, as if they were impromptu affairs, but in fact his moves were carefully prepared and brilliantly staged. Timing was of the essence. De Gaulle would not act until all the pieces were in place: a nuclear capability must be visible, the Algerian war had to be concluded, an electoral endorsement of the direction he was moving was a necessary prelude to the final action. And not least in importance was the need to complete the arrangements before old age caught up with him. Most of these preparations took place during the early years of Lemnitzer's tenure; the major blow occurred at the very midpoint, and coping with the repercussions occupied much of his final three years as SACEUR.

In fact, French rejection of the NATO Council decision of 1957 to deploy nuclear weapons in Europe was made in the last days of the Fourth Republic, but it was carried out fully under de Gaulle. IRBMs could be placed on French soil only if shared under a dual-key arrangement, as with Britain, and only if France then received the necessary technical assistance to produce its own missiles. When negotiations on this matter finally collapsed in 1959, Norstad noved 250 American Supersabre fighter-bombers from French to British and German bases where they would have access to tactical nuclear weapons.[25] Also before Lemnitzer assumed command, the French fleet in the Mediterranean in 1959 and in the Atlantic in 1963 had been removed from SHAPE's and SACLANT's authority respectively. In neither case was there an advance warning; the French government in June 1963 simply eliminated France's Atlantic ships from an Annual Review questionnaire asking which vessels would be available for NATO in the following year.[26]

In 1965 France ostentatiously refused to participate in "Fallex '66," a military exercise for Allied general staffs proposed by Lemnitzer as early as November 1963 to test Allied communications networks and alert systems. But because the exercise was intended to implement the American flexible response approach that de Gaulle had rejected, it was unacceptable to him. The most that Lemnitzer could rescue from this situation was an agreement with Gen. Charles Ailleret, French chief-of-staff, to keep a few French officers in the exercise.[27]

It is hardly surprising, then, that the SACEUR in letters written in the spring of 1965 to two correspondents should characterize French relations as turbulent. He noted that when he took on the SACEUR assignment, he was well aware of the problems ahead, yet he was particularly concerned over "a certain element of vindictiveness creeping into Franco-American relationships, particularly in the political field."[28] And he found it to be an American as well as a French problem. "There is entirely too great a tendency in the U.S. to consider that all decisions made by the French Government are made for the sole purpose of being anti-American, and vice versa. I hope something can be done to reverse this trend, because it is damaging to the interests of both countries and NATO."[29] But the temptations to yield to paranoia must have been difficult to resist when de Gaulle ordered all French members of the French integrated staff at SHAPE to boycott preparations for the fall 1965 annual military exercise. The order, given by Defense Minister Pierre Messmer, was described as "the severest blow yet struck by France against Gen. Lyman L. Lemnitzer's Supreme Headquarters, the embodiment of the alliance's principle of integrated command."[30]

Still, with all the problems posed by French behavior between 1963 and 1967, there was never a sense that de Gaulle's attitude toward Lemnitzer contained any *ad hominem* animosity. Perhaps there was an element of condescension in the relationship, but if so it was reflective of the French president's attitude toward any American. Whatever truth may be assigned to de Gaulle's reported statement that he "had never heard of the man," his pique over Lemnitzer's appointment had little to do with Lemnitzer himself. According to the pundit Henry J. Taylor, de Gaulle displayed "a remarkable schizophrenia" during Lemnitzer's first six months in Paris. On the one hand, his opposition to SHAPE as the symbol of integration increased in this period; on the other hand, he showed cooperation and support in every instance where he dealt personally with the SACEUR.[31]

This cordiality was more than *politesse*, or so it seemed to Lemnitzer even as life in de Gaulle's France grew more difficult. In the course of farewell ceremonies marking the removal of NATO forces from France in March 1967, de Gaulle personally awarded the SACEUR the Grand Cross of the Legion of Honor. Earlier he had written Lemnitzer of "the great esteem that I hold for you because of the eminent military qualities of which you have given proof in the exercise of your command and the sincere friendship that our excellent relations inspire in me in your regard."[32] In his letter de Gaulle professed to have been "touched" by Lemnitzer's sentiments about his experiences in France. Certainly the SACEUR himself was touched by de Gaulle's personal presentation of the Grand Cross with the sash and the statements that followed in the luncheon at the

Elysée Palace. "In everything he said," Lemnitzer wrote his family, "he made it clear that the decision to evict U.S. and NATO headquarters from France had nothing whatsoever to do with his feelings toward me personally. This I have always understood, because he had made this very clear in my frequent contacts with him during the past six months."[33]

While de Gaulle's personal attitude may have produced some psychological balm for the wounds inflicted, most of Lemnitzer's American peers did not even have that to sustain the shock caused by de Gaulle's letter to President Johnson of 7 March 1966. Similar letters were presented to heads of states or governments in Britain, West Germany, and Italy on 9 March. At the end of that month, memorandums to all the Allies announced that France was withdrawing from the military organization and expected prompt removal of NATO forces from her soil.[34] If it was a shock, it may have been, as U.S. Permanent Representative to NATO Harlan Cleveland suggested, because de Gaulle had spoken so often about such an outcome but had taken only piecemeal steps until then. Or perhaps his previous press conference of 21 February seemed to imply that nothing definitive would take place until 1969 when, according to Article 13 of the North Atlantic Treaty, any party may withdraw one year after it has given notice to the Allies.[35]

Even when the letters were delivered, ambiguities about France's stand remained. The initial language of the press conference spoke of normal attributes of sovereignty in that any foreign army on French soil would have to be under French command alone. In Foreign Minister Maurice Couve de Murville's explication of 9 March, it was made clear that France would not denounce the Treaty in 1966 or in 1969. The action involved France's role not in the Alliance as such but in NATO's organization and in particular with regard to French forces in SHAPE and the stationing of Allied forces on French territory.[36] Only on 29 March did a French memorandum specify a timetable for the transfer of American and NATO commands out of French territory as well as for the termination of all French personnel in NATO commands.³⁷ The date 1 July 1966 was set for the latter, and 1 April 1967 for the former. The April deadline had some slight measure of flexibility for the more complicated moving operations, since the expulsion order involved supply depots, warehouses, and headquarters buildings, among other military installations. Moreover, special provisions were to be made for allowing the United States to continue the use of the vital oil pipeline from Donges on the Atlantic to Huttenheim in Germany. Additionally, an offer would be made to West Germany to continue the stationing of French forces in that country, not under SHAPE provenance but under the Paris-London Agreements of October 1954 whereby West Germany entered NATO.

Nonetheless, the expulsion order held special problems for the United States inasmuch as bilateral accords had included, as the de Gaulle note of 12 March specifically pointed out, "warehouses at Deols-La Martinerie, American headquarters at Saint-Germaine, pipelines, supply lines, and the placing of certain air bases and installations in France at the disposal of the United States command."³⁸ Much of the burden of living with the implications of these problems would fall on Lemnitzer, both as SACEUR and as CINCEUR.

But before he could respond in either of his roles, the United States government alone and with its Allies had to come to grips with the kinds of responses that should be made to this unilateral eviction order. This was not easy, if only because the French language was at one and the same time painfully clear in its immediate objective and delphically elliptical in its projection of future relationships in the Alliance. Whatever the fairness or accuracy of the reasons de Gaulle offered—which ranged from the refusal of the United States to adjust the organization to new circumstances, to the charge that the United States exploited NATO for its own imperial purposes, to the assumption that the Cold War and the Soviet threat had altered significantly since 1949—his action evoked confusion, hesitation, and even agreement among some of the Allies.

Portugal, for example, acclaimed the note of "realism" in de

Gaulle's behavior, according to *Diario de Noticias*. The Salazar government had become increasingly upset with its allies' unsympathetic views concerning Portugal's colonial problems in Africa and used the Gaullist attack on NATO to express its own frustrations with the Alliance. French Quebec acted as an inhibition on a forthright response from Canada, which attempted to behave as if nothing had happened. The West Germans and the Belgians, seeking some hopeful signs of reconciliation and rapprochement in the disarray, found them in de Gaulle's exclusion of the political side of the Alliance from his expulsion order and in his recognition of the value of the Treaty itself. They consequently urged caution in replying to the French demands in the hope of minimizing offense to their sensitive ally.[39]

While anger and outrage were also expressed, particularly in the Netherlands and Britain, the most emotional reactin appeared to have been in the United States, the country most directly under attack by de Gaulle. To well-known critics of NATO, such as Sen. Mike Mansfield and others who fretted about Europe's negative reaction to America's Vietnam War, the challenge was a welcome reminder that something was wrong with NATO. In their opinion change should come, perhaps even to the point of withdrawing American troops not only from France but from all Europe as well. Indeed, as Mansfield was reported to have said, de Gaulle may have performed "a needed service: by providing an occasion to reduce American obligations and to place greater responsibility on the European allies for the defense of Europe."[40] Within the Pentagon there was even an echo of this sentiment from McNamara's circle, which felt that the prospective loss of French participation was of limited military significance and hence could be used to streamline with cost savings the NATO defense system.

But these were not the dominant reactions in Washington. Another viewpoint in the Pentagon was that the United States should challenge the legality of de Gaulle's cancellation of bilateral agreements that provided two years' notice before termination. This position was supported strongly by such

"Atlanticists" in the State Department as Undersecretary of State George Ball, who purportedly informed Allies in Paris that the United States would challenge the legality of eviction, ignore deadlines, and deny France access to intelligence sharing and to NADGE (NATO Air Defense Ground Environment).[41] In his memoirs Ball remembered his annoyance with de Gaulle's exploitation of France's geographical position between West Germany and the Atlantic, "knowing that whatever he did, his country would be protected by American power," which permitted a shameless flaunting of France's sovereignty. In his view this deserved a strong rebuke.[42]

Yet President Johnson's response turned out to be remarkably mild, considering the provocation and considering the advice he received. Ambassador Harlan Cleveland noted that while his "private references to General de Gaulle stretched his considerable talent for colorful language," he "imposed an icy correctness on those who had reason to discuss French policy in public." John M. Leddy, the assistant secretary of state for European affairs, recalled the draft of a stiff letter of protest prepared for the president by Secretary of State Dean Rusk with the advice of U.S. Ambassador to France Charles Bohlen, Dean Acheson, and Ball. Johnson altered the tone on the grounds that de Gaulle was not going to change his mind whatever arguments might be made. "He's asked us to get out of France. We'll get out of France." Leddy recalled an ambassadorial lunch—without the French ambassador—at which Johnson said: "Well, when that old man talks I just tip my hat to him, tip my hat. When he comes rushing down like a locomotive on the track, why the Germans and ourselves, we just stand aside and let him go on by, then we're back together again." Gen. Andrew Goodpaster suggested that Johnson's composure was not shaken because he was not personally engaged in a confrontation with de Gaulle; it was a confrontation rather between two nations.[43]

As a result of these internal American deliberations as well as the variety of views among the Allies, ten days were required before the other fourteen members of the Alliance could come up with a public statement on NATO without France. Four formal meetings as well as informal debate preceded the declaration.[44] Whatever the differences between the approaches of Britain, which took the initiative in proposing new Alliance machinery, and Canada, which blamed the United States' lack of nuclear sharing for spurring de Gaulle's actions, the Allies agreed on the importance of continuing NATO's functions. According to Cleveland's judgment, the fourteen produced, on the basis of a British draft, "a declaration of admirable clarity and, considering it was produced by diplomats and politicians, remarkable brevity"—fewer than 150 words. "The North Atlantic Treaty and Organization are not merely instruments of the common defense. They meet a common political need and reflect the readiness and determination of the member countries of the North Atlantic Community to consult and act together."[45]

Rather than emerge demoralized and divided from the experience, the NATO political leaders appeared energized by the crisis. Bohlen suggests a manic quality to the reaction, as if the Allies had foiled the French by not begging for a delay or dragging their feet or raising objections at every turn or by not behaving, in short, "in a rather bitchy fashion," which the occasion might have warranted.[46]

On the strength of a new resolve and of a unity forged by the absence of French dissent, reform and modernization of the defense system seemed to have better prospects after 1966 than before. A Nuclear Planning Group could now look toward a new European role in the defense of Europe. A Defense Planning Committee (DPC) need not deal with French rejections, as the French delegates would stay away from Council sessions involving organizational problems. A new military representative system would replace the old Standing Group in Washington. France's departure from Rocquencourt brought initiative and élan to Casteau, the Belgian successor headquarters, and to the Brussels suburb of Evére to which the political headquarters was moved on 26 October 1966. It is worth noting that while the French did not want to lose the political headquarters, this was the price they had to pay for their action against SHAPE. To their credit they did so gracefully. The French mission quietly moved from Paris to Brussels with their NATO colleagues.

NATO's euphoria over coping with France's withdrawal could not endure. The very real problems arising from translating de Gaulle's order into reality guaranteed this even without a close look at the character of the defense posture of Europe without France. And nowhere was reality more in evidence than in the activities required of the SACEUR in Paris. The blessing in efficiency of the DPC's transfer of the Military Committee from Washington to Brussels in November and the organization of an integrated International Military Staff (IMS) as the executive agent of the Military Committee would bring long-run benefits to the SACEUR. But they did not help much in the short run. Lemnitzer had to meet deadlines which his political superiors bravely accepted, and he had to meet them quickly and effectively. In less than a year's time, before 1 April 1967, SACEUR had to oversee the removal of his SHAPE headquarters, along with the headquarters of his American command (EUCOM), to a still-unknown location. Along with these changes would be the physical relocation of hundreds of bases and installations and depots scattered throughout France that served NATO and/or American needs.

It may be noted in retrospect that de Gaulle's France shrewdly eased some burdens that would have been impossible to overcome: the May 1966 agreement to allow continued operation of the oil pipeline from the Atlantic to Germany and the agreement after some negotiations to permit continuing flights of NATO planes from Britain to southern Europe over French air space. Had de Gaulle continued a ban on all bilateral overflight rights that had been previously given to France's NATO Allies with virtually automatic annual renewal, the identification of France with Austria and Switzerland would have created a neutral belt of nations—an "Elysian Curtain," as C. L. Sulzberger called it[47]—splitting NATO into two parts and reducing flexibility of troop dispositions. For a time after May, the American authorization for thirty-nine categories of overflights was subjected to monthly and then almost daily clearance. The question, however, was satisfactorily resolved in a meeting in November of that year between Lemnitzer and General Ailleret on the future status of military relations between France and its Allies. The overflight reviews were modified, and American military flights were permitted again on an annual basis as of 3 August 1967. These privileges were extended to all the other NATO members the following month after another meeting between Lemnitzer and Ailleret.

In exchange, the French made sure that they would enjoy the benefits of the NADGE air alert system, essential to French security. Although this NATO Air Defense Ground Environment would be an integrated as well as improved air defense system, it was important enough for French security to justify France's contributing a share of the costs (12 percent of the total) and to keep a French company as a member of the consortium chartered with constructing the sysem.[48]

Similarly, French national interests managed to contain the potentially explosive issue of a French military presence in West Germany. While West Germany was unwilling to accept the 1954 terms of admission to NATO as grounds for continuing French troops in place, neither the Germans nor the other Allies wanted the French alternative: full withdrawal of the French military presence in Germany. Rather than persist in the claim that France could station troops in Germany only within a NATO context and under NATO authority, the Germans sought instead to retain a bilateral French commitment to West German security. The result was first an interim agreement allowing the temporary stationing of French forces after 1 July 1967 pending a definitive arrangement. This was satisfactory to the French as long as the NATO mission they served was not integrated within SHAPE. The matter was settled through an exchange of letters on 3 December 1966 between Couve de Murville and Willy Brandt, foreign minister of the new German coalition government. The legal issues were solved by an understanding that the 23 October 1954 convention on foreign forces in Germany did not rule out the continued presence of French troops.

Having won the point, France then permitted the flying of both West German and French flags over French bases, and German liaison officers posted with the French forces would be informed fourteen days in advance of any troop movements at or above the regimental level.[49] Thus, France was able to maintain its troops in Germany on its own terms free from Alliance obligations and free, for that matter, to leave whether or not the Germans wanted them to go. The NATO Council was an unwilling observer of these arrangements because no clearcut military agreements had been made to bring French forces under a NATO command in the event of a war alert. The most that Lemnitzer was able to extract from his 23 November conversations with Ailleret was agreement on the missions that might be assigned to French troops if France decided to join in NATO's common military actions. Joint contingency plans could be made, but no automatic commitment.[50]

Such was the nature of the burdens falling on the SACEUR. They had far-reaching implications that would affect SHAPE's sense of effectiveness as well as its organizational arrangements for the balance of Lemnitzer's tenure as SACEUR.

Lemnitzer's most immediate and pressing responsibility resulting from the French activities of 1966 was how to respond to the expulsion order. Unlike the secretary-general and the political headquarters, which by implication were exempted, SHAPE and its subsidiary headquarters as well as the U.S. Command in Europe (EUCOM) had no choice but to move and to move quickly. When secretary-general Manlio Brosio also departed for Belgium in October, it was a consequence of NATO's (and particularly America's) initiative, not France's. As mentioned earlier, while the decision was made by the fourteen NATO Council members without France, the French delegate announced that France would move to Brussels with the others in full cooperation with its Allies. No deadline was set by France for the departure. Compared with the SACEUR's position, these circumstances seemed leisurely and almost comfortable. Even though the Council could afford to defer until October the question of moving the International Staff and the secretary-general's office, it could not delay beyond its June meeting a decision on where to move the military headquarters.[51] While the choice of the new host country for SHAPE was settled on 21 June when the Belgian House of Representatives approved the transfer of SHAPE to Belgium, the specific location of the military headquarters and the conditions under which it would be built remained under negotiation throughout the summer of 1966.

The removal of the lagest subordinate headquarters of SHAPE, Allied Forces Central Europe (AFCENT), from Fontainebleau was even more problematical since it was not known as late as 1 July whether its destination would be the Netherlands or West Germany. As Lemnitzer noted, he "was getting very concerned about the delays that are being imposed, because it would be most difficult to move either one of these headquarters in a year, and now we only have nine months left before April 1, 1967."[52] NATO's military headquarters was not his only concern; as CINCEUR he had to find a new home for EUCOM as well. Spacious and comfortable facilities then used by the U.S. Seventh Army were found in Stuttgart despite Lemnitzer's recognition that it was economic reasons that dictated the move to a location "much too far removed from SHAPE in Belgium."[53] But if Stuttgart was considered to be too far from SHAPE, the ultimate location of SHAPE itself was also considered to be too far from the political headquarters in Brussels. Or so Lemnitzer believed. He felt that the most reasonable location would be the old Belgian military base in Evére in the eastern suburbs of Brussels and neighboring the international airport. This suitable facility, however, became the home of the secretary-general and the political headquarters.

Lemnitzer had made it clear "as a result of our studies that from the military communications point of view, as well as other factors, there is only one feasible location of SHAPE, and that is in the Brussels area."[54] He wanted a site at least as close to the Belgian capital as his former headquarters had been to Paris, and preferably within ten miles to the south or east of the city. In his opinion, any further distance would damage the effectiveness of his headquarters.[55]

Despite this strong advice, the Belgian government offered Lemnitzer two sites far from the capital and unsatisfactory in almost every respect. Both were in southern Belgium in the vicinity of Casteau and were offered because they were the only large acreages belonging to the State. Furthermore, according to Count Charles de Kerchove, who headed a special Belgian commission on the issue, other desirable sites would be either too expensive to acquire or too time-consuming to manage within the time span allotted. The problems of appropriation, building new roads, laying water and electric mains, and building a telecommunications network would be too forbidding. Beyond these considerations, de Kerchove observed that the initial Belgian invitation made clear that other buildings or sites nearer to Brussels would be excluded because of the government's unwillingness to relocate SHAPE in an urban area. At least at Casteau and Chievres some of the infrastructure was available and the rest ready to be worked on immediately.[56]

Lemnitzer recognized that he had little choice. Casteau ranked slightly higher than neighboring Chievres because it was on the main highway to Brussels. Had he pressed too hard for a better location, it might have fed Gaullist charges of American domination. Indeed, his vigorous attempts to locate in Brussels had already resulted in some sniping from the Belgian defense minister that was aired in the Belgian popular satiric journal *Pourquoi Pas*. Reputedly, Lemnitzer refused to accept the minister's offer of either Chievres or Casteau and instead insisted on touring the Waterloo region on his own and "not for its celebrated historical associations." The magazine then built on Defense Minister Poswick's annoyance to suggest that the real reason for Lemnitzer's reluctance to move to suitable quarters an hour and a quarter from Brussels was not the distance from the airport but rather the opposition of the families of SHAPE's senior officers, whose wives would be inconvenienced by living fifty kilometers from the capital. As for Lemnitzer's concern for suitable housing for families of staff, this was trivialized as a concern as to whether suitable household help would be available in a rural area.[57]

That economic considerations came into play was obvious; the depressed Hainaut province would benefit from the presence of seventeen hundred SHAPE families. This issue was more to the point than Belgian fear of SHAPE as a lightning rod for enemy attack. But these questions were essentially irrelevant because SHAPE would have to make the best of what was offered. Some of the strains were relieved by the Belgian promise to spend $500 million in readying Casteau for occupation and in building a road system to Brussels that would respond to Lemnitzer's objections about distance from the capital. The results, for the most part, spoke for themselves. Within the allotted time limit, 31 March 1967, less than six months, the new headquarters opened. Much of the construction was done in winter, but even with a reasonably mild winter, as Lemnitzer noted, it was a "tremendous accomplishment to transfer operations from Rocquencourt with minimal difficulty."[58]

The relocation of families and the construction of support facilities were more troublesome. The SACEUR himself lived in the Bachelor Officers' Quarters for over four months while his and other families remained behind in Paris. But at the end of August 1967, Lemnitzer could write to a friend that a large housing program as well as a renovated chateau for the SACEUR was well under way.[59] Less than a year later, he could report that the new headquarters was a more efficient organization than its predecessor in Paris. A new SHAPE community had been created on the headquarters site, encompassing six hundred family housing units, a complete shopping center, a sixty-bed hospital, three clubs, theater, chapel, and gymnasium. Not all the problems were solved, among them his own housing, but the SACEUR had reason for satisfaction.[60]

A little over a year later, Lemnitzer could report with even more satisfaction to the North Atlantic Assembly in its meeting at Brussels "that these tremendous relocations have been completed successfully without the loss—even for a moment—of the command and control so vital to the security of all Allied Command Europe."[61] In a long letter filled with reminiscences of his career he noted that:

> I never expected to stay in this job as long as I have, but when the decision was made by the Government of France to evict all NATO and non-French military activities in France which were under my command, I was determined to see this job through. As you can well imagine, it was an enormous undertaking and involved the movement of over 100,000 U.S. and NATO personnel and over one million tons of supplies and equipment of all types.... We had less than six months to complete enough of the headquarters so we could shift our operations from France by 1 April 1967. We shifted the operations on 31 March 1967, thereby beating the deadline to everyone's surprise. I was very pleased that the relocation from France, which involved a great many difficult negotiations and dislocations, was accomplished smoothly without any real crisis.[62]

Lemnitzer's success won him deserved commendation from his colleagues and superiors in Washington, but there were distinct differences between the conclusions Lemnitzer drew and those of Secretary of Defense McNamara and his colleagues. The SACEUR was only too aware that there were serious problems in SHAPE's capacity to fulfill its mission that resulted from France's withdrawal. In contrast, McNamara regarded the dispatch with which the removal was conducted as an augury of other accomplishments. For too many persons in the Defense Department, the relocation provided an opportunity to regroup and to reshape American forces in Europe in order to make them more efficient and less costly. As Assistant Secretary of Defense for International Security Affairs John T. McNaughton noted in April 1966, it would be very expensive to move all the United States forces and facilities; hence, the Department was looking for "alternatives which would make efficient use of modern logistic knowledge and equipment, including various alternative configurations of U.S. forces and facilities and of NATO facilities which bring the costs down."[63] A year later McNamara could announce that considerable savings had been achieved as a result of relocation, ranging from annual foreign exchange savings of over $100 million annually, to $50-60 million in the expenses of new bases in Britain and Germany. The latter were due in part to "retreading" American bases already in being. Many of these cost-cutting measures resulted from returning troops to the United States, along with accompanying dependents, and reducing foreign nationals to four thousand from the fifteen thousand employed in France. All told, the reduction in personnel associated with U.S. military operations in Europe would be fifty thousand.[64]

It is apparent that the Defense Department used France's action to put into place ideas reflecting its concern about waste and excessive costs of equipment, manpower, and supplies in the European theater. De Gaulle unwittingly accelerated McNamara's reforms, which might have required much longer to put into effect without the sudden changes imposed on SHAPE.

The most spectacular of them was reported in a press statement on 2 May 1967 announcing a new arrangement for West German financial support to offset American foreign exchange costs of its forces in Germany by means of a $500 million Bundesbank investment in special medium-term U.S. government securities. Additionally, the United States proposed the redeployment from Germany to the United States of up to thirty-five thousand military personnel. None of the redeployment would involve a lessening of the American commitment to NATO, for even after the Twenty-fourth Infantry Division was returned to the United States, at least one brigade would remain in Germany at all times. Similar plans were intended for air force units, and both air and army forces would be together in Germany for exercises once a year.[65]

These actions were postulated on an assumption that the removal of France from SHAPE would be "in no way disabling" to the military posture of the Alliance. French territory was not necessary for the defense of NATO; "neither the United States nor its allies have ever contemplated a way in which falling back upon French soil through the battlefield of Germany was an acceptable strategy for the alliance." The key was forward defense, which means at the West German frontier.[66] Thus, while French cooperation was desirable, in McNamara's opinion it was not vital to NATO's military planners.

Neither the projected reforms nor the rationale on which they were made impressed the SACEUR in the same manner as they did his superiors in Washington. At one point Lemnitzer was moved to comment about the putative opportunities to be derived from de Gaulle's action that "one more benefit of this sort and we will be out of business."[67] What the military leadership had to face was the continued commitment to a forward defense of all European territory, a promise reaffirmed by Secretary McNamara in June 1966, "which means, in central Europe, a defense at the frontier of West Germany."[68] But this involved a commitment of manpower and equipment at a level belied by the reduction of U.S. troops in Europe and the concomitant reluctance of European partners to sacrifice more for the common cause than they already had done. On the American side, McNamara's reforms encouraged Senator Mansfield to demand larger withdrawals of American troops, to the point where the secretaries of both state and defense publicly opposed the "substantial reductions" contained in the Mansfield resolution.[69] Restlessness in Washington fed European discontent, of which the British complaints about their balance of payments expenses in Germany and the German resentment against special assessments for the upkeep of Allied forces could possibly contribute to an unraveling of NATO without any prodding from the Warsaw Pact observers.

But more than troop levels were involved. The line of NATO communications, while remaining open after the bilateral U.S.–French negotiation as far as overflights of French territory and the maintenance of the oil pipeline were concerned, still involved a major transformation. From an east-west flow from France to Germany, they had to be changed to north-south as supplies were transferred to German ports. The irony, of course, lay in the fact that the Berlin crisis of the early 1960s had revealed the old north-south military supply line to be painfully vulnerable; it was to have been remedied by locating the supply sector as far west as possible, near the Atlantic.[70] Even if this dislocation was only a temporary problem, the military men on the ground were faced with the fact that "the disrepair of American military arrangement is apparent." In other words, SHAPE could only be adversely affected by the French withdrawal, as communications, infrastructure, and defense agencies had to be adapted to a new situation. Despite advances in technologoy that might permit some redeployment of combat garrisons without reducing their effectiveness, the preservation of their organizational integrity came under question.[71] Such were the somber conclusions of a Senate subcommittee in March 1967, which doubtless caused Lemnitzer much concern.

To maintain credibility in the face of change, Lemnitzer made it clear that NATO must recognize that France's actions had done damage and NATO must be prepared to cope with the consequences. Paradoxically, rather than assuming new obligations, the Allies seemingly were being lulled into a false sense of security through the application of new management techniques and through the relative ease of the move from France to Belgium. In an address to the North Atlantic Assembly in November 1967, Lemnitzer noted that potential enemy military capabilities remained substantial and were growing. He posed the question as to what happens to deterrence when the Allies reduce their term of military service, redeploy troops to the United States, cut back on military budgets—and still expect the armed forces to conduct an effective forward defense in the event of aggression? The way out of this dilemma in the immediate future would be through one of two alternatives: to "thin out the already marginal resources available in Central Europe" or to provide more units for its defense. But in the absence of the latter decision, he pointed out that the Alliance must recognize the possibility of "earlier employment of selected nuclear weapons." "No matter how one rationalizes it," he said, "the French withdrawal from NATO's integrated organization makes ambiguous what help its land or air forces would provide the center region of ACE; it affects not only operations but also flexibility to carry out operational missions." He concluded, "This potential loss is from a vital area—one [in] which I considered the existing forces to be only of marginal strength before this action was taken."[72]

Lemnitzer was under no illusion that his own success in responding to France's expulsion order did more than provide a measure of damage control. NATO's ability to respond to hostilities in a crisis and, even more seriously, to deter a crisis from occurring was weaker in 1967 than it had been in 1965.

Lemnitzer relinquished his command on 1 July 1969, having served in that post longer than any of his predecessors. But he did not retire from his service to NATO. In the first months of private life, he continued to express his concerns about relaxation of efforts in the face of what he called "the most formidable conventional armed forces in the world today."[73] His role may not have been as a conceptualizer or as a strategist or as a political leader—others have made their contributions in these areas. His role was as a manager who could contain crises and turn them on occasion to the advantage of the Alliance. Although Lemnitzer does not trumpet his experience with the crisis of 1966-67 as his crowning achievement, his greatest service to NATO was to take up the challenge imposed by France's demands upon its Allies and to lay it down four years later with minimal damage.

6. Goodpaster
Maintaining Deterrence during Détente

LEWIS SORLEY

Gen. Andrew J. Goodpaster became SACEUR on 1 July 1969. Two months earlier, following an example that General Lemnitzer had set when he succeeded General Norstad, Goodpaster had assumed the complementary duties of CINCEUR. That gave him two months to make an initial round of calls relating to that post and to establish himself with that staff before taking on the duties of SACEUR as well.

Goodpaster was, especially given the times, an almost ideal choice for the post of SACEUR. He was in a sense coming home, having served in NATO in its earliest days under Generals Eisenhower and Gruenther. As he says in his introduction to this book, Goodpaster had in fact been the staff officer who drafted General Order Number 1 by which the newly activated SHAPE assumed operational control of those Allied forces dedicated to the defense of Western Europe. And, of course, he had been very close to Eisenhower during his presidency, serving as staff secretary in the White House. That association was not lost on the Europeans, who retained their wartime regard for Eisenhower and their appreciation of his contribution to the establishment and early development of SHAPE.

Goodpaster had enhanced his own professional reputation as well while serving the president. He was widely perceived as an honest broker, a man to be trusted, one who was fair and discreet and enjoyed Eisenhower's total confidence.[1] This reputation was very helpful to him as SACEUR and helps to explain his performance as the head of the Alliance's military organization in a time when there were abroad so many potentially disruptive forces. Had he not maintained the confidence of so many key Alliance leaders, they could have damaged very seriously the solidarity that was so crucially important, something that Goodpaster knew full well and that every SACEUR emphasizes at every opportunity.

Thus, his early NATO-related career was to serve Goodpaster well when he arrived in Europe, particularly since he came directly from serving under Gen. Creighton Abrams as deputy commander of U.S. forces in Vietnam since the previous summer. The deteriorating public support for continued American involvement in the war, particularly in the wake of the Tet 1968 offensive and the later domestic political repercussions, was strongly echoed throughout Western Europe. It was a measure of the regard for Goodpaster and for his earlier associates that he reported experiencing no personal antagonism, either public or private, when he arrived in Europe to take up his new post. In fact, as he later recalled, at the governmental level the attitude was just the opposite, although European leaders were not going to say so publicly in the atmosphere of that day.[2]

Soon after arriving at SHAPE, Goodpaster, as had become customary, set out to visit key individuals in each of the NATO nations, including foreign ministers, defense ministers, and heads of state. With each he attempted to establish the Terms of Reference for later dealings by asking what they thought the consequences would be if, for some reason, NATO suddenly ceased to exist. He was typically answered with a nervous laugh and the observation that fortunately that was not something one would have to contemplate. But when Goodpaster persisted and urged his colleagues to contemplate exactly that, he found their answers to be serious and thoughtful.[3] While expressed in a variety of ways, they amounted to the same thing: admission that without NATO, they would be living in terror if they were living at all. Having obtained this key admission of NATO's worth, Goodpaster would say, "That's right and I think that's the basis on which we can and should work together." He went on to stress his belief, as he did at every opportunity, that "NATO represents an enormous net 'plus' to every member-nation when its costs in resources are weighed against its benefits in peace and security."[4]

The SHAPE that Goodpaster took over was one that had undergone considerable challenge and buffeting in recent days. President Nixon later stated flatly his view that at that point "NATO was in disarray."[5] Not only were there continuing effects of the disruptive and difficult move from France and the continuing problems associated with relocation of facilities and especially elements of the infrastructure, as recounted in the previous chapter, but also other problems. Without discounting the valiant efforts of Lemnitzer and the remarkable achievements in relocating headquarters, troop units, and support facilities, it was apparent that shifts in the Alliance's stance and structure continued to pose problems for the SACEUR. Not the least of these was the opportunity that French withdrawal from the military organization provided to certain elements in the United States to intensify their efforts to reduce the American commitment to NATO, especially in terms of U.S. troop strength there.

Senator Mansfield, in particular, had been agitating since at least 1966 for a reduction of troops in Europe. While the invasion of Czechoslovakia in 1968 by Soviet and Warsaw Pact forces had temporarily dampened these efforts, by the time of Goodpaster's accession, Mansfield was back at it with a vengeance. This time he found some additional allies in the ranks of those who opposed American actions in Vietnam and who wanted to reduce American involvement in foreign affairs and American military capabilities elsewhere in the world as well. One result was that during the period 1963-69 U.S. forces in Europe were reduced from 408,000 to 300,000, a process later characterized by Henry Kissinger as "thinly disguised withdrawal."[6]

Strong pressures for additional reductions were mounting as Goodpaster took over as SACEUR. In some quarters near hysteria prevailed. In October 1969 a correspondent for the journal *Nato's Fifteen Nations*, writing in the "Letter from London" feature under a heading "The American Puzzle," offered this view: "I cannot close this letter without mentioning the curiosity—not to say anxiety—arising in Britain over the foreign and defence policy of the United States in the near future. To many minds the big question is not whether the Americans are going to pull out of Europe, but whether they have not already gone."[7] Then, at a mid-October meeting of NATO Parliamentarians in Brussels, where Goodpaster "urged the nations to pay the modest costs of peace to avoid paying the terrible costs of war," he was undercut by some attending Senators who, as Goodpaster soon reported to the assembled U.S. Army senior commanders in Germany, made it clear that they intended to press for further reductions in the U.S. commitment to NATO.[8]

In November an "Anti-NATO Congress" was held in Amsterdam, attracting some fifteen hundred young people. Organized by left-wing youth groups from the NATO memberstates, the gathering ignored the recent Soviet invasion of Czechoslovakia. Instead, it was reported, those attending "talked of atrocities in Angola, Greece and Vietnam."[9] By December U.S. Senators were back on the scene, with Fulbright, Mansfield, and Kennedy appearing at a NATO Council meeting in Brussels, where they asserted "that forthcoming considerable cuts in American forces in Europe were inevitable." This pronouncement, it was reported, "came like a cold water shower upon the heads of NATO Defence Ministers already worried by... impending Canadian withdrawals, and trying to patch up NATO defences by some haphazard measures."[10] The following summer the debate on defense expenditures in Congress was characterized by the *Washington Post* as "the most widespread assault on all kinds of military activities ever made on Capitol Hill."[11]

President-elect Nixon had at the beginning of 1969 sent a warm letter to European leaders, including Secretary-General Brosio, reaffirming his intention to give priority to strengthening Atlantic ties. Nixon's first foreign trip as president was to Europe, only a month after his inauguration. Henry Kissinger, who accompanied him, later recalled the difficult situation they encountered:

> There was uncertainty about the future of Europe. The attitude to the common defense was a curious mixture of unwillingness to augment European efforts and fear of American withdrawal. European leaders were urging us toward detente with the East—but we had the uneasy sense that the principal motive was to lift the burden of difficult decisions from European shoulders. And Vietnam confronted European governments with a dilemma: they felt the need to respond to domestic pressures, but for their own security they feared an American humiliation or defeat and shrank from any step that would contribute to it. It was clear that all our perceptions and planning were now about to be tested.[12]

Besides force reduction pressures, there were a number of other problems in the context of the times, many deriving in one way or another from the war in Vietnam. One of the most troubling was the sharp decline in the readiness, and hence in the capabilities, of U.S. forces in Europe as an outgrowth of the war. Despite the massive amounts spent to support operations in Southeast Asia, still other assets required were obtained by stripping and then under-resourcing American military elements elsewhere in the world. In Europe this resulted in units that were grossly understrength; wracked by continual, massive turnover in those who were assigned; plagued by widespread problems of drug abuse, racial disharmony, dissent, and indiscipline; and thus, not only much reduced in operational capability, but also poor examples for the NATO Allies that the U.S. was trying to get to contribute more and better forces to the Alliance. Goodpaster was very candid in discussing these matters with military leaders of the other Alliance nations, telling them in late 1972 that the problems were "serious, and deep-seated," being rooted "in the present condition of the American society of this generation."[13] It is a tribute to Goodpaster's personal prestige and influence that this state of affairs apparently did not undermine his moral authority in dealing with the other nations and their military establishments.

These were also interesting times in terms of the evolving nature of the military threat faced by NATO. In the wake of the Soviet invasion of Czechoslovakia, there were more Soviet divisions in Central Europe than at any time since World War II. Growing Soviet nuclear capabilities and a blue-water navy were emerging capabilities directly related to NATO's concerns. By 1970 the Soviets were to conduct three major military exercises (DVINA in March, OKEAN in April, and COMRADES IN ARMS in October), each the largest of its kind since World War II.[14]

Even before assuming his duties in Europe, though, Goodpaster encountered a critical challenge to the continued viability of the Alliance's military forces, and hence their ability to maintain deterrence in this evolving context. Having been called back from his duties in Vietnam to provide counsel in the early days of the Nixon administration, he was at a dinner at the White House at which the president introduced him to Prime Minister Pierre Trudeau of Canada. As Goodpaster came through the receiving line, the president told Trudeau that he was looking forward to having him talk with Goodpaster. Then as soon as the line broke up, the president went to Goodpaster and said he'd like to have him talk to Trudeau because he seemed to be rather down on NATO. Goodpaster, of course, followed up on this, encountering a rather blustery Trudeau who began by saying, "You should know that we don't think much of NATO in Canada, my government doesn't think much of NATO." Goodpaster responded that Canada had gotten a lot of good out of it and that this was something he would want to come and talk about.[15]

The question was more than academic, for there was pending a proposed Canadian reduction of their NATO forces by half. It was quite apparent to Goodpaster that if the Canadians made this reduction, there were going to be strong pressures from other nations to reduce their forces as well. All were experiencing similar budgetary and internal political pressures that went in that direction. Having analyzed the situation and the likely consequences, Goodpaster and his staff came to the conclusion that they should take the initiative by proposing that, after doing everything possible to limit the Canadian reduction, other member-nations should make up the losses and that the SACEUR would make some recommendations as to where those augmentations should come from.

This occasioned some "fluttering" at the NATO political headquarters at Evére, even among the Americans, and someone passed to Goodpaster a copy of a message that had been sent back to the Pentagon suggesting that he be straightened out on the role of the SACEUR in such matters. Goodpaster responded by contacting the chairman of the Joint Chiefs of Staff, then Gen. Earle Wheeler, telling him that he understood one of the responsibilities of the SACEUR was to analyze such matters and make force recommendations. He buttressed his case by observing that when he was a staff officer there under Eisenhower, the operation had been set up that way, and he saw no reason why it should not continue to be done. Finally, Goodpaster observed that it was a matter of sufficient importance that he wanted to talk to the president about it if there was going to be any difficulty; Wheeler came back and assured him that there would not be.[16]

Having thus established his right to weigh in on the matter, Goodpaster set about trying to undo the potential damage to the Alliance force structure. He began by visiting the military forces of all the contributing nations. Then, having firsthand knowledge of them, he could speak to an issue the Canadians were about to raise publicly. He arranged a call to Canada to talk to the prime minister and the defense minister about their proposal to cut their NATO forces in half. He had been told they were going to make a statement to the parliament that the Canadian forces were of no real value in Europe. Goodpaster, having just visited those forces, knew that they were highly trained and had an excellent professional standing. He told the defense minister that if anyone publicly said Canadian forces were of no value, he would contradict it publicly. So they backed away on that statement, and then, having said the reduction decision was one that had been made and could not be changed, they negotiated a considerable change. This amounted to increasing by 50 percent the forces they planned to keep in Europe, undertaking to purchase tanks and reequip their mechanized brigade, and agreeing to leave their air units in place (although they did terminate the nuclear role of those forces).[17]

Even though the Canadians did go ahead with cuts in their deployed forces, the full extent of the proposed reductions had been moderated, and other forces were found to make up most of the shortfall thus created, so the command was able to deal with the situation without a significant reduction in overall strength. It was a crucial test for Goodpaster's leadership right at the outset, one that he later recalled as "kind of a fast start for me in NATO."

It was apparent to Goodpaster that it was not going to be much fun just being the recipient of such proposals for reductions in forces, funds, and support for his new command. His instincts were, in any case, attuned to taking the offensive. An opportunity to set this in motion soon came along. It had been the custom for some time for the key principals to take turns hosting a monthly luncheon at which the secretary-general, the SACEUR, the CINCHAN, the chairman of the Military Committee, and so on would get together, each accompanied by only a single assistant. At those luncheon meetings, which might run on for another two hours after lunch, they could talk candidly about what was going on in NATO, what they should be concerning themselves with, and what they should do about it.

At one such luncheon soon after Goodpaster arrived he said that he didn't like just being on the receiving end of all these proposals to reduce, to cut back, and so on, and that he felt they should assess their situation and come up with what they thought ought to be done to put NATO in the best position and to make the most effective use of its resources. The latter point Goodpaster viewed as particularly important because they were constantly hearing complaints from the United States that NATO had more manpower than the Warsaw Pact and was spending more money, and yet it was still inferior in combat power. Goodpaster, as a strategist, believed such formulations were ignorant of the strategic realities deriving from NATO's defensive posture, the geography of reinforcement, and other asymmetries inherent in the relationship between NATO and Warsaw Pact forces.

This was one of the themes he wanted to address, taking the analytical initiative, so to speak. The secretary-general at this time was Manlio Brosio, a diplomat much respected by Goodpaster, who viewed him as astute and able, really "a wise old fox." Brosio was quick to pick up on Goodpaster's idea. The result was the initiation of a study that came to be known as "The Study of Alliance Defense Problems in the 70's," or AD-70 for short. Before the conduct and results of this study are described, something should be said about how NATO's strategic requirements had evolved over the preceding period of five years or so.

NATO had adopted a revised strategy, known as MC 14/3, in December 1967. It was the outgrowth of a changed perception that had gone back at least to the early days of the Kennedy administration, the essence of which was that massive retaliation was bankrupt as a strategic concept and that something offering a richer range of options in the event of hostilities was needed. As discussed in the preceeding chapters, the new approach, known as flexible response, had become a part of the American strategic doctrine early in the 1960s. The implications of the new strategy, which also institutionalized for NATO the idea of forward defense, were very significant in terms of the forces and the support facilities required. Most important from the American viewpoint was the need to raise the nuclear threshold which in turn required increased and improved conventional forces. This was particularly pressing because in the year immediately following adoption of the new strategy, the Alliance had actually experienced a *reduction* in the number of readily available combat forces, the result not only of U.S. redeployments but also of redeployments by Britain, reorganization of forces by West Germany, and restructuring of forces by Belgium.[18] Besides the force implications, adoption of the strategy contained in MC 14/3 greatly increased the requirements for infrastructure support. These included improvements in various elements of support for conventional warfare forces, to include protection of airfields and aircraft, expansion of command and control facilities, and increases in reinforcement capabilities. Given that failure to make progress in these areas meant the nuclear threshold would be lowered, that there would be a heightened prospect of early use of nuclear weapons in any conflict, the importance and urgency of the task were apparent.

It was against this background that work on AD-70 was undertaken, with the primary effort taking place in SHAPE. The staff worked with the ministries of defense in the various NATO countries and with the various NATO subordinate commanders and their staffs to develop a priority list of the things that should be worked on. This set of priorities was important and played a significant part in focusing the efforts of planners in the years ahead, in effect giving focus to the multinational dialogue. But another significant result of the study was that it served to a degree to turn the discourse around, to change the terms of the dialogue, so that NATO planning took on more of a positive, rather than just a damage-limiting, aspect.

The AD-70 study was comprehensive in that it examined the political and strategic factors in East-West relations as well as the military balance. It concluded that at the strategic nuclear level, the West had the means of inflicting devastating damage on an aggressor. At the tactical nuclear level, it held that adequate forces existed at that time, although improvements in the weaponry would be desirable. But at the conventional level, serious deficiencies were found to exist in the relative strengths of NATO and Warsaw Pact forces.[19] It was here, then, that the emphasis in the immediate future was to be placed.

Goodpaster was realistic about the practical results of AD-70, observing that "in true NATO style, you have to measure in millimeters,"[20] but there were clearly tangible benefits in addition to the psychology of restructuring the dialogue. Goodpaster as SACEUR had continued a long-standing practice of carrying on a card in his pocket his "hit list," the handful of major problems he thought he should be dealing with. During his tenure as SACEUR, the list remained substantially the same, with the strength and effectiveness of the collective force at the top, and for obvious reasons. Also perennial entries on the list, although the order of importance might shift about from time to time, were the role of tactical nuclear weapons, working out a relationship with the French, logistics support in its many manifestations, and communications. These concerns showed up in AD-70 in a variety of ways.

Some of the emphases deriving from the study were, of course, continuations of long-standing concerns. Augmentation of the infrastructure was one such, along with improvements in communications and airfield protection. Emphasis on armor and antitank weaponry, air defense, and antisubmarine forces was also included. But beyond the practical aspects of the forces and their support, and perhaps even more important, was the way in which the study's results served as a vehicle for recommitment to maintaining the Alliance as a viable entity. The study addressed equitable burden-sharing, for example, and maintenance of a level of effort, postures that were not givens in light of the experiences of recent years.[21]

The results of the AD-70 study were taken up by the North Atlantic Council at ministerial meetings in Brussels in December 1970. These meetings culminated a year of work and resulted in "decisions... taken both in NATO and in the European context which [had] the effect of continuing the American presence in Europe undiminished, providing an increment of effort by the Eurogroup countries which assumes a greater share of the overall burden, and defining areas where further work to strengthen [the] defense is needed."[22] The key actions taken at Brussels, stemming from approval of the AD-70 study recommendations, were arresting the downward trend of forces that had been occurring for several years, inaugurating new augmentation of the common infrastructure and focusing effort on specified high-priority areas such as communications and airfield protection.[23] The first priority in guidance issued by the ministers for preparation of force proposals for 1971-75 was improvement of conventional forces, and this in itself was a significant step, as there were European elements within the Alliance which feared that any increase in conventional capabilities could serve to reduce the willingness of the United States to commit nuclear forces should that be necessary. This was, of course, not a new problem.

There is a tendency, in evaluating accomplishments in implementing the results of AD-70 and other NATO plans of this period, to concentrate on the shortfall between what was achieved and the stated requirements. It is necessary to address that gap, of course, but it is also important to recognize that the requirements had been greatly increased, especially in areas having to do with support for conventional forces, by adoption of the new strategy of flexible response and by concurrent increases in the magnitude and nature of the threat posed by Warsaw Pact forces. The change in strategy, as small as the evolving threat, compounded the resource demands caused by the necessary restructuring precipitated by France's earlier withdrawal from the Alliance military structure. It resulted in altered force requirements as well as the relocation of headquarters, troop units, support facilities, and elements of the common infrastructure. There was a conjunction of factors, all having major resource implications, that had to be dealt with during Goodpaster's tenure, and an international context (political and psychological, about which more will be said shortly, as well as economic) that made it all the more difficult to obtain political support for provision of the assets required. Thus, while substantial progress was made, the gap between what was put in place and what was thought necessary also remained substantial.

Among the areas of genuine progress was that of airfield protection. The program for physical protection of airfields had been briefed during the first CLOUD COVER conference in 1969. Three years later, Goodpaster was able to report to that same conference that more than six hundred shelters had been completed and that construction was under way, or soon would be, in all the countries of ACE.[24] Air defense was another area reflecting real progress. The plan called for eighty sites for air defense radars and computers designed to integrate the elements of nine national air defense systems into a single unified system. By late 1972 more than sixty of the planned sites had been accepted, with all scheduled to be finished by the middle of 1973. In reporting these achievements, the SACEUR also sought to put the issue of burden-sharing in perspective, pointing out that in the European area America's other Allies contributed 90 percent of NATO's manpower, 80 percent (in numbers of vessels) of its naval power, and 75 percent of its airpower.[25]

Goodpaster, like his predecessors, concentrated unflinchingly in his classified reports and presentations on the shortcomings in Alliance capabilities and support and the resultant risks. And occasionally, when he wanted to share with an audience some of his frustrations over the sometimes glacial pace of improvements in NATO, he would use the analogy of the slow bicycle race to make the point.

The slow bicycle race was a sport that had a certain popularity in England a few years ago. The rules were simple. The course was quite short, about thirty yards across the beautiful green lawn of an English country estate. Each one of the riders, who were mostly attractive young ladies..., was required to stay in lane. The object of the race was to go as slow as possible without actually falling off the bicycle or touching a foot to the ground. The last girl across the finish line won. The contortions were many, the gyrations extreme. Sometimes, in my more pessimistic moments, it seems to me that some at least of the NATO nations are engaged in a similar competition—trying to go as slowly as possible without actually falling out of the Alliance.[26]

Yet, reflecting his constant emphasis on the importance and benefits of Alliance solidarity, Goodpaster believed, as he once wrote to French strategist Gen. Pierre Gallois, that "even though we were often dissatisfied with the tangible results of the nations' working together in NATO, I for one was always sure that it would be far worse to have them split apart, quarrelling and even threatening each other, as has been the unfortunate experience in the past."²⁷

Goodpaster also tried to deal with détente in a way that would be constructive rather than disabling for the Alliance whose military forces he led. He believed that "a sound defense capability works for a true and meaningful detente, rather than against it as is sometimes assumed."²⁸ He understood very well the importance of outlook and morale on performance as well as on what is viewed as possible and attainable. He observed in this regard late in 1970 that "in the socio-psychological field, so basic to stability, confidence and firm forward-looking action, we see attitudes that approach the neurotic toward the needs of defense, toward the 'military-industrial complex,' and toward the man in uniform."²⁹ Thus, well before the high-water mark of what he later called "the euphoria of detente,"³⁰ Goodpaster wanted to deal with the phenomenon in a way that would preserve the Alliance's viability. He did this first by assimilating the legitimate goals of détente, making them his own, so that he began to state that he classed among the key NATO objectives not only the longstanding goals of deterrence, defense, and solidarity, but also détente.³¹ But the central point was that détente was a goal to be pursued *in addition to,* not instead of, deterrence, defense, and solidarity. In this view he had the full support of Secretary-General Brosio.³²

Détente was, of course, not a single and easily identifiable phenomenon but the product of a number of events taking place more or less simultaneously. Among these were West Germany's overtures toward the Eastern bloc, referred to collectively as "Ostpolitik," under Chancellor Willy Brandt. One result was nonaggression agreements with the Soviet Union, Poland, and Czechoslovakia, as well as recognition of the Oder-Neisse as the eastern border of the Federal Republic.³³ There was the impact of the long-running Conference on Security and Cooperation in Europe (CSCE) at Geneva. There were the Strategic Arms Limitation Talks between the U.S. and the Soviet Union and the resulting SALT II treaty. But most important and most challenging for NATO in general and ACE in particular were the negotiations on Mutual and Balanced Force Reductions (MBFR) being convened in Vienna. At perhaps his first meeting with assembled U.S. military leaders in Germany after assuming the duties of SACEUR, Goodpaster had told them, referring to MBFR, that "of paramount interest to those charged with maintenance of NATO security is that the realities of defense are not submerged in overzealous attempts at negotiation."[34]

Goodpaster's strategy was to embrace MBFR and seek to ensure that its outcome would not endanger NATO's abilities to achieve its other enduring goals. The 1972 theme of SHAPEX, the annual conference of ACE, was thus "to examine the defense of Allied Command Europe in a context of mutual and balanced force reductions." The following year the theme was "continued NATO security against a background of change," while in 1974 conference participants examined "new challenges for NATO."

Goodpaster's willingness to consider and to attempt to turn to positive advantage the potential of MBFR surprised some observers. Many of them had expected SHAPE to oppose it, with talk suggesting military opposition to what was a politically appealing opportunity. But Goodpaster had asked his staff to analyze the implications of MBFR, and they had come to the conclusion that—if you could really achieve in MBFR some mutual and balanced results—they could support this. A key point, however, was their conclusion that balanced results would necessarily mean *unbalanced* reductions, with the Warsaw Pact forces making greater reductions than NATO, to accommodate the strategic asymmetries between the two.

Initially, Goodpaster recalls, there was some panic among a number of the ministries of defense, where he had been expected to oppose MBFR categorically. But when he was called on by representatives of the various governments, and they sat down and talked the thing through, he was able to show them that—if they would hold to the key provision for the enduring asymmetries—MBFR could indeed be in the interest of what

NATO's Supreme Commanders meet in Paris on 19 June 1951. Front row, left to right: Adm. Sir Patrick Brind (U.K.), Gen. Lauris Norstad (U.S.), Lt. Gen. Augustin Guillaume (France), Field Marshal Bernard Montgomery (U.K.), Gen. Dwight D. Eisenhower (U.S.), Air Vice Marshal Hugh Saunders (U.K.), Adm. Raoul Lemonnier (France), Adm. Robert Jaujard (France), and Adm. Robert Carney (U.S.). Second row: Gen. Wilhelm von Tangen Hansteen (Norway), Lt. Gen. Maurizio de Castiglioni (Italy), Lt. Gen. Alfred Gruenther (U.S.), Maj. Gen. Ebbe Gortz (Denmark), and Maj. Gen. Robert K. Taylor (U.S.). Wide World Photo.

General Eisenhower confers with President Truman on 5 November 1951 shortly before assuming his duties as SACEUR. Courtesy of the Eisenhower Library.

Above, General Eisenhower with French President Vincent Auriol and Minister of Defense Jules Moch (behind Auriol) at the opening of SHAPE headquarters, 23 July 1951. NATO photo. Below, a view of the house and grounds at Marnes la Coquette, France, in 1951. This was the official residence of SACEURs Eisenhower, Ridgway, and Gruenther. SHAPE photo.

Right, General Matthew Ridgway in battle dress, including hand grenade, a photo that aroused controversy at the time of Ridgway's appointment as SACEUR. Below, Generals Gruenther and Ridgway confer while both were at SHAPE. SHAPE photos.

Above, President Eisenhower presents the Distinguished Service Medal to General Gruenther on 28 December 1956. Mrs. Eisenhower, Mrs. Gruenther, and John Foster Dulles look on. National Park Service photo, courtesy of the Eisenhower Library. At left, General Norstad greets his civilian counterpart, NATO Secretary-General Paul-Henri Spaak. SHAPE photo.

Above, President de Gaulle presents General Norstad with the Legion of Honor on 20 December 1962. Below, a September 1986 view of the SACEUR's current residence near Casteau, Belgium. SHAPE photos.

At left, General Lemnitzer meets with Secretary of Defense Robert McNamara at SHAPE. Below, General Lemnitzer, like his predecessor, received the Legion of Honor from President de Gaulle. They are shown here at Les Invalides, Paris, 1966. SHAPE photos.

Above, General Goodpaster is shown with officers and civilian officials at SHAPE during his tenure as SACEUR. Courtesy of General Goodpaster. Below, General Goodpaster and his successor, General Haig, hold a press conference at the time of Haig's assumption of command, 15 December 1974. SHAPE photo.

General Haig enjoyed visiting NATO troops in the field, as seen here. SHAPE photo. Below, General Rodgers, left, Admiral Lee Baggett, Jr., center, and Admiral Sir Nicholas Hunt, right, take part in a chiefs-of-staff meeting at NATO headquarters in December 1985. NATO Information Service.

they were there to do. This enabled Goodpaster to take the stance of supporting MBFR, which turned out to be very useful given the disruptive potential had he opposed it.[35]

In the event, of course, the MBFR talks dragged on interminably, with no concrete results to affect NATO one way or the other. What turned out to be more of a challenge were the attitudes spawned by hopefulness over the outcome of this and other negotiations under way. And again the most serious threat was to Goodpaster's first priority goal, maintenance of the strength and effectiveness of the collective force.

Efforts to reduce national contributions to the NATO military forces, always a potential just under the surface when not being actively pursued, were fueled by the effects of détente. Détente raised hopes on the part of many that military requirements could be reduced, while it provided an excuse to demand such reductions on the part of others who opposed military expenditures on other grounds. Kissinger viewed these pressures in the United States, embodied in the Mansfield amendment, as "a serious threat to our entire foreign policy."[36]

Goodpaster took an active role in seeking to head off further reductions in the level of U.S. forces in Europe. Before taking up his post as SACEUR, he had had long talks with the president, talks that left Goodpaster confident that they shared views on NATO which were essentially identical. It was, in Nixon's words, the cornerstone of U.S. foreign policy and of its security policy. When the subsequent attempts to reduce further U.S. forces serving the Alliance in Europe reached a critical stage, Goodpaster was called home by the president to assist in mounting a counterattack. At one point, so urgent was the situation that Goodpaster left his own dinner party in Belgium to fly back to counter the current version of the Mansfield Resolution. He talked to a number of senators, always stressing his conviction that "a balanced American military contribution in place in Europe, not substantially less than we have [there] today, is essential to the continued effectiveness and viability—and credibility—of NATO." There were, at the time, some 300,000 U.S. troops in the European area.[37]

Goodpaster also stressed to the senators with whom he met a kind of formula he had developed, more like a set of syllogisms, that went like this: NATO or something like it is essential to the security of the United States, the force in being in Europe is essential to a viable NATO, and a U.S. contribution not substantially less than what we now have is essential to continuance of an adequate force. Goodpaster even talked briefly with Senator Mansfield, who agreed with him on the first two points but refused to address the third, simply telling Goodpaster that he had to realize that they were looking at things differently.

Having served in Europe when the NATO military organization was first put in place, Goodpaster had concluded that the four additional American divisions then provided had been what put the glue into NATO. "I thought that was true then, and I think it remains true," he told the senators who were contemplating the possibility of reducing the American commitment.[38] As it turned out, further cuts were not directed, thus avoiding setting an example that could have started a stampede of imitative initiatives on the part of other members of the Alliance. But while the problem had been dealt with for the time being, it did not go away. Indeed the next year an American observer was telling NATO members that "in candor, the message seems clear; the American forces in NATO Europe will be reduced" and that, therefore, "NATO nations must recognize the new mood in [the U.S.] Congress—particularly the Senate—and adjust their thinking and expectations with regard to the future American role in the alliance."[39]

While fighting hard to prove inaccurate these continuing predictions of force cuts based on expectations of détente, or on Vietnam-induced disenchantment with U.S. involvement overseas no matter where it took place, Goodpaster was faced with a challenge to the U.S. force levels based on a different set of concerns: the high cost in terms of the balance of payments resulting from support of the European contingent. In the autumn of 1973, this concern found its way into legislation in the form of the Jackson-Nunn amendment to the defense procurement and manpower authorization bill for the following year. Sponsored by two respected legislators who could in no way be accused of being anti-defense, the measure provided for reduction of U.S. forces in Europe proportionate to the extent the United States was unable to recover the balance-of-payments deficits attributable to those forces from its European Allies. While this was not a function of détente, it did represent an additional challenge to the maintenance of adequate NATO forces on the ground at a time when support for doing so was already under considerable strain as a result of détente in its many manifestations.

All things considered, NATO forces under Goodpaster seem to have withstood remarkably well the challenge to their viability represented, at least potentially, by détente. Activities in furtherance of the new conditions, previously described, went forward, although certainly not at the level the SACEUR might have wished. (One estimate had it that new infrastructure initiatives were funded at only half the desired level during the first half of the decade.) It is probably not possible to disaggregate the complex of factors having an impact on the various resource decisions taken by the Alliance during this period so as to allocate an appropriate weight to considerations of détente, economic factors, domestic politics, antiwar movements, and the like. What is clear, however, is that through all of this Goodpaster did keep the Alliance intact and moving ahead on the course it had set for itself.

There were, however, other troubles ahead, ones perhaps more difficult and potentially more damaging even than the possible impact of détente. Speaking to an academic conference in Washington in the summer of 1973, Goodpaster returned to his familiar concern with Alliance solidarity. It is "through solidarity the NATO nations rise above the quarrels, the ancient hatreds, and the mutual conflicts of the past which have exhausted them and twice this century in the two great world wars have nearly destroyed them," he emphasized.[40] But only a few months later, in the events of the 1973 Middle East war and the Arab oil embargo, that solidarity was to experience one of its severest challenges, one it almost failed to survive. If the crisis of détente had involved negotiations between adversaries, the new crisis rang a change on that theme. Speaking to the Council on Foreign Relations on the topic "NATO in an age of negotiation," Goodpaster ruefully pointed out that, in the wake of the events of October 1973, "the crucial negotiation has come to be in good part a negotiation within NATO to keep it alive, and the testing is now to see if NATO can survive the disputes and recriminations that have arisen from the Mid-East crisis."[41]

This was one of his most remarkable presentations. Coming scarcely a month after hostilities had broken out in the Middle East, it reflected the deeply held disappointment and anger he obviously felt. At a time when a crisis outside the NATO area had affected the security interests of all the members of the Alliance, they had acted unilaterally instead of pulling together to devise a coordinated and coherent response. He regarded the results as self-serving and self-defeating, especially on top of "negotiations—MBFR, CSCE, and SALT—which were already difficult and demanding enough in themselves."

Among the manifestations of NATO's "inglorious and inadequate response to the Mid-East crisis" cited by Goodpaster were West German demands that shipments of American arms out of Bremerhaven on Israeli ships be stopped, sharp complaints of inadequate consultation when American forces in European countries were placed on alert, "national responses to the oil tactics of the Arab producers characterized by individual nations trying to save their own skins," and the fact that, "at major stages of the developing crisis.... the Europeans chose to sit on the sidelines, while demanding a voice in calling the plays." Summing it up, he told his audience that in his view "the overall performance of NATO...was such that to call it ignominious would be to indulge in unwarranted flattery."[42]

His concern went beyond the stresses of the moment, however, for he continued by analyzing how the experience of reacting to the current crisis revealed what he called deep-seated weaknesses and shortcomings in NATO. These included tendencies on the part of its member-nations to emphasize short-term over longer-term considerations, self-interest over the common interest, and the dictates of internal party politics over more enduring if less visible needs. Perhaps no single event since the Suez crisis of 1956 put so great a strain on the Alliance. Goodpaster's sharp and unsparing assessment of the performance of individual member-states was no doubt stimulated in large measure by the challenge this represented to his cherished concern with solidarity. Instead of pulling together when faced by a crisis of common concern, the Allies went their separate ways in what could only be viewed as an alarming demonstration of just how fragile their commitment to shared concerns really was. "We had hoped that 1973 might be a year for the strengthening of NATO," Goodpaster told another audience soon thereafter. "Instead,... we saw disunity, disarray, disagreement, and mutual recrimination."[43]

If the effects on the Alliance of the Middle East war were the most divisive, they were far from the only strains on solidarity experienced during Goodpaster's tenure as SACEUR. Indeed the spectacle of two NATO members engaged in armed conflict with one another was in many respects even more shocking, but that was exactly what Greece and Turkey did over their disagreements about Cyprus. In Greece after the "colonels' regime" had been overthrown, the successor regime was very hostile toward NATO and toward the SACEUR himself, alleging that they had propped up the colonels and kept them in power. But regardless of these strained relations, when it came to intra-Alliance armed conflict Goodpaster again reaffirmed solidarity. He remained in touch with the Greek defense minister throughout the affair and passed the word that while he understood the problems on Cyprus, there was also reported to be tension on the border between the two countries, and there simply could not be any clash between Greek and Turkish forces. Goodpaster implied that if that were to occur it would be very costly to both countries.[44] Similar problems for the Alliance occurred when a coup took place in Portugal, resulting in overthrow of the military regime. Meanwhile, yet another troubling situation was building— the Watergate break-in and its protracted aftermath. While not affecting the Alliance directly (indeed, many European leaders professed to wonder what all the fuss was about), the preoccupation of the American leadership and its eventual disablement as results of these events inevitably meant deflection of its attention from affairs abroad, including Europe and NATO. Goodpaster at one point went beyond just the leadership to refer to Watergate and "its saturation of American attention."[45]

On top of détente in its many manifestations, the combined events of the Middle East war and oil embargo, the coup in Portugal, another in Greece and the conflict between that nation and Turkey over Cyprus, and domestic upheaval and eventual paralysis in the United States would have made for a full enough plate for any SACEUR, even without a hostile Alliance to be concerned about. It is little wonder that, writing to an old friend in the spring of 1974, Goodpaster referred to "this time of trouble and turmoil for NATO."[46] Yet these were troubles the Alliance endured and outlasted, perhaps not least because of the man serving as SACEUR at the time. As recounted before, in an earlier assignment in the pressure cooker known as the White House, Goodpaster had impressed a younger colleague as "the calmest man under pressure" he had ever seen.[47] In his dealings in NATO, he exhibited not only that quality in abundance, but also a concern for the long haul that transcended day-to-day preoccupation with the crisis of the moment. In this respect, he reflected the best instincts of the strategist (perhaps as contrasted to the tactician), a capacity that was central to his success as SACEUR.

It is commonly said that the role of SACEUR is essentially a political one, and one can see why that would be believed.[48] But given the events of his tenure and the way in which he responded to them, it would be difficult to characterize Goodpaster's quintessential role as SACEUR as other than that of strategist. NATO had had a change of strategy not long before he assumed command, but it is probably fair to say that his predecessor had been somewhat distracted from the military implications of implementing the new strategy by the necessity to deal with the multiple and pressing problems that followed the relocation from France of the Alliance's headquarters, troop units, and support facilities (a job for which he deserves great credit, as detailed in the preceding chapter).

Thus, it was largely left to Goodpaster to devise ways of implementing flexible response. In addition, he had AD-70 and the continuing questions of troop strength, the deployment of those troops, and the utilization of them, along with questions of tactical nuclear weaponry (whether it needed to be modernized, how it was going to be designed, particular types of nuclear weapons, and their political acceptability). President Nixon, in discussing the situation in Europe at the end of his first year in office, began by recognizing the "fundamental change in the strategic balance" that had taken place there over the past decade.[49] And then there were the multiple events described above that pulled the Alliance in every direction.

If a strategist was what was needed, Goodpaster could claim to have been to the right school. He broke in during the last months of World War II when he served in the Pentagon with the likes of "Abe" Lincoln and Thomas Handy under George C. Marshall as army chief-of-staff. Goodpaster remembered it as "a pretty good school, a strong school there." Subsequently, of course, he served not only in the White House but as assistant to the chairman of the Joint Chiefs of Staff and later as commandant of the National War College.

Perhaps as a result of the latter assignment, while he was SACEUR, he enjoyed making frequent visits to the war colleges and staff colleges in a number of countries, where he found that the students' questions were instrumental in keeping him from getting too much in a rut in his thinking. Often he would return to his headquarters and ask his staff to go to work on one or another of the questions that had been posed to him by some student.

Goodpaster himself believed that strategy was at the heart of the enterprise: what to do, how to do it, and what to do it with—those three things.[50] He also realized that the course of battle was not predictable and that not everything could be worked out in advance Thus, he considered that one of his main chores as SACEUR was to emphasize flexibility of operations to his subordinate commanders (not all of whom were so inclined if left to their own devices). One of his main thrusts in exercises and war games was to try to get commanders to command, to (as he put it) "wield the force." This meant his using the assigned forces as though he had a weapon in his hand, not relying on set piece responses that might have little real relevance to the situation as it unfolded.

Knowing that in any conflict, being by definition on the defensive, NATO forces would be faced with a mobile defense task in which quick analysis and evaluation of enemy thrusts would be absolutely vital, Goodpaster sought to train his commanders to deal with that situation. If the enemy could choose the time, the place, the mode, and the weight of the attack, NATO commanders had to be able to respond to that and then take advantage of what NATO would take to be a set piece plan on the Soviet side. Success in this calculus would depend on being able to bring to bear more command flexibility, agility, and adaptiveness. Goodpaster particularly liked the term "agility" to express this concept; he had adopted it from André Beaufré and he found it a good one.[51]

There were many other matters to occupy a strategist's attention. One of the most important was tactical nuclear weapons and their role in Alliance defense. Goodpaster recalled that all through Secretary McNamara's tenure a common statement was that we had no plans for the use of tactical nuclear weapons. The first time he heard that, and it was both a time and a place where the matter was critically important to him, was while he was in command of the U.S. Eighth Infantry Division in Germany. The concerns he had then stayed with him when he returned to Europe as SACEUR.

Goodpaster was not, of course, anxious to have to resort to

the use of nuclear weapons, tactical or otherwise. In fact, one of his overriding concerns was the improvement of conventional forces so as to raise the nuclear threshold. But he also wanted to strengthen deterrence by ensuring that there was—and was perceived by the Soviets as being—some alternative beyond conventional forces short of resort to an all-out strategic nuclear exchange. That meant so far as he was concerned working out plans for the judicious use of tactical nuclear weapons and working on the improvement of the available weapons to reduce collateral damage effects and in other ways make it more feasible to employ them, especially on Allied territory. Again his thrust was not to make their use more likely, but rather to increase the strength of deterrence by making it possible to use such weapons should conventional defense fail without having to suffer unduly in the course of doing so. It was the same view he had, as staff secretary to the president, expressed in a memorandum to President Eisenhower some fifteen years before: "An effective atomic capability is indispensable to a maximum deterrent and essential to defense in Western Europe."[52]

Goodpaster recognized that this was a very sensitive area, and so the plans that were worked out were very tightly controlled, limited, and constrained. He also recognized, and strongly agreed with, the reality that whether such weapons would ever be employed was a matter that rested with the top policymakers. But he believed that having the capability, with the Russians knowing that such a capability existed, was a powerful addition to the deterrent. Developing the planning approaches that supported this capability was a key concern of Goodpaster throughout his tenure as SACEUR. In this he was at one with Henry Kissinger, who argued that "it was a counsel of defeat to abjure both strategic and tactical nuclear forces, for no NATO country—including ours—was prepared to undertake the massive buildup in conventional forces that was the sole alternative."[53]

Another strategic concern that occupied Goodpaster personally was working out an arrangement with the French, who had, of course, withdrawn their military forces from the NATO organization, a step that Robert Osgood said at the time "called into question the viability of the whole institutional superstructure."[54] That was how serious knowledgeable observers considered the situation to be. Goodpaster's observation when he arrived was that NATO was still in somewhat of a state of shock over this. He found his staff was constantly talking about what could be done to bring the French back, what could be done to work with the French, and so on. Goodpaster put that on his agenda, but quickly concluded that it was a loser. As he put it, if we were to take initiatives along those lines, we would wind up buying the same horse quite a number of times, and it would turn out always not to be there. So he decided that the thing to do was to reshape NATO planning on the basis of being able to operate without the French, but with provision made that if the French should come in and associate themselves with the Alliance forces (as Goodpaster always believed was very likely in the case of a real threat developing), then that could be done effectively.

In working out a policy paper along these lines, Goodpaster the strategist reverted to his earlier role as Goodpaster the consummate staff officer, writing the paper himself because, as he later recalled, his staff just yearned to try to talk to the French and see if they couldn't get this and couldn't get that. Essentially, then, he said we will do this, we will let the French know what we've done, and we will tell them that we will respond cooperatively to anything they are interested in doing to improve their ability to work with us when the time comes. But the initiative is going to have to rest with them. And so it was done, clearing away a lot of distracting "what ifs" from the NATO planning scene and making very clear-cut the terms under which future work would be done.

There was one collateral aspect in which Goodpaster also took a personal hand to good effect. A plan had been worked up by the Central Army Group staff, headed by a German officer and with an international staff, for cooperation with the French in the event of hostilities. It was premised on their forces being associated with NATO when the NATO defense had failed.

Goodpaster called them and suggested that, as military men, they consider this: Wouldn't it be much better to have as the premise that this plan would be used whenever the French forces are associated with NATO forces, on the understanding that it would really be better to do so before NATO had failed? The change was made, and to Goodpaster's mind it was a crucial step. After that the contingency planning was on a sound basis.[55]

Of course, the French had a military mission with NATO, whose senior officer was viewed by Goodpaster as very good and who was honestly carrying out his country's policy but at the same time was aware of the military implications. Other French officers were equally realistic. Gen. Vernon "Dick" Walters, then U.S. military attaché in France, told Goodpaster of an experience he had had after the French had run an exercise of conducting a French-only war in Europe. A senior French officer came to Walters and said that they had done this and afterward agreed that it was nothing but "military nonsense."[56]

Goodpaster's strategic outlook made him sensitive to the complex of external influences, mostly nonmilitary, that shaped the climate in which defense strategy was examined by the NATO countries. We have already stressed his overriding interest in promoting solidarity within the Alliance, something he considered so important that he told a congressional committee that he viewed a threat to this solidarity as "a threat to the very basis of the Alliance."[57] But the lack of solidarity, or at least the immaturity of a genuine commonality of interests, also frustrated one of his most favored initiatives, cooperation in terms of standardization and commonality of equipment and supplies. He looked at cooperation in the fields of military research, development, and production as "the most rewarding single area of effort for improving alliance defense in the next few years." Admitting that "NATO's record in this regard has frankly been less than good," he advocated a bold step, "creation of a NATO common armaments fund that would be used for common procurement and ultimately for the operation of a common logistics system."[58] As matters then stood, the SACEUR had no funds that he controlled, other than for the common infrastructure, to provide the logistic support he deemed necessary. (Nothing has changed in this regard). NATO's philosophy on logistics has been that it is a national responsibility, with each nation responsible for the logistical support of its own forces. This had led, as Goodpaster noted, to "such anomalies as planes which cannot re-arm at airfields other than their own, ammunition that does not fit the guns of neighboring Allied units or the weapons brought in by external reinforcing units, and ships at sea which require additional oilers because they use different kinds of fuel."[59] As a result, he added, "our scarce resources are being expended on varieties of equipment which reduce the flexibility and capability of our forces and increase their logistic problems."[60]

Unfortunately, this was an area in which little progress could be made, given all the "headwinds," the "institutional rigidities and opposition" that stood in the way. When it was all over, Goodpaster viewed the lack of progress in achieving a greater degree of commonality and standardization as one of his two greatest disappointments as SACEUR (the slow progress in getting an adequate communications system into effect being the other).[61] His strategist's sense told him of the critical importance and potentially high payoff of these two areas, but the realities of the "slow bicycle race" intruded to prevent accomplishing what he would have liked to leave in place for his successor.

Goodpaster was very aware of his "tutorial" role with respect to the strategic imperatives of the Alliance, the rationale for its existence, and what was required to keep it vital and viable. He sought to remind Americans that, as President Kennedy had said on a visit to Germany, the security and freedom of Western Europe are essential to the security of the United States, and "that's why we're here."[62] That was an important point to remember in an era of concentration on possible force reductions, burden-sharing, and the like. And he never failed to remind Alliance leaders that in the final analysis, "the forces in being are what count."[63] Early in his assignment as SACEUR, Goodpaster had told a professional military audience, in one of his most detailed public explications of his outlook and philosophy on the responsibilities of his position, that "we live at a time when a valid understanding, broadly shared, of security problems is of tremendous importance. These problems are complex, difficult, burdensome—some irksome—and they are, in important areas, obscure and hard to define and to grasp."[64] He worked hard throughout his tenure to increase understanding of these problems and to find workable and attainable solutions to them. A remarkable consistency runs through his interactions with the political leaders of the NATO countries, the military officers in his own headquarters and throughout the Alliance, and the public audiences in Europe and the United States. He was committed to deterrence, defense, solidarity, détente. He fought every threat to reduce the forces in being and developed an active approach to defining priorities to improve their capabilities and support, thus shaping the dialogue and eventually, to a very significant degree, the outcome.

Relinquishment of his command as SACEUR was not a happy event for Goodpaster. What should probably have been an occasion of great personal and professional satisfaction in looking back over more than five years in this capstone assignment to an outstanding career was somewhat soured by his perception that he was being pushed out prematurely in order to make room for his successor. Having been told earlier by then-army chief-of-staff Gen. Creighton Abrams that the intention was to keep him in the post until the summer of 1975, Goodpaster learned sometime in 1974 that he was to be retired at the end of that year. This left him with less time than expected to make the round of farewell calls and visits that he had planned and that he viewed as essential parts of a graceful conclusion to the assignment. There was some personal animosity toward his successor, and this made the transfer of command a bit awkward.

Nevertheless, any fair-minded assessment of Goodpaster's period of stewardship would have to award him very high marks indeed for holding the Alliance together in the face of divers disruptive influences. He stemmed the tide of diminishing resources allocated to its defense needs and did not just "hold the line" but made important improvements in obtaining commitments to the Alliance's military capabilities from its constituent members, in formulating long-range plans for upgrading especially critical areas, and in forcefully reminding members of the Alliance of the central importance of solidarity in the face of the numerous temptations to disintegration.[65] He had served during a time of exceptional turbulence, both internationally and in the United States, and his steadiness and strategist's outlook had served him and the Alliance well.

7. Haig
The Diplomacy of Allied Command

MORRIS HONICK

On Sunday, 15 December 1974, responsibility for the defense of the NATO nations of Europe, and for command of the vast array of Allied military forces which those nations had pledged to place under the authority of the SACEUR in an emergency, passed to Gen. Alexander M. Haig, Jr. In unusual but appropriately formal indoor ceremonies at SHAPE, Gen. Haig succeeded Gen. Andrew J. Goodpaster, thereby becoming the seventh United States officer to hold that position since Eisenhower assumed command in April 1951.[1]

If the 1974 ceremonies were less auspicious than those that had taken place on six earlier occasions—many of which had included nearly day-long observances, thundering fly-pasts, and additional plane-side departure formalities—they lacked none of the other elements of colorful military ceremony, nor the appropriate drums and trumpets, which, on that relatively rare occasion, were provided by a Belgian gendarmerie band seated in concert formation on the stage of the cinema-theater at SHAPE.[2]

The bleak winter day's inconveniences appeared to be of less interest to the 702 guests than did the continuing discussions of the events that had led to the change of command itself, discussions that combined the usual myriad of national and international factors with curiosity and, not least, some doubt. Such public puzzlement prevailed even though, once again, as had been the rule during all of the nearly twenty-five years since the establishment of SHAPE, an American officer had been designated with the approval of the North Atlantic Council in the customary manner. The diplomatic, political, and military representatives attending the unusual assembly also were aware that Goodpaster, the last of the Eisenhower generation of SHAPE planners, was relinquishing his office somewhat earlier than had been expected.[3]

The two men exchanged salutes, and in their remarks each was careful to disabuse the audience of possible misconceptions concerning a reported mutual disaffection, and each dutifully, carefully, and with dignity awarded the other commendation and professional respect.[4]

The overall tone, however, was described thus by one qualified observer:

> The atmosphere became even more glacial. Haig seemed to sense it. He began to speak with a firm voice, without manuscript, off the cuff, and with insistence. He gave a brief outline of his mission, soberly.... He presented himself as a man who knows what he wants and is sure of himself. The guests came under the spell of his voice. Many a guest asked himself whether he hadn't been mistaken about that general. Yet no one was prepared to admit that much. When Haig ended his speech, applause was thin.... After a few days eulogies were coming from Haig's staff: the General was giving new dynamism to the planning. He was negotiating with the Chiefs of governments whom he had known from his days at the White House. He was skilled, flexible, animating. The staff was on his side....[5]

As related in the preceding chapter, three months earlier, in September 1974, the NATO Defense Planning Committee had agreed to a proposal from Pres. Gerald Ford to release Goodpaster from his assignment as SACEUR prior to his retirement from the United States Army and to appoint Haig as his successor.[6] Haig was more than nine years junior to the veteran SHAPE planner he was to succeed.[7] But he brought unique and internationally acquired qualifications to his new position. His prior experience included service as a deputy commandant of the U.S. Military Academy at West Point; as a senior military adviser to the secretary of state; as vice chief-of-staff of the army; and as chief of the White House staff during a traumatic period in the history of the United States.[8] And yet, curiosity and some doubt persisted. Was the general who alone had successfully carried the staggering burdens of national stewardship during Watergate merely a political general? Was there justification for the reticence that was expressed in some official quarters of the NATO nations about the nomination, notwithstanding Haig's combat service and the successful diplomatic missions he had undertaken on behalf of Pres. Richard Nixon?

To dispel that doubt, only a few hours after the ceremonies and their accompanying social amenities, Haig startled some veteran NATO observers by turning immediately to his new tasks. Within only a few minutes of Goodpaster's departure, he convened a command-level conference with senior officials of ACE and his new staff and impressed upon them his intention to be a "take-charge" general. On another occasion he was determined to rejuvenate the value of a major NATO combat effectiveness report, which was sent annually to higher NATO authorities but which had been bogged down in compartmentalized and somewhat routine handling by the individual Major Subordinate Commands of ACE. Haig summoned the NATO major subordinate commanders themselves to his office, ordered his office door closed, and announced, somewhat to their surprise, that "we are not leaving here until we all agree on this thing." In the discussions that followed, in which the SACEUR aimed not only at upgrading the report's value within NATO but also at ensuring its validity in relation to the United States' Single Integrated Operating Plan (SIOP), "there was a lot of hollering and 'horse-trading,' " observed one senior adviser to SACEUR. "But, by golly, when it was all over, and the smoke had cleared [literally], they had agreed," on new procedures and on their individual participation and mutual support.[9] Not only did the new SACEUR enhance the participation level of his office, he also acted as a catalyst to reinvigorate, where needed, all of ACE.

Even before his assumption of command, Haig was very much aware of the challenge that détente presented to NATO.[10]

It was at this time that détente, that element of the dilemma with which Haig would wrestle durng his entire tenure but which he would continue to insist was the fruit of and not a substitute for strength and unity, became a fundamental policy consideration in the Western Alliance as a whole.[11] Essentially, the reasons for the pursuit of the policy were contained in Secretary of State Henry Kissinger's congressional summary in which he pointed out the "paradox [that] confuses our perception of the problem of peaceful coexistence...," namely:

If peace is pursued to the exclusion of any other goal, other values will be compromised and perhaps lost; but if unconstrained rivalry leads to nuclear conflict, these values, along with everything else, will be destroyed in the resulting holocaust. However competitive they may be at some levels of their relationship, both major nuclear powers must base their policies on the premise that neither can expect to impose its will on the other without running an intolerable risk. The challenge of our time is to reconcile the reality of competition with the imperative of coexistence....

Some fundamental principles guide this policy: The United States cannot base its policy solely on Moscow's good intentions. But neither can we insist that all forward movement must await a convergence of American and Soviet purposes. We seek, regardless of Soviet intentions, to serve peace through a systematic resistance to pressure and conciliatory responses to moderate behavior.

We must oppose aggressive actions and irresponsible behavior, but we must not seek confrontations lightly. We must maintain a strong national defense while recognizing that in the nuclear age the relationship between military strength and politically usable power is the most complex in all history."[12]

If paradox continued to confuse the perception of peaceful coexistence for some, it did not for Haig. Within five months of assuming his new post, he visited every capital of the NATO nations except those of Iceland and Greece. He discussed détente along with many other matters which he termed parts of a "socio-economic crisis," and gained an "overriding impression...that there is a growing realization that the common nature of this...threat, which is the same in each capital, and differs only in degree, demands the collective pooling of our best energies and our best resources in the same cooperative way in which we have worked in the past to cope with more stereotyped, purely military threats."[13] He, along with Secretary-General Joseph Luns, perceived the threat to NATO in a global as well as a regional context.

He conveyed these impressions in May 1975 in his first address to the Assembly of Western European Union (WEU). In the discussion that followed, Haig was challenged to explain: (1) whether the United States would accept a "joint collective decision as to what arms they should have for the United States Army" (since all the SACEURs had placed such emphasis on support for standardization of weapons); (2) why he had omitted mention of the indefensibility of Berlin, only recently the subject of a renewal by the United States of its pledge to stand by West Berlin; (3) whether recent European members' defense-budget reductions indicated a decrease in the will and awareness of the need for vigilance. Obviously, members of his audience were trying to pin Haig down on the specific current issues. More challenges followed.

Other parliamentarians queried: (4) In view of the fact that his command would continue to depend upon supplies of oil, minerals, and indeed, reinforcements from overseas, and in view of the military and economic threat he had described as well as the danger from the lack of willpower to resist, was Haig satisfied about the degree of priority given to the protection of the sea lanes and his cooperation with SACLANT? (5) Was "it now time to think of putting almost all our naval strength under the water instead of its floating on top?" (6) Had the heavy battle-tank exhausted its usefulness, in view of the lessons of the Yom Kippur war? (7) Were all the types of strike aircraft then flying fully justified? (8) What were the greatest dangers in Central Europe? (9) Had he new thoughts about weaknesses on the northern flank of his command and the disintegration of certain relationships on the southern flank? (10) What about strategic balance? The force balance? Where did NATO now stand in relation to the Soviet Union's preponderance of conventional power?

Haig moved quickly to describe the credibility, vitality, and viability of the American guarantee, insisting that he "would not be where I am if I had any doubts about that." He pointed out that recent events in the United States had intensified American awareness of the importance of its obligations and the mutual benefits derived by Americans as well as Europeans from the American presence in Europe.

He asserted that no one who had studied the strategic environment and the literal explosion of Soviet naval strength and consequent mobility (including the range and durability of the latest Soviet Delta class submarine) and who also considered the recent energy finds in the North Sea, could fail to be concerned about the likelihood of a growing problem on NATO's northern flank. NATO's rapid reinforcement of that area in time of crisis or conflict—which involved "the great imperative of warning" and the development of a political consensus to take steps before a conflict started—contributed to Haig's discomfort, especially as a recent force review in Britain had concluded that British reaction forces in the North should be reduced. But this reduction was compensated in part by improving United States and Canadian rapid reinforcement capacities.

As for the détente dilemma, Haig said, two questions arose: whether détente was a one-way street and what its psychological impact was. Wondering "whether we are providing the East with technological assets that it would take the East decades to get, in return for very little," Haig noted that this was the concern of a number of American experts, and he suspected that the question would be "politicized" in the days ahead. As for the psychological impact, had it "put the West to sleep"? It surely was contradictory to the requirement for continued defense expenditures. But "detente is with us and...as we wrestle with this difficult question we must always be prepared to cope with the alternative: the obligations and burdens of a return to confrontation politics."[14] Haig acknowledged that communication with the East was still preferable to isolation and polemics, which eventually could only be sterile. "Some of the rhetoric of the past promised more than perhaps detente could ever provide and it should be toned down to more realistic language," he said. Although Haig saw no fundamental erosion of will, he did perceive some confusion about what the problem was.

More specifically and in relation to the force balance, Haig called attention to the Soviet strength in Central Europe of approximately fifty-seven first-echelon divisions with another thirty immediately reinforceable and to an Allied "M-Day" posture substantially below that. Thus, in purely quantitative terms, NATO's most severe shortfall was in conventional ground defense capability. Nonetheless, in his view the strategic balance was essentially equivalent and the theater (European) nuclear balance was in NATO's favor. But he warned, "We tamper with our current capability only at the greatest risk, not only in purely security measurements, but in terms of that very unity, self-confidence and solidarity" he had referred to earlier.

As for naval matters, Haig was gravely concerned with the growing capability of the Soviet naval forces to interdict the North Atlantic sea lanes as well as to conduct more sophisticated operations that subsurface launching platforms provided. He pointed out that in World War II over 93 percent of the Allies' supplies had come across those lanes. In a major conflict, possibly 90 percent would still have to be carried through the same areas. His concern was that if the Allies' naval strength deteriorated beyond its current level—and the margin was very slim—NATO would be faced with a situation in which those military forces would have to focus first on the elimination of the submarine threat. In World War II the Allies had been confronted with some fifty submarines. In contrast, the number NATO would now face was 100, "and they are far more sophisticated and far more capable," he pointed out.

Haig had good reason, and valid authority, to be concerned about naval matters. SHAPE was not only an air/land command; it was also a naval command. Indeed, as chapter 1 recounts, from its inception ACE had been a major naval as well as land and air command. Its sea area, which extended along its entire periphery encompassing the land mass of continental Europe, totaled more than one and one-half million square miles. The responsibility in peacetime entailed planning, organizing, and training for the use of all the elements of his command including major naval forces. These measures would doubtless have to be accomplished under crisis conditions, and therefore, in the case of naval forces, such measures would include a forward maritime defense, protection of NATO shipping, and the deployment of naval forces in support of the land and air campaigns. SACEUR was, thus, indeed a major naval commander.

As for his view of undersea warfare, Haig noted that a recent major Soviet naval exercise indicated that the Soviets were not aiming at "any tricky gimmick of shifting all of their assets to undersea." In fact, precisely the opposite was the case. "They are looking for a balanced naval force which can cope with American convoys and American undersea submarine-launched vehicles, which can undertake a submarine killer role, and which can handle the great burdens and problems of the exits of the Baltic, the Bering, and the Mediterranean [seas]."

Turning to the utility of the tank on the modern battlefield, Haig pointed out that SHAPE studies had confirmed that the majority of the tank kills in the Yom Kippur conflict had been the result of tank-inflicted wounds; indeed, 80 percent of the tanks were knocked out by other tanks. Thus, the tank remained essential on the modern battlefield. He also, however, asserted that he was not an "anti-missile man." Missiles had "done a very good job in the Yom Kippur conflict." The greatest danger he saw was that by cutting back expenditures, "we risk bringing about an imbalance in that force structure for which we will ever after have to pay the price." He saw the tank as "a very fundamental part of the conventional ground battle in Europe tomorrow as well as today."

While he saw no fundamental changes in combinations of strike aircraft, Haig felt compelled to point out that the Soviet Union had been moving in the previous two years progressively toward increasing the duration of flight and toward improving the load-carrying capability and range of its tactical aircraft, which only enhanced its offensive capability.

In summary, Haig laid out clearly at the outset of his tenure his views on the important policy issues facing the Alliance. But frustration lay ahead in his vigorous efforts to maintain momentum in many of the programs he foresaw as necessary to remedy the shortfalls in NATO's readiness, reinforcement capabilities, and rationalization of resources—that series of shortcomings or problem areas that acquired the inevitable short title, the "3-Rs."

In 1974, prior to Haig's tenure, legislation had been passed in Congress concerning troop levels, burden-sharing, and tactical atomic weapons policy in Europe. As a result, on 5 August 1974 President Ford signed a bill that called for a reduction in the ratio of noncombat to combat troops in Europe. A section of the act (302[a] of PL 93-365) required the secretary of defense to reduce headquarters and noncombat military personnel located in Europe by eighteen thousand as of 30 June 1976 but authorized the secretary to increase the combat component by a comparable amount if necessary. The secretary had to submit a semiannual report to Congress on all actions taken to improve the combat proportions of U.S. forces in Europe.

As for balance-of-payments difficulties, Ford reported to Congress a few days later that the NATO Economic Directorate had concluded a study showing that the payments for military-related items from the NATO Allies, other than the Federal Republic of Germany, would amount to approximately $1 billion, which was a figure slightly more than the difference between the estimated American deficit for 1974 of $2.1 billion and the German offset figure for 1974 of $1.2 billion. Later in the year, on 18 November 1974, the president reported to Congress that preliminary figures on American defense expenditures included in the United States' international balance of payments during the fiscal year 1974 and estimates relating to military purchases in the United States by European NATO Allies anticipated that costs of U.S. forces assigned to NATO would be fully offset by the German–U.S. Offset Agreement and by military-related purchases of other NATO Allies in the United States. This met the congressional requirement that retaining U.S. forces in Europe at current levels could only be possible if the Allies made up any balance-of-payments deficit that this might incur.

The Military Procurement Authorization Act for fiscal year 1975 also had imposed a freeze until 30 June 1975 on the total number of tactical nuclear warheads located in Europe except in the event of hostilities. It also called for the secretary of defense to report on the overall concept of the use of tactical nuclear weapons in Europe. Congress further had asked for an assessment of standardization-of-weapons actions that could improve the overall nonnuclear defense capability or save resources for NATO as a whole.[15]

These congressional actions highlighted a major factor in NATO defense planning: the fact that no known instrument or document committed member-nations of NATO to the permanent stationing or pledging of a specific number of their forces in or for Europe—with some exceptions.[16] In the past several nations (France, Britain, and the United States) had withdrawn for one reason or another portions of their military forces stationed on the Continent: France during the upheavals in Algeria, Britain in 1967-68 upon the announcement of cuts in government expenditures and the withdrawal of all British forces from the Far East and from the Persian Gulf, and the United States in announcing its policy of the "dual-stationing" of some of its forces assigned to Europe.

Indeed, special provisions concerning national withdrawals of forces, when carried out at a time other than during the normal NATO Defense Planning Review, were contained in approved NATO political documents. Thus, it was not only the nonspecific commitments that confronted Haig, but the circumstances that could arise from so-called out-of-cycle tampering with the tenuous arrangements already in existence. Such tampering did not enhance the sense of interdependence he continued to stress—the concerted Atlantic community action that would obviate the "tendency to seize on one or another aspect of our strategic situation, dissect it, and draw from it sweeping conclusions concerning new requirements and even new doctrines."[17]

The tendency that Haig warned against consisted of those instant analyses that did not stand the test of time but that, while they predominated, threatened to do serious damage. To him it was more important to step back and examine more broadly the key elements of the strategic situation in which the Alliance found itself in the mid-1970s. That environment had changed substantially since the formation of the Alliance in 1949. A bipolar world that arrayed the Free World against a monolithic threat centered on Moscow had given way to a multipolar world with three competitive centers of influence: one in Moscow, one in Peking, and one in the revolutionary Third World. Strains among these centers were accompanied by increasing "centrifugal tendencies" within the Soviet sphere of a sort that had historically induced efforts to divert attention outward.

Despite a growing imperative for Western interdependence, a countertrend of nationalism was on the rise. The "unique hegemonic power that formerly permitted the United States unilaterally to manage global crises on bahalf of all Western nations [had] declined," he found. At the same time, Western Europe, recovered from its post–World War II exhaustion, no longer was content to assume a junior role in Alliance affairs. Strains in the West were intensified by a growth in the real and perceived power of the Third World where Western dependence upon resources was complicated by the widespread existence of dictatorial governments of the right or left which were capable of precipitous shifts in policy and alignment. Meanwhile, the West's ability to deal with this problem collectively was complicated by a socioeconomic crisis in which fiscal problems and limitations on raw materials were accompanied by "the anguishing challenge facing Western leaders as they seek to distribute the products of the success of industrialized societies in a just and responsible way."

From this necessarily overgeneralized capsule appraisal of the contemporary strategic environment, as he termed it, Haig drew several conclusions: (1) that the West would enjoy "the advantages of multipolarity only to the extent that it is perceived as relevant, reliable, and consistent" by each of the centers of influence he had cited; (2) that the requirement was the more pressing in view of developing strains within the Warsaw Pact and the Soviet Union itself, which increased the danger that the Soviet Union might look outward as a diversion from its own problems; (3) that "we will meet this requirement successfully only if we are able to forge a new conception of Western partnership, based on cooperation rather than competition; (4) similarly, that if the West wished to deal effectively and responsibly with the emerging Third World, it must do so as "a collective consumer."

The modern imperative for the West, therefore, was interdependence in the political, economic, and security spheres. Concerted action of this kind, he stressed, could be realized only under "an umbrella of continued confidence in our security arrangements."[18] The principal threat to that confidence derived from the relentless growth in sheer Soviet military power, Haig said. It was not the result of some sudden or precipitous shift in Soviet policy but rather of a persistent long-term effort dating back at least to 1962 and perhaps earlier. Real annual Soviet increases in defense expenditures of some 4 to 5 percent and a total annual expenditure representing approximately 11 to 13 percent of the Soviet Union's gross national product were evidence of this.

While this allocation of resources might suggest a relative Soviet inefficiency in defense production, it clearly confirmed to Haig the priority the Soviets attached to defense—in "a nation whose GNP was less than 40 percent of our own." Military authorities, he warned, must not be diverted by debates over dollar–ruble differentials, but rather should focus their attention on the military capabilities which Soviet expenditures provided in terms of hardware and resources on the ground.

Haig's comparison of capabilities became an analysis of "our Triad of Central Systems [i.e., strategic], theater nuclear forces, and conventional land, sea, and air forces." He characterized the central strategic balance as "rough equivalence." Since 1962 the Soviets had erased what amounted to a ten-to-one inferiority in ICBMs through a long-range building program that continued unabated. He pointed out in 1976 that during the two years of his command, the Soviet Union already had added four new land-based ICBMs to its inventory, three of which carried independently targeted reentry capabilities, and all of which were more accurate than similar weapons that had preceded them. The Soviet Union had already begun to deploy a forty-two hundred nautical mile "SS-N-8" missile on its Delta and "Stretched" Delta submarines, weapons that were capable of targeting the United States, Europe, and much of China from patrol areas in the Barents Sea. And even as the SS-N-8 missile entered deployment, a "MIRV'd" follow-on weapon, the "SS-NX-18," was under development.

In Haig's opinion the character and magnitude of the Soviet programs, together, reflected a trend toward strategic capabilities far in excess of any reasonable deterrent need. "Indeed," he insisted, "these programs, including a continuing attention to Civil Defense, suggest that the Soviet Union has not entirely assimilated the prevailing Western view that a nuclear war can have no winner, and that strategic systems are therefore exclusively political in character."[19]

As for theater nuclear forces, here again the trends were "highly dynamic." The quantity and quality of ground-to-ground rocketry; a nuclear capability for a new self-propelled field artillery type of equipment; a reconfiguration of the Soviet tactical air arm, from an air defense to deep penetration; a pending deployment of the SS-X-20, a "MIRV'd" solid-fueled ground-mobile IRBM capable of striking targets throughout Western Europe from sites in the Western extremities of the Soviet Union, and other trends all suggested to Haig increased Soviet concern with theater nuclear warfare.

But the most worrisome aspect of the military balance, he said, was the improvement in Soviet conventional land, sea, and air forces. Soviet military strength had increased by a million men during the previous decade, and in NATO's central region alone, Soviet divisions had been augmented by 130,000 men, by about 40 percent in tanks, and by between 50 and 100 percent in artillery. While the West had been occupied with "tooth-to-tail" ratios (e.g., combat force and its logistic support), the Soviet Union had improved both the mobility and the sustaining capabilities of ground formations and had added large numbers of new armored personnel carriers, trucks, and helicopters, while substantially upgrading their support base. In 1975 alone, he asserted, the Soviets had demonstrated an enhanced airlift capability by rotating over 100,000 Soviet troops in Eastern Europe by air, while at sea Soviet naval forces had evolved from what was once an essentially coastal defensive force into a blue-water navy capable of worldwide power projection.

Finally, although some in the West took comfort from what traditionally had been a Western qualitative advantage and although the Allies did retain a technological edge, the trends, Haig warned, were not reassuring. In particular, the Soviet Union was embarked on a research-and-development program nearly twice the size of the West's.

From this assessment of the military threat, Haig drew two conclusions. First, the assessment confirmed that what was once an essentially continental Soviet military capability had become a global capability that provided the Soviets with a global power-projecting potential. Coping with this expanding Soviet military threat, therefore, had become a major task for the West. In a period of rough strategic equivalence, that task would place increasing importance on regional balances worldwide, "of which NATO is clearly the most central," he noted.

Second, upon examining Soviet allocations of military manpower and resources, it was clear to Haig that the Soviets still assigned priority of effort to the forces facing NATO's Central Region. Yet he foresaw no direct military challenge in that area in the near future. But in terms of conflict, he considered that the NATO nations were far more likely to be faced with a continuation of ambiguous, "ambivalent" situations on the flanks and periphery, challenges resulting from Third World dynamics which might not even result from deliberate superpower instigation but which could easily induce confrontation.

"Managing these situations," Haig thought, clearly would require NATO to maintain a "military balance flank-to-flank."

Thus, NATO was confronted with an unprecedented security challenge. Moreover, to those persons who discounted the deterrent value of nuclear weapons and "who would therefore have NATO place virtually complete reliance on a conventional capability to defeat an aggressor on the battlefield," he confessed that he shared their desire to improve the conventional forces. Indeed, it was currently—and continued to be— "our priority focus of attention." But Haig also warned against "the facile proposition that we can simply ignore our nuclear capabilities in the face of an opponent whose own concern with nuclear warfighting is clear beyond doubt. No posture could successfully deter if it forfeited an entire range of capabilities to the potential aggressor, and, in so doing, promised to confine the costs of aggression to the victum of that aggression. Nor could it maintain the confidence of Allies who would be the first to suffer from its failure," he insisted.

Haig clearly differentiated among NATO's strategic forces, "the ultimate measure of our commitment and the ultimate demonstration of our determination"; theater nuclear forces, "the least understood in terms of their contribution to the integrity of our strategy"; and the Allies' conventional forces, "absolutely critical to the successful deterrence of aggression in Europe, not because conventional forces replace nuclear elements of our Triad, but because they are an utter prerequisite to their credibility." But he insisted that the components of the three were not mutually competitive. On the contrary, in his view they were mutually essential. No one could replace another, nor could improvements in one be considered to lessen the need for all of them. Improvement of NATO's conventional forces, therefore, became "our first priority," not because theater or strategic forces were any less important, but because conventional force deficiencies were the most serious. In this respect, Haig was reiterating a theme echoed by his immediate predecessors. As this analysis reveals, Haig conceived of the SACEUR's role as that of sketching out the broad geo-strategic picture of the West vis-à-vis the Soviet Union in order that his subordinate commanders and other specialists could then address the more specifically military aspects.

He defined NATO's three-pronged force improvement program as being designed "to increase the readiness of our in-place forces, to rationalize our forward defense posture, and, finally [to] enhance our capacity to rapidly reinforce from within and outside the theater"; in brief, the "three Rs": readiness, rationalization, and reinforcement. They must, however, be linked to better short- and long-range planning, and in support of this view, the Department of Defense had arranged with the RAND Corporation to conduct during the period 1973-76 three studies. The first study was to determine how to adjust NATO's defense posture in the event an agreement was achieved in the MBFR negotiations. A second study concerned the rationalization of the defense posture, which would be built on the planning already under way at SHAPE and on national initiatives concerned with force-restructuring programs. The third study considered Alliance defense in the 1980s and proposed a long-term program to provide an integrating framework for meeting critical needs.[20]

Furthermore, at the heads-of-government summit meeting in London in May 1977, President Carter proposed that the NATO Allies combine their efforts to achieve, on a high-priority basis, short-term measures to show renewed Alliance resolve, to design a long-term NATO program, and to cooperate more closely in armaments—a part of the program to which the president pledged more of a two-way street between the United States and Europe. He also invited the other NATO heads of government to review what had been accomplished in these areas at another summit meeting in the spring of 1978. The substantive content of the Long-Term Defense Program (LTDP), as it emerged, was not at all that new, at least in the opinion of Robert W. Komer, an adviser to the U.S. secretary of defense. For the most part, it simply built on many previous proposals long seen as essential to cope with the evolving threat, but now the program was injected with Haig's intensity of purpose. What the LTDP concept really added was a coherent management framework for pulling together key NATO requirements, already largely analyzed and widely accepted, so that all Allies could see clearly what was needed and thus could commit themselves to respond.

Both American authorities and Haig recognized that not all proposals would be fully acceptable to all the NATO Allies. Some measures would have to be extended to a longer term than others, some might have to be changed completely because of costs, and some might have to be restudied. It was here that an "agonizing appraisal" confronted Haig: how to accommodate a NATO DPC decision that set a target of a 3 percent annual increase in national defense budgets as well as newly "managed" commitments with the slow but steady command-diplomacy he had pursued in applying already established and accepted procedures for encouraging the Allies to remain on course in their defense efforts. If the pace and cycle of the annual Defense Planning Reviews were interrupted, would the defense requirements that had been approved by governments be subsumed in a "stretched-out," "syncopated," new system that might wipe out the previous progress?

If Haig's first reaction to the new tasks was less than enthusiastic and indeed impelled him to consider making a stand against them, several extensive "sounding-board" sessions with his senior advisors and careful reflection—and, not least, a comprehensive review of the meaning and possible achievements of the program when measured against the shortfalls that threatened to remain—convinced Haig that his authority and command belonged fully in support of LTDP. Using those around him as a sounding-board so that he could analyze a problem verbally was characteristic of the SACEUR. Consequently, as he approached the end of his fourth year as SACEUR, Haig energized the LTDP process as only he could. This was reflected in the observation of a former Danish minister of defense that Haig had provided "great impetus within NATO and had been of tremendous help in getting the LTDP going."[21]

Also during Haig's tenure, on 3 January 1978, for the first time in the history of ACE, the post of a second deputy SACEUR was established, and a senior West German officer was designated to occupy it. According to Gen. Gerd Schmuckle of the Federal Republic of Germany, the additional post was established because of a certain imbalance between the contribution of the West German armed forces and the German posts within the NATO structure, particularly in the higher commands and posts within the commands. In effect, the Germans had been underrepresented for some time, said General Schmuckle.[22]

But the background to the appointment was not a simple matter of review and direction for Haig, particularly in view of his responsibilities toward the Military Committee, chaired at the time by British Adm. of the Fleet, Lord Peter Hill-Norton, from whence the SACEUR's Terms of Reference emanated,[23] and the fact that a British DSACEUR would continue to serve in the same capacity, albeit each with distinctive responsibilities. There also was some internal, political-military maneuvering among West German officials. A few years later, Schmuckle reflected:

> The Germans criticized the Alliance. For years they were complaining that they did not have enough military command positions in NATO. Attempts to increase German representation had been unsuccessful. Since I did not know exactly whether our reproaches to NATO were really justified, I had my staff count the number of general stars of the senior NATO military and give a breakdown by nationality. But they were to count only the "golden stars" of the respective Commanders-in-Chief, their deputies, and the Chiefs of Staff, for it was there that the real decisions were taken.

To Schmuckle the result spoke volumes. "In the Alliance, American generals wore 73 stars, British generals 66, German generals 24. Yet the Federal Republic provided more forces to the Alliance than the UK. The star arithmetics proved the manpower management skills of the British and the inability of the Germans." He then recounted:

At the next Ministerial Meeting I showed the result to Georg Leber [Federal German defense minister]. He took action immediately without asking anyone. He had the allotment of general stars made public by one of his officer aides. General [Harald] Wust, the Chief of Staff/Federal Armed Forces, who had succeeded the [late] Admiral Zimmerman, was furious. He felt that the time had not yet come for the Germans to claim the manning of NATO posts of such calibre. He accused me [of having] given wrong advice to the Minister. The next day, contrary to his prognosis, we had an enthusiastic press. The simple breakdown by stars was more convincing than all the general statements of the past. General Haig asked Georg Leber to suggest to him as his deputy a German four-star general. Haig's offer was not free from risk. For 30 years a British general had been Deputy SACEUR. Haig intended thus to break away from tradition. The demand that only a British soldier could be the deputy of the Supreme Commander in Europe had allegedly been made by Winston Churchill himself. This was a clever political calculus: via this point Great Britain would alone be able to exercise influence upon the American "Supreme Allied Commander Europe." The stubborn Field Marshal Montgomery had been designated by Churchill as the first DSACEUR.[24]

Schmuckle was appointed DSACEUR in January 1978. Haig's issuance of specific terms of reference to him was followed by the addition of two special tasks. One was command and control updating, i.e., developing computer-based command and control systems for the future. One result of this task was the implementation of a West German system for all air-defense operation centers in the Central Region, not, Haig hastened to note, because of Schmuckle's nationality but because it was the only system available. "We succeeded in developing a study for a common system for the armies in the year 1990 to the year 2000," Schmuckle said; in the meantime, SHAPE was developing a means for interoperability in this field.

A second task was the establishment of a basis for American rapid reinforcement in time of crisis. This was one of Haig's chief initiatives after a study group had helped him to conclude that it was possible to "move twice as much in half the time." In fact, Europe was not prepared to receive such large reinforcements in an emergency. "We found regulations, for example, in which it was very complicated...to move from Holland to Germany without having to be checked by Customs [authorities], which was ridiculous in a crisis."[25] One big element was host-nation support so that the European receiving nations could free American authorities from supporting tasks which could be executed by Europeans. For example, it was unnecessary for Americans to bring butchers, bakers, barbers, and truck drivers to Europe. Another element was the stocking of American materiel. Here, Haig encouraged Schmuckle to draw on the help of U.S. command and control authorities. Haig's policy stipulated that pre-stocking should not be concentrated on German soil alone; rather, it should take place also in the Benelux countries and in other areas. He especially viewed Norway as a region where pre-stocking in support of possible amphibious operations had taken on greater importance, partly because of the Soviet naval buildup in the Kola peninsula. A consequence of the Haig-Schmuckle rapport was a growing satisfaction among American authorities with the progress made in the 1978-80 period in this important "R."

Another of Schmuckle's accomplishments was an initiative which he referred to as industrial mobilization, e.g., the ammunition and manufacturing resources that would be needed in a crisis or war. Discussions with industrialists, proposals to the Federal German government, and conferences within SHAPE and with Haig (and later with Gen. Bernard W. Rogers, Haig's successor) established requirements for additional reserves of such raw materials as chrome and copper. Similar efforts had been undertaken to establish such reserves in Britain and the United States, while particular emphasis was placed on a capability to increase the production of "some dormant factories" and to have enough trucks at depots available in Europe.

Finally—but not the sum of the tasks which the SACEUR had given the new DSACEUR—Haig introduced a special project: how to improve the "readiness of forces," one of the three principal elements of the campaign that he had been leading for adapting the new factors affecting NATO Europe's defense.

In mid-summer 1979 as his tenure was drawing to a close, Haig reflected on the challenges that NATO faced and the measures that remained to be implemented.[26] He had continuously pointed to the relentless growth of Soviet military power over the previous fifteen years. He recalled the steps NATO had taken to strengthen conventional military capabilities. Among them were: SHAPE's so-called flexibility studies, which, like earlier ones, had produced hundreds of recommendations for improvement; the follow-on "3-R Program," which was intended to increase the readiness of in-place forces and to improve their timely reinforcement by active and reserve forces from within and outside the theater; and attempts to achieve interoperability, i.e., to rationalize the capabilities of "diverse multinational air, sea and land forces to work together." He recalled the exercises, particularly AUTUMN FORGE, which were practically open to public view, that had been created during his tenure and had served as a driving force to implement improvements.

The short-term measures of LTDP, which at first had appeared to threaten an interruption of the annual force planning process and which he initially had viewed with some alarm, were now essentially completed. These had included ACE's improved anti-armor capabilities, greater theater reserve stock levels, the readiness of in-place forces, and the Allied ability to reinforce more rapidly and thereby enhance crisis-management capabilities. Long-term programs now permitted projection of NATO needs at least a decade ahead. Meanwhile, the NATO nations had agreed to aim for the annual increases in their defense spending of approximately 3 percent, and all these efforts had provided a framework for dealing with the buildup of Warsaw Pact conventional military capabilities in Central Europe. But with an experienced eye toward previous performances, Haig warned of the dangers of failing to follow through on the programs developed and the commitments made. Not following through, he said, not only implied that important Third World countries might be less pro-Western, but also would have grave consequences harmful to the security of the North Atlantic Alliance itself.

Complicating these issues was the evaporation of American strategic nuclear superiority. Where it had been for almost three decades "the ultimate arbiter in any local or regional crisis which found the United States in direct or potential confrontation with the Soviet Union," the emergence of a new strategic equation in the early 1970s had eliminated this ultimate arbiter, and instead regional military balances had assumed a far greater importance. The increasing Soviet capacity for intervention had become more politically significant while the Soviet propensity to intervene had become more difficult to deter. "The developments reinforce the need for a concerted Western approach to the management of global Soviet activities," he continued to stress. The West needed well-coordinated regional policies which encompassed Western political, economic, and security assets as integral components of a comprehensive, balanced global strategy.

Haig's global analysis served to underscore the one he had presented to the WEU Assembly in Paris four years earlier.[27] He had observed then that Allied planners' assessments of Europe, and especially of the North Atlantic Alliance, suggested that the Alliance was in far worse shape than its worst fears. Allegations that the Alliance, which had provided over twenty years of security for the West, had lost its vitality, or worse that it had lost its future potential in a changed strategic environment, had been serious and worrisome questions. The momentum injected into the Soviet Union's expansion program, especially after the traumatic events of the U.S.–Cuba confrontation in 1962; continuing disagreements between the Western Allies on the one hand and the Soviet Union on the other in attempting to settle remaining problems in Central Europe; and, of capital importance, the Soviet Union's increasing nuclear capabilities in both strategic and tactical-type weapons had dramatically changed the entire strategic environment. The difficulties that NATO nations were experiencing on the flanks of ACE, particularly in the Mediterranean area, where Greece and Turkey still differed on solutions to their mutual problems, and where in the Middle East continuing unsettled conflicts threatened to spill over into NATO's direct area of interest, formed a major part of any calculations of NATO's strength.

In Haig's view three broad challenges remained urgent: (1) the need to modernize theater nuclear forces; (2) the need to strengthen NATO's southeastern flank; and, most importantly, (3) the need to recognize the implications to NATO of global Soviet activities. Often referred to as matters "beyond NATO's borders," or "out-of-area factors," that affected NATO members' participation in NATO, Haig highlighted "the necessity to deal with the interrelationship between events occurring outside NATO's geographic boundaries, and the security of the Alliance, itself."

There were ample precedents for calling attention to this kind of concern, notwithstanding the absence of direct encroachment by an aggressor upon the territories of any of the NATO nations. In close proximity, if not on NATO's immediate periphery, there had occurred the upheavals in the Middle East; the invasion of Hungary; the occupation of Czechoslovakia, which brought for the first time Soviet forces along the extended frontier of a NATO nation in Central Europe; the Cyprus crises and Haig's efforts to reintegrate Greek forces into NATO; and a surfeit of incidents in air corridors and incidents at sea in the North and in the Mediterranean.[28] The 1978-79 period alone had witnessed the appearance of new pro-Soviet governments in Afghanistan, South Yemen, and Ethiopia; the growth of Soviet involvement in southern Africa; and the invasion of Cambodia and North Yemen by Soviet-sponsoed proxy forces. Western nations could not afford to ignore even the short-term consequences of "untended, illegal Soviet adventurism in the Third World," he insisted. Such adventurism posed threats to Western sources of raw materials and provided the Soviet Union with bases that could threaten lifelines of Western commerce.

Shortly after, Haig pointed out that the United States had

learned in two great conflicts that there was no American security without West European security. But it was increasingly important, he observed, that in Japan and in the Pacific through to the North American continent and onward to "our West European Allies," there should be recognition that "there can be no security in their sphere if they continue to ignore the activities going on outside the specific sphere of the Alliance." One observer asked if he was proposing some new kind of institution. "That," Haig said, "is for the politicians to settle." But he agreed that his job had its political dimensions, not least because of its multinational nature; and he recalled that President Kennedy on taking office had issued a directive requiring the U.S. military to provide political assessments of given situations.[29]

In retrospect, as early as 1977, only a little more than twenty-four months after becoming SACEUR, Haig's skills in articulating and characterizing his programs within combined political-military parameters had won him growing professional respect as well as active Allied support. Although some elements in the new United States administration, in the Pentagon, in the press, and among the public continued to criticize him, he maintained his sense of humor.[30] His success in winning over the doubters, who had kept an unsure distance at the outset of his tenure, suggested that his efforts had had positive results. That he was the first of the "new era of SACEURs" who had not inherited the aura of the NATO "founding fathers" had in no way served to diminish the respect he had wrung from them as they acknowledged that he had genuinely—indeed, exceptionally vigorously—achieved notable progress.

His previous national, political, and military offices, and his subsequent experience among the highest authorities of NATO, led some observers to conclude that he was "destined for even higher office." Thus, on 29 June 1979 in a colorful outdoor parade-ground SHAPE ceremony, Haig passed the SHAPE standard to Gen. Bernard W. Rogers.

CONCLUSIONS

What Can We Learn from the NATO Experience in Multinational Military Leadership?

ROBERT S. JORDAN

In a 1942 letter to General Marshall, Eisenhower commented with obvious frustration: "The sooner I can get rid of all these questions that are outside the military scope, the happier I will be. Sometimes I think I live ten years each week, of which at least nine are absorbed in political and economic matters."[1] Ten years later, of course, he found himself back in the same situation that he was deploring earlier, and, as the record shows, no SACEUR can avoid the political and economic aspects of NATO defense.

Given the fact that the true deterrent in NATO has remained largely in American hands, even though there has been over the period recounted in this book much maneuvering on the part of the Allies to share more fully in nuclear affairs and much maneuvering on the part of the United States to minimize such sharing, the essential role of the SACEUR must be seen as twofold. In one direction, as with the secretary-general, he must at all costs maintain an effective dialogue with the United States. This can prove difficult not only because of such irksome matters as nuclear command and control or weapons and/or budgetary burden-sharing, but also because often the United States government itself does not behave as a unified policy-making entity. And with the approach of presidential elections, this latter situation can often become almost intolerable for a SACEUR, especially if the presidential office changes parties. White House politics figured directly in the NATO careers of Eisenhower, Ridgway, Norstad, Lemnitzer, and Haig, and indirectly in those of Gruenther and Goodpaster.

In another direction the SACEUR must retain the confidence of the Alliance's European members, in particular the Germans.[2] From the very beginning of NATO, the question of a West German military contribution has been present. It had been part of the strategy of the defense of Western Europe even before NATO. The Brussels Treaty (Western Union) defense ministers had declared in 1948, for example: "In the event of an attack by Russia, however soon it may come, the five powers are determined to fight as far east in Germany as possible. ... Their preparations are therefore aimed at holding the Russians on the best position in Germany, covering the territory of the five powers in such a way that sufficient time for the American military power to intervene decisively can be assured."[3]

Even after German participation had been achieved, "the main political problem [for the SACEUR] was to reconcile the French demand for controls over Germany with the German demand for equality."[4] Every SACEUR has had to grapple with this problem of the German contribution to NATO, whether from the angle of EDC or of MLF, or of various diplomatic proposals for East–West disengagement, East–West German neutralization, etc. As one observer put it, Eisenhower took NATO to the Rhine, Ridgway crossed the Rhine, and Gruenther went to the Elbe, which committed his successors to geopolitical constraints that made it very difficult for them to construct a defense-in-depth military strategy for prevailing in Central Europe if deterrence were to fail.

In other words, "questions outside the military sphere" are what the SACEURs have had to deal with, which is the leadership challenge that faces any coalition commander. But as General Rogers pointed out in his preface, having to do so in peacetime makes the job that much more difficult. Nothing shows this more clearly than the constant discussion over troop levels. At Lisbon, Eisenhower got pledges from the member-states that his successor, Ridgway, was unable to collect on, and which in turn Ridgway's successor, Gruenther, had to formally acknowledge were unachievable. For one thing, the Soviet

Conclusions

leaders proved uncooperative at this time by engaging in a post-Stalin "thaw" in the Cold War, which tended to undermine the sense of urgency and sacrifice that had prevailed earlier in Western Europe. Also, the change in the American posture away from large conventional forces to reliance on American-controlled tactical and strategic nuclear weapons as the backbone of the deterrent was a political disincentive for Europe to extend conscription or to build up reserves.

While this did not result initially in a drawdown of American ground forces, it meant that the American buildup would not continue. In fact, even during Gruenther's tenure in the mid-1950s, it was expected that the United States would be able to turn over more of the responsibility for the defense on the ground of NATO to the European Allies. Shortly thereafter, however, two major European Allies, the French and English, after the Suez crisis of 1956, preferred to insist on retaining national nuclear forces, thus complicating the symmetry of the assignment of roles and missions for the SACEUR. Instead they imposed on him the continuing problem of how to keep NATO's conventional guard up in the face of domestic political pressures everywhere in Europe in the late 1950s—including West Germany—to minimize these contributions.

By 1963 a new element had intruded: the addition of West German to British and French pressures for access to the "nuclear club." As was said about German motivations for supporting MLF: "Three principal motives lay behind the German policy on the MLF. First, it would bring Germany indirectly into the business of strategic nuclear weapons, in a way that would minimize the political risks and costs. Second, it represented a move toward military integration... as, whatever its shortcomings, the most imaginative proposal since the European Defense Community. As such it would offer a framework within which the British and French nuclear forces might ultimately be incorporated. Finally, the argument most frequently voiced by the Germans..., it would bind the United States more closely to European defense."[5]

In this, as in other cases, the SACEURs have been compelled by political necessities to advocate causes that have tended to complicate rather than to simplify their efforts to carry out their responsibilities. Supranational control over an important segment of the armed forces potentially at his disposal, as embodied in the still-born European Defence Community/European Political Community, for example, could hardly be expected to arouse the SACEUR's enthusiasm, if the truth were told. Also, the endless maneuvering over weapons procurement and standardization has made more difficult the formation of an integrated NATO force, although for other reasons, primarily those of national interest in terms of conceptions of protecting their own arsenals, the SACEUR's have not been able to do much about it.

Information-sharing on nuclear matters has been another constant area of concern for the SACEURs, and in this case they have had virtually to be a supplicant with the United States on behalf of the nonnuclear member-states, as well as of the secretary-general at times, to share more information, since control was not going to be widespread. Also, when SACEURs have found themselves advocating an Alliance position at variance with the current thinking in Washington, as Norstad learned, they have sometimes found themselves unwelcome in circles where it was crucial that they be accepted. Whatever the political motivations for the appointment of a SACEUR— and it is quite clear that Washington politics have played some role in virtually every selection—the SACEUR's capacity to speak for the Alliance in Washington and to interpret Washington to the Alliance must remain unimpaired.

In Gruenther's case, of course, the fact that he might be briefing a congressional committee during the day and playing bridge with the president that evening in the White House could not help but enhance his overall prestige in both SHAPE and Washington. It also did not hurt him that at the time of his appointment at SHAPE, he was viewed as a serious future candidate for at least the post of chief-of-staff of the army. Conversely, the generally low expectations that accompanied the appointments of Lemnitzer and Haig made their jobs, at least initially, more difficult. It was an open secret that the Kennedy administration wanted Lemnitzer out of Washington partly to make way for an officer not presumably tainted by the Cuban fiasco; it also was no secret that the Ford administration wanted Haig out of the public eye because of his close link to Nixon (and the army did not want him contending for the post of chief-of-staff because he was viewed as a political general who had not earned his stars "the hard way"). In this sense, as with Imperial Britain's governors general, the post of SACEUR was a convenient prize to be awarded at Washington's pleasure and according to Washington's needs.

Except for Eisenhower, whose appointment as SACEUR preceded the creation of the office of secretary-general, all SACEURs have had to share their place in the "NATO firmament" in varying degrees with the secretary-general. Ridgway, in this respect, was at a disadvantage because he had made his career mark in the period after World War II outside of Europe. Also, he was not a product of the Anglo-American Combined Chiefs-of-Staff wartime operation that provided so strong a tie, persisting in fact through Goodpaster's tenure.

Lord Ismay, for example proved an especially efficacious choice, partly because he had worked so closely during the war with Eisenhower and those closest to the new SACEUR. In short, he was almost the perfect counterpart to Eisenhower. As Churchill's right-hand man, Ismay "supervised [as deputy secretary (military) of the War cabinet] the running of the military Committees and their relations with other interests; as a member of the Chiefs of Staff's Committee, he took his share of responsibility in its decisions, and geared the machine to its demands; as Chief of Staff to the Minister of Defense, he acted as the link between the machine, the Committee and the Minister, and as the link for the Committee with Washington and for the Prime Minister with allies and with commanders."[6] Eisenhower paid Ismay this tribute: "Ismay's position...was, from the American point of view, a critical one because it was through him that any subject could at any moment be brought to the attention of the Prime Minister and his principal assistants. It was fortunate, therefore, that... his personality was such as to win the confidence and friendship of his American associates."[7]

There was no doubt, in other words, that the creation of SHAPE along with the creation of a civilian international staff headed by a secretary-general was at least initially a re-creation of the Anglo-American wartime collaboration. The presence in SHAPE of Field Marshal Lord Montgomery reinforced this perception—especially by the French, who viewed themselves as outsiders.

As an eminent historian has commented: "Between 1940 and 1945 London was, as it had never been before or since, a great international capital.... So those who returned to the Continent from London after the war already constituted a certain kind of community which survived into the post-war years and made the creation of NATO, when it came into being, infinitely easier. Officers of all three services from many of the countries concerned had already got to know one another working side by side during the war. It was all the easier for them to take up the threads again."[8]

All the SACEURs—especially Eisenhower along with his deputy, Lord Montgomery, who were the foremost personal military symbols in NATO of the Allied victory over Germany—went out of their way to reassure the Germans that they were welcomed as true allies rather than as defeated former enemies. Nonetheless, the *esprit* created in the founding years of SHAPE was uncontestably reflective of the rekindling of wartime memories and of postwar political/military/diplomatic careers that had brought high national office and international recognition to persons who later were to play leading roles in the creation of NATO.

This could be both a benefit and a liability to the secretary-general. In Spaak's case his somewhat patronizing attitude toward Norstad was reflective of his view that only a person who had held high public office in his own country could operate truly effectively, in a political sense, in NATO. Spaak viewed

Conclusions

himself more like a prime minister, with the NATO Council as his cabinet of political inferiors, than as the servant of the Council, as Ismay had somewhat misleadingly characterized himself. The reaction was strong resentment among the permanent representatives and, to some extent, a turning away from Spaak toward Norstad. Ironically, Norstad's more quietly persuasive manner proved more effective in a public relations sense than Spaak's more demanding demeanor.[9]

Spaak's successor, Stikker, while laboring under the impossible burden of the Franco-American rift of the late 1950s that had also plagued Spaak but had now intensified, also failed to establish close relations with the Council. For one thing, he was seen as being too closely identified with the United States; Norstad, in contrast, during this terminal period of his incumbency, was openly not in Washington's pocket. Thus, paradoxically, whereas in Gruenther's time the SACEUR's close association with the president of the United States helped him in his political role as SACEUR, Norstad's increasing alienation from Washington, intensified when Kennedy came to office, helped him win sympathy in Europe. Ridgway, not being an Eisenhower protégé (as were both Gruenther and Norstad) had little political currency outside the formal structure of the office itself to draw upon; his patron, General Bradley, had fallen out with Eisenhower over Eisenhower's perceived failure to defend General Marshall after Sen. Joseph McCarthy's attack on him, and in any case was himself too strongly identified with Truman and the unpopular Korean War.[10]

Lemnitzer's arrival at SHAPE in the early 1960s was not auspicious. He was perhaps viewed as the least promising SACEUR at the outset of his tenure. But his modest ways and his determination to make the best of a bad situation brought him respect and even affection by the time he left. His old-soldier manner, not unlike Ismay's, won him friends because it conveyed a sense of goodwill and reliability that was hard to resist. It did not do him any harm, in those days, either, to appear to be a victim without complaining of French (or, more precisely, Gaullist) displeasure. As one former American diplomat termed it, "I know full well that the French in some ways wrecked the military structure, but the alliance as a force, nonetheless, continues to exist."[11] To Lemnitzer must go a good bit of the credit.

He also was helped inadvertently because Stikker took upon himself, with some political bravery, to attempt to get the Alliance to face up to the problem of nuclear sharing, command, and control. Much of the emotional as well as *realpolitik* national considerations were, therefore, directed at the secretary-general rather than at the SACEUR. Stikker's successor, Manlio Brosio, continued to serve as the dominant, though less visible, figure in NATO. He shared this role, as far as United States–NATO relations were concerned, with the U.S. permanent representative, Harlan Cleveland, who had succeeded another strong political figure, Thomas Finletter, whose own political fortunes had gone down with President Johnson's final burial of MLF.

A rift occurred between Brosio and Lemnitzer over the question of NATO's proper attitude toward the Soviet Union at the time of the Czechoslovakian crisis of 1968. In Lemnitzer's view Brosio was too fearful of NATO's apppearing provocative. Lemnitzer was especially annoyed when Brosio advocated successfully that SHAPE shift its scheduled military exercises from West Germany to Britain.[12]

In other words, by the late 1960s the civilian side of the Alliance was capturing more of the political attention in the national capitals, especially Washington, than the military side. Unfortunately for Goodpaster, he also had the difficult task of providing political/military leadership during a period when there was a relaxation of tensions in Europe and when America was distracted by Vietnam. It is not inaccurate to observe that, as to nuclear affairs and détente, Brosio also could only chase after events that were being set in motion elsewhere, and his successor, Joseph Luns, was faced with the same dilemma. The major themes in NATO strategy continued to have their origins in Washington, leaving it to the SACEUR and the secretary-general to argue for their implementation.

Conclusions 183

The domestic political unrest in Europe, partly reflecting the domestic turbulence in the United States at the height of the Vietnam period, added to the general perception that perhaps NATO was obsolete, a Cold War relic that only bureaucratic inertia kept afloat. Although this was manifestly a caricature, nonetheless, it presented Goodpaster and Luns, in particular, with a challenge not faced by their predecessors.

This was because the intrinsic value of the Alliance had been generally accepted, even by France under de Gaulle (who merely used the security it provided for more openly nationalist purposes) until the late 1960s and early 1970s. But by then West Germany's desire to form a real and lasting rapprochement with East Germany signaled that the Adenauer policy of winning from the West, through multinational commitments, as much as possible in the way of national restoration, had largely run its course, and therefore the time had come to look to the East for concessions. The ultimate price, of course, was the negotiation in the mid-1970s of the Helsinki Accords, by which West Germany abandoned the notion of German reunification or the restoration of the so-called lost provinces at least for the foreseeable future. The reward was the prospect of closer ties and friendship between the two Germanies.

These fundamental shifts in the political currents of European and Atlantic relationships made it extremely difficult for either Luns or Goodpaster to argue that the threat from the East was real and imminent and, concomitantly, that military budgets should not be cut. Unfortunately for them, the United States military budget was itself being cut, and there was, in general, an antimilitary bias in the United States that spawned a host of speculative writings and books dissecting the end of NATO, although it had not been formally buried. It is instructive to take note of how President Ford viewed the situation. "Of all the problems NATO faced in the late spring of 1975, perhaps the most serious was psychological. In the wake of Vietnam, would the U.S. remain firm against Communist aggression elsewhere? Could our old allies still depend on us?

Democratic Senate leader Mike Mansfield and others had been calling for us to withdraw many of our troops from Western Europe. Understandably, the leaders of the NATO countries wanted to know whether this new mood of isolationism would prevail or whether we would honor our commitments abroad."[13]

Afghanistan proved a great boost for NATO with the Carter administration's belated realization that military spending must go up even if it ran against the domestic political tide. The sharp increase plus an Alliance commitment to increase all NATO spending by 3 percent annually after inflation represented what former pessimists now called a resurgence for NATO. Luns's warning that détente was merely a Soviet trap to beguile the Allies began to sound more credible, even though domestic opinion in Europe, especially among the youth (the so-called successor generation), remained skeptical.

Haig, somewhat inauspiciously succeeding Goodpaster, proved an effective advocate of rearmament; his earnest, spontaneous, almost theatrical style was more reflective of Luns's style than had been Goodpaster's more retiring, cautious, and scholarly demeanor, and so he and Luns were comfortable with each other. Paradoxically, although both Goodpaster and Haig earned their high military rank in part by serving as loyal aides in the White House, Haig came across in NATO as a real soldier's general—he was careful to be seen showing concern about the welfare of his troops, and he was soldierly in his bearing, as befitted a West Pointer of the old school. He was determined to overcome the skepticism of his fellow generals (including Goodpaster), and his style and manner soon overcame the cynicism in NATO that had accompanied the announcement of his appointment. By the time of his departure, Haig had won widespread respect throughout NATO that was in contrast to the, by then, more matter-of-fact acceptance of Luns. This was partly because Luns had remained in his post the longest of any secretary-general, and inevitably such length of tenure brings on a tendency, perhaps unfairly, to take the incumbent for granted.

CONCLUSIONS 185

Over the years, there have been some problems in maintaining political control over a military command. An illustration of how national political pressures concerning the high-level staff positions of SHAPE can be employed in the interests of a particular nationality can be found in the following letter from Gruenther to Lt. Gen. Sir Nevil Brownjohn, then chief staff officer to the British minister of defense.

As I explained to the British Chiefs of Staff and you at Greenwich last week, we intend to replace Brigadier General John M. Schweizer, Jr., U.S. Air Force, about mid-May.

In your letter of February 11th, you suggested that the position of Deputy to the SHAPE Director of Intelligence should be filled by a one-star officer, and in this instance by a U.K. officer. I informed the Chiefs at Greenwich last week why I considered it inadvisable to fill the Deputy post at this time. I wish to reaffirm now, what I said then, namely, that I have not ruled out the idea of a Deputy. On the contrary, there are many considerations which make it highly desirable that we fill that post. However, for reasons which I outlined last week, I do not think that it would be appropriate to make such an appointment at this time.

You also make reference in your letter to the British concept that the appointment of a U.S. officer as Director of Intelligence now should be made without prejudice to the nationality of the officer appointed later to succeed him. With this point of view I agree wholeheartedly.[14]

The problems that Ridgway had in defining the various maritime commands, as recounted in this book, is another example. Whatever military logic might dictate, it simply was necessary that the various European maritime member-states, proud of their respective naval traditions, be given national recognition through the parceling out of command roles and missions. On the ground, we have merely to recall the difficulty that Norstad had in obtaining acquiescence, if not enthusiastic endorsement, for a German to succeed a Frenchman to command the forces concentrated in West Germany.

Then there is the problem of whether the SACEUR should intervene in connection with a political position that one of his senior officers of another nationality might have taken that was at variance with the SACEUR's position. Two examples come to mind, one in which the SACEUR did intervene and one where he chose not to. In the first instance, the deputy SACEUR at the time, Field Marshal Lord Montgomery, had made some remarks at the NATO Defense College in 1955 concerning his views about eventual German reunification which, because of Montgomery's having also discussed them with the publisher of the London *Observer*, got into that paper. Gruenther wrote to Montgomery: "I consider that we in SHAPE should be especially circumspect in discussing any aspect of this problem which involves the neutralization of Germany in any form. Your remarks at the NATO Defense College on this subject, were, in my judgment, unfortunate, and I earnestly request you not to air such views again—at least until you and I have had a chance to talk about the matter."[15] The matter was smoothed over, but not without the leader of the Alliance's most influential member-state being appraised of it. Gruenther was able to report a happy ending to Eisenhower. "You will recall that I told you I was displeased with Monty because of his NATO Defense College talk and because of his off-the-record interview with the publisher of the Observer—both on the status of Germany (viz: What kind of a deal should we accept?). I wrote him a letter expressing my unhappiness. When I returned yesterday I found this contrite letter awaiting me. So please dont [sic] say anything to Anthony [Eden] when you see him next week."[16]

When it came to French Marshal Alphonse Juin's having come out against EDC while he held a major NATO command, Gruenther took a different tack, as he reported to Eisenhower in April 1954:

You may be interested in the JUIN [sic] case. After he made his talk against EDC a week ago today he was directed to appear before [Premier] Laniel and [Defense Minister] Pleven. He refused; not once but twice; not orally but in writing; not politely but arrogantly. He said he would not be treated "like a corporal." So they bounced him from his remaining French assignments.

Then came the question of his Central Command. No one has

known how to handle that. My contention is that this also is a matter between French Govt and Juin. Pressure has been brought to bear on me to take action. I have declined.

The feeling with respect to EDC is very intense in some quarters and I feel if NATO or the U.S. gets off base in this controversy EDC will suffer. Juin came to see me Thursday to say that if I had lost confidence in him he would resign out of consideration for me. I told him that this was a French Govt–Juin affair and that I had not lost confidence in him.[17]

The really delicate aspect of this incident was not confined to the SACEUR's relationship with a major commander of another nationality, but also involved the SACEUR's relationship with the French government itself. As Gruenther went on to recount: "Bidault asked me to see him today. He hinted twice that if I had any influence with Juin that a letter of apology from Juin would still save the situation. But Juin will not apologize—at least not today. I said that I did not feel that I should be a national negotiator in a matter of such national delicacy."[18]

In sum, the SACEUR, almost willy-nilly, cannot at times avoid being drawn into intense political debates involving his most senior commanders or staff officers not only over NATO policies but also over a policy conflict with his own government. Norstad's example is the best to cite.

Finally, there is always the dichotomy over what the SACEUR is empowered to do in the exercise of his command authority in peacetime as against what he is empowered to do in wartime. In peacetime he is required to be a negotiator, a publicizer, and almost an abstract symbol; in wartime he is to be a field commander in the classic coalition sense, marshaling and employing forces contributed by member-states to the coalition. Yet even though a national of the largest and the most powerful member in real terms, he has nonetheless been limited in what he can accomplish. Although his command authority was considerably expanded in the years between Eisenhower and Rogers, there are still areas of significant command and control over which he has limited authority even in wartime to assign priorities or to commandeer resources.

The reservations insisted upon by Denmark and Norway on the northern flank and by Greece on the southern flank are two examples.

For all of these reasons, the rationale that justified Ridgway's appointment proved short-lived; a truly battlefield general has not been what has been needed. An officer skilled in planning, negotiating, articulating, and conciliating is what has been required; and in most of the incumbents, this is what NATO has received.

Without a doubt, Eisenhower's decision to form a truly international staff, rather than merely a staff of seconded officers, contributed greatly to the *esprit* and the real control that a SACEUR could obtain at his headquarters. By directly assigning officers from the member-states to SHAPE, the headquarters could be accurately termed an international headquarters, and over time, as a result, SHAPE has developed an ethos and identity unique to itself. As to the type of officer that succeeds best in such a setting, one of the first cadre that set up SHAPE made this comment. "In resolving problems which have arisen, the SHAPE staff has found it necessary to make the approach a very flexible one, taking patterns and procedures which might not be applicable to the complex situation which it has faced. In consequence, our methods have undoubtedly seemed very fluid to many of our officers. Particularly, they have been a strain on those officers lacking inflexibility [sic] and habituated to a full set of regulations, standing procedures and doctrine, the appropriateness of which it was not their task to question."[19] Doubtless these traits were necessary for the SACEURs, as well. In particular, as was said for the role of George Washington in the founding of the new United States, NATO was indeed fortunate to have Eisenhower as the first SACEUR.

Professor Michael Howard put his finger on the main objective of the North Atlantic Treaty at the time of its signing, at least for the Europeans, when he observed that "the West Europeans still saw the problem as psychological, not military. What they required was reassurance rather than deterrence; not necessarily precise military commitments and evident, well publicized and well backed-up military plans, but simply the certainty that the United States had aligned themselves with Western Europe and regarded themselves as involved in Western European affairs."[20]

Eisenhower's personal prestige and magnetism, along with the obvious political influence that he could exercise to good advantage, and an image of the office, although unfillable by his successors, helped the Europeans to overcome the natural nationalistic resistance of the member-states to any outside influence or international innovations. And matters concerning defense—how to build it and how to pay for it—were vital areas of national politics, regardless of the size or strength of the military forces involved. As one observer stated flatly, "Without Eisenhower there would be no European defense."[21] This was a tribute to the man as much as, if not more than, to the country he came from.

No other SACEUR could command the instant recognition that came to Eisenhower, although of his successors perhaps Norstad came the closest, followed by Haig. But neither of these men was as visible in his own country as in Europe, nor could either arouse the kind of reaction described by John Gunther:

Eisenhower's popularity is phenomenal even in France, a country not strongly given to the admiration of exterior heroes. Early last year [1951] the General made one of his rare trips into Paris, to attend a dinner given to Miss Margaret Truman by President Auriol. After dinner at the Elysee the company went to a performance of Antigone at the Comedie Francais, the formal brittle shrine of French dramatic art. The blase audience paid only the minimum of polite attention to Miss Truman and the President of the Republic; then, a few seconds later, Eisenhower entered the presidential box. There had been no announcement that he would be there but he was instantly recognized, and the entire house rose spontaneously and cheered. No greater tribute could be paid in France to *any*body.[22]

Ridgway was fairly stiff in his personal relationships; as SACEUR he discontinued the informal discussion luncheons that Eisenhower had with his staff. Instead he would spend most of his spare time at home with his wife and young son.

Although the Eisenhowers were very private people, not inviting persons to their quarters very often and entertaining only as officially necessary, they conveyed an image of open friendliness that helped to mold the international military staff into a more unified group.[23] Gruenther appeared more open, approachable, and even a bit too extroverted for European tastes. But he had a gift for putting people at ease and was able to continue building the camaraderie that Eisenhower had begun and that he was fortunate to have reinforced through the personality of his civilian counterpart, Lord Ismay.[24]

Norstad, slim and good-looking in a Nordic way, with an equally attractive wife, appeared the embodiment of the dashing, even flamboyant, air force officer. He also had the advantage that while his career was on the rise in NATO, increasingly NATO was relying on tactical and strategic air operations, and so he symbolized the true source of NATO's defensive/offensive capability. Both General and Mrs. Norstad were assiduous in their entertaining responsibilities, even though at heart he was not naturally gregarious.[25] It is quite true that in diplomacy a reputation as a good host can enhance one's influence, which is one reason why Norstad could obtain easy access to high political figures. An example was provided by Spaak in his *Memoirs:*

> In August 1959 and September 1960 I met [Adenauer] in the villa which Stikker—at that time the permanent delegate of the Netherlands to the Atlantic Council—owned at Menaggio on Lake Como. It was a magnificent place in a splendid setting, and combined the beauties of the Italian landscape with traditional Dutch comfort. There was a splendid view of the mountains and the lake, a well shaded terrace and lovely garden. Cool drinks, the wise views of trusty friends—the master of the house, as well as Andre de Staerck, General Norstad and Ambassador Blankenhorn—all these were there for the asking.[26]

Access to governments, of course, was a *sine qua non* that Eisenhower had insisted upon and that has proven continually essential for any SACEUR. He has at times been characterized, because of his two-hat position, as beholden to the American

CONCLUSIONS

Joint Chiefs of Staff and at the same time to the North Atlantic Council and/or the Military Committee (later also the DPC) composed of the chiefs-of-staff. Ismay put it thus: "The Council have considerable responsibility toward the military authorities. In each country there is a government whose military advisers are the Chiefs-of-Staff, and these in turn direct the commands. On that analogy the Council are an international cabinet. Their military advisers are the Military Committee, which in turn gives directions to the Supreme Commanders."[27]

By and large, the SACEURs have been careful not to appear to exceed the limits of their office in this respect. At one time a member-state whose parliament was embroiled in an acrimonious debate over its defense budget asked Gruenther to testify before the appropriate parliamentary committee, but he wisely declined on the ground that he could not be made subject to the parliamentary desires of the member-states. He reasoned not only that his time would be literally eaten up if he were required to respond to every request to testify whenever a NATO parliamentary body so desired his presence, but also that he could not allow himself as SACEUR to be viewed as being accountable to any purely national political authority.

This does not mean, however, that the SACEUR has not at times addressed various legislatures, but in each case the circumstances were carefully defined so as to be construed as part of an official visit in response to a formal invitation from the host government. He has not infrequently been called upon by his national counterparts in the United States government to testify before congressional committees, but on these occasions he has made it clear he was doing so as CINCEUR and not as SACEUR. Obviously, the appearance of the SACEUR in this guise was intended to lend prestige and authority to the Defense Department's budgetary requests, but the distinction was important and was carefully maintained. Especially concerning the recurrent attempts in the Senate to force reduction of U.S. troops in Europe, the SACEURs have been called at times on very short notice to come to Washington to lobby or to testify against these attempts.

Often, the SACEUR has combined an official visit to a

member-state with an appearance before a private gathering in order to advance whatever policy appeared significant at the time. These appearances are often widely reported in the national press and sometimes have caught international attention. For these reasons, the ability of the SACEUR to be an effective public speaker has enhanced his capacity as SACEUR. His speeches have to combine substantive policy issues with more general rhetorical flourishes, usually affirming faith in the Atlantic idea (whatever it may be at the moment) and calling attention to the Soviet threat.

The personal security of the SACEURs as they have pursued a seemingly endless round of public appearances in the member-states has seldom been a major cause of anxiety. They have, as befitting their very high rank, the usual logistic and protocol protective elements that minimize personal danger. Only since the 1970s has vulnerability to terrorist attack become an additional security consideration. The famous episode of the bombing attempt on Haig, when his car was almost destroyed, focused public attention on this problem. As a consequence, the SACEUR is now more closely restricted in his personal appearances. Personal courage, perhaps, has become more significant as a result.

Out of the various observations derived from the historical record that comprise the contents of this book, can we discern some uniquely multinational aspects of military leadership? From the foregoing, it is clear that a multinational military leader must have strong political instincts. These traits can be refined through national career experience, but also there is no doubt that the immediacy of World War II enabled NATO to draw upon an exceptionally talented group of senior officers experienced in coalition warfare whose careers otherwise would probably have not been particularly noteworthy. Events had combined with talent to produce this generation of leaders.

Failing this combination, it appears to be important that future SACEURs should have extensive professional exposure to international political conditions, including serving on interna-

Conclusions

tional staffs and, if possible, commanding multinational military forces. They also should be proven planners because NATO remains a peacetime defensive Alliance with war fighting the result of the failure of the SACEUR, and the Alliance in general, to fulfill his/its primary mission of deterrence. In peacetime, planning for war must never cease, and good planners are not easy to find. The member-states, especially the United States, should make every effort to reward generously those officers willing to devote a significant portion of their careers outside the normal national military career channels in order to serve on international planning staffs or commands.

Multinational military leaders need to be exceptionally articulate, not only in motivating troops to their maximum effort, but more importantly perhaps, in conveying a concept of collective military preparedness to national publics. By the very nature of the political processes in most of the member-states, a public dialogue accompanies virtually every parliamentary action, and this dialogue is only partly accessible to the SACEURs and their colleagues. They must be careful not to appear to be interfering in the domestic politics of the member-states even while advocating positions that in their judgment require a high level of discussion in order to marshal public support for the collective requirements of the Alliance. This is a delicate tightrope to walk, and every SACEUR has come close to slipping off. Even though Ridgway faced the most determined domestic opposition, none of his peers has been immune from partisan domestic political attack.

Endless patience and tolerance for NATO's cumbersome decision-making processes and machinery must be the lot of the SACEURs. It is almost considered a truism in some quarters that by the time NATO makes a decision as to what to do about a crisis, the crisis will be largely resolved, most likely to NATO's disadvantage. How is it possible to make urgent military decisions through levels of political committees? Alternatively, exactly how much unilateral decision-making authority can be given to the SACEUR to respond to a crisis without risking his usurping the political responsibilities of the North Atlantic

Council and its subordinate bodies? Careful contingency arrangements have been negotiated and are in place, but every SACEUR must be sensitive to the possibility that he might be accused of acting outside his authority if he responds too precipitately to a crisis.

The capacity to win the confidence of national politicians without himself appearing too political is a desirable asset. Norstad bordered on being viewed as too political, and Ridgway came to be viewed as not political enough. How much is too much, and how much is not enough? A lot depends on the personality of the SACEUR, but also much depends on the overall international political climate in which he operates. In the early years, the SACEUR had much to offer the European Allies in a material sense; after Norstad the Europeans felt less dependent on the United States, and so this element of the SACEUR's authority began to diminish. Additionally, if the overall political climate is laden with East-West tensions or with a high level of domestic and political uncertainties, then the SACEUR might be better able to speak out forcefully on political subjects and to carry some influence. If the East-West climate is more accommodating and domestic political conditions are on the whole more stable, then the SACEUR will probably be less likely to be listened to. Unfortunately, national and international apathy is a real factor with which every SACEUR has had to contend.

Regardless of the circumstances surrounding his appointment, it is clear from the survey of the SACEURs contained in this book that each incumbent has had wide latitude in overcoming any initial liability and in setting his own mark on the office. Haig's appointment, for example, was viewed with skepticism bordering on cynicism, yet by the end of his tenure he was viewed as a dynamic, committed SACEUR retaining the confidence of the European Allies, even if not perhaps his compatriots in Washington. Furthermore, the SACEUR need not become a captive of his office even though by the time of the Kennedy administration the power enjoyed by the World War II generation of coalition generals was being pulled back.

Conclusions

Secretary of Defense McNamara and his "whiz kids" and those Pentagon civilian leaders who followed them did not share the ingrained deference of their predecessors to the military notables of World War II. This deference had worked not only to the benefit of Eisenhower, but also more or less to that of Ridgway, Gruenther, Norstad, and Lemnitzer.

Nonetheless, the SACEUR still stamps the office with his own personal characteristics, and he can have an effect on the overall political/military environment. In this respect, it is interesting to contrast Haig and Goodpaster. Although both generals came to prominence through working directly within the bureaucracy of the White House rather than within the normal military career ladder, Goodpaster developed a keen appreciation for staying within the system in his exercise of high military office, whereas Haig developed a flair for appearing to transcend the system. As a result, Goodpaster as SACEUR was remembered as a low-profile, "straight-arrow" but somewhat detached incumbent, while Haig was remembered as a high-profile, firmly engaged incumbent.

Although national states are still the central element of international politics and national interests are considered more enduring than friendships, the SACEUR can help to shape those persisting interests in the direction of multilateral collaboration. He need not sit helplessly by and watch unilateral national actions overwhelm him. One example, small but in its way significant, was the French refusal to have a French band perform at the flag-raising ceremony to celebrate the West German entry into NATO. As Gruenther described the situation in a letter to Eisenhower:

> We have a major flap trying to arrange a flag raising ceremony for the German entrance at SHAPE tomorrow. At first the Council rules "No ceremony at SHAPE," but Friday night they reversed that decision and we are following the pattern for the ceremony you put on for the Greeks and Turks on March 1, 1952. This involves playing the German national anthem as the flag is raised... and that is causing some Frenchmen great agony. The French finally decided late yesterday that they did not want a French band to perform, so now we shall use a

British band which happens to be in town. I was sorry to see the French act that way.[28]

Then Gruenther went on to explain why, in his view, the flap had occurred. "They are in a super-sensitive mood at present about Indo-China, about North Africa—about the Mid-East; in fact about everything."

Certainly one of the most significant examples—if not, *the* most significant—of how a SACEUR need not be a captive of unilateral national actions was the dignified yet determined way in which Lemnitzer handled the relocation of SHAPE from France to Belgium, and of EUCOM from France to West Germany. The vigorous attempts by all the SACEURs to resist troop withdrawals and to advocate effective conscription policies are but two other examples. When unilateral national actions of these sorts occur, whether large or small, the SACEURs must adapt or respond to these actions with grace even if they are duty bound to oppose them.

Finally, it is noteworthy that every occupant of the SACEUR's post, regardless of how frustrating or even disappointing his experience may have been, has come away a dedicated advocate of multilateral military leadership. The loyalty to NATO that all of them have exhibited subsequent to their tenures is remarkable. It is indicative not only of their suitability to have held the post of SACEUR, but also of their appreciation of the inherent worth of this high office.

NOTES

INTRODUCTION

This chapter, with slight editing, is reprinted from *International Organization* 9, no. 2 (May 1955): 257-60, by permission of the MIT Press, Cambridge, Massachusetts; © 1955, World Peace Foundation. It is General Goodpaster's personal, not official, recollection.

1. EISENHOWER

1. "The Future of NATO," *International Conciliation*, no. 565 (Nov. 1967), as cited in Robert W. Clawson and Lawrence S. Kaplan, eds., *The Warsaw Pact, Political Purpose and Military Means* (Wilimington, Del.: Scholarly Resources, 1982).
2. Six years later at an international conference for officers and officials (St. John's College, Oxford University, 15-27 July 1973) Professor Buchan did not reflect conclusively on these earlier views.
3. France in 1966 (and Greece, briefly, later) announced the withdrawal of French military forces from the Allied integrated military command structure of NATO, but did not withdraw from the North Atlantic Alliance nor renounce the Treaty (see chap. 5 of this book).
4. Greece, Turkey, the Federal Republic of Germany, and Spain.
5. Eisenhower, remarks at Command Post Exercise One (CPX 1), SHAPE, Rocquencourt, France, April 1952 (SHAPE Historical Section files).
6. Eisenhower, acceptance speech, 20 Jan. 1957 (SHAPE Historical Section files).
7. Eisenhower, remarks at SHAPE, 3 Sept. 1959. With keen foresight, Eisenhower, as SACEUR-designate, had established a historical program—unique, as it was the only official international program of its kind—even before the official activation of his command. His reasoning for this action was that "if we succeed, [the Alliance] can be a model for future cooperation; and even if we fail, we must know every reason why we failed" (Eisenhower, interview with Lt. Col. R. Lamson, U.S. Army, historian, SHAPE, Paris, March 1951, SHAPE Historical Section files).

8. DDE Diary series, 6 July 1960, Ann Whitman file, Eisenhower Library (EL).
9. DDE Diary, 28 Oct. 1950, EL; Eisenhower to Hazlett, 1 Nov. 1950, 1652 file, EL.
10. DDE Diary, 28 Oct. 1950, EL.
11. Dwight D. Eisenhower, *At Ease: Stories I Tell to Friends* (Garden City, N.Y.: Doubleday, 1967), 366.
12. Lauris Norstad interview, EL.
13. Eisenhower, memo of conversation with Salazar, 17 Jan. 1951; in Copenhagen, 12 Jan. 1951; Eisenhower to Selden Chapin, 13 Jan. 1951, and to Harriman, 14 Jan. 1951, all in 1652, EL.
14. Eisenhower, memo of conversation with Pleven, 24 Jan. 1951, 1652, EL.
15. Eisenhower, press conference notes, 20 Jan. 1951, 1652, EL.
16. Eisenhower to Lovett, 25 Sept. 1951, 1652, EL.
17. Eisenhower, notes, Executive Session, 2 Feb. 1951, 1652, EL; *New York Times*, 2 Feb. 1951; Robert E. Osgood, *NATO: The Entangling Alliance* (Chicago: Univ. of Chicago Press, 1962), 78-79; Walter S. Poole, *The History of the Joint Chiefs of Staff*, vol. 4 of *The Joint Chiefs of Staff and National Policy, 1950-1952* (Wilmington, Del: Michael Glazier, 1980), 222-23.
18. Sen. Robert A. Taft, *A Foreign Policy for Americans* (Garden City, N.Y.: Doubleday, 1951), 89 and *passim*.
19. Ibid., 100. The withdrawal of American troops was to remain a vain hope, even in 1955, when the focus of peril shifted back to the Far East.
20. Lt. Col. J.D. Hittle, *The Military Staff, Its History and Development* (Harrisburg, Pa.: Military Service Publishing Co., 1944), 147.
21. Lord Ismay, *NATO: The First Five Years, 1949-1954* (Paris: NATO Information Service, 1954), 38. For an account of the formation of NATO in the early years, see Robert S. Jordan, *Political Leadership in NATO: A Study in Multinational Diplomacy* (Boulder, Col.: Westview Press, 1979), and idem, *The NATO International Staff/Secretariat, 1952-57: A Study in International Administration* (London: Oxford Univ. Press, 1967).
22. Gen. of the Army Dwight D. Eisenhower, *First Annual Report of the Supreme Commander, Allied Powers Europe* (Paris: Public Information Division, SHAPE, April 1952), 14.
23. Gen. H.J. Kruls, "The Defense of Europe," *Foreign Affairs* 30, no. 4 (Jan. 1952): 265.
24. Ibid., 266.
25. Eisenhower, *Report* (1952), 13.
26. Gruenther, address to John Carroll Society, Washington, D.C., 7 March 1954. Quoted in the society's *Quarterly* 4, no. 2 (Summer 1954): 9.
27. *United States Department of State Bulletin* 26, no. 656, 21 Jan. 1952, 79.
28. Adm. Robert B. Carney, *First Annual Report of the Commander-in-Chief, Allied Forces, Southern Europe* (Naples, Italy, 3 July 1952), 1.
29. Ibid., 1-2.
30. Ismay, *First Five Years*, 73.

31. Eisenhower, *Report* (1952), 15-16. (Italics supplied.)
32. Carney, *Report* (1952), 3-4.
33. These additions brought total American strength to the equivalent of six divisions and British strength to four divisions.
34. Eisenhower, *Report* (1952), 17. Notes 18-34 reflect text drawn from the following: George Eugene Pelletier, "The Ridgway Regime at SHAPE: A Preliminary History" (Master's thesis, Georgetown University, March 1955), 47-59.
35. Eisenhower, notes on conversation with Belgian minister of defense, 10 Jan. 1951, Brussels, during Eisenhower's early survey tour of the NATO nations, prior to his assumption of command on 2 April 1951 (SHAPE Historical Section files).
36. The "national points of view" representation later was vested in the individual NMRs at SHAPE.
37. Gruenther, informal notes of conference, 8 Jan. 1951, Hotel Astoria, Paris. (NB: The Hotel Astoria, since demolished, was the initial temporary location of SHAPE on its establishment on 2 April 1951.) WUDO, the Western Union Defense Organization, was the short-lived military headquarters that had been established in Western Europe as a result of the Brussels Treaty of 1948. It had been headed by Field Marshal Montgomery as chairman of its Chiefs-of-Staff Committee. Montgomery later became the first deputy SACEUR upon the establishment of ACE and SHAPE (SHAPE Historical Section files).
38. Lemnitzer, closing remarks, SHAPEX 69, May 1969 (SHAPE Historical Section files).
39. SHAPE chief-of-staff to USNMR re: "Review of U.S. Staffing of NATO," 10 April 1974 (SHAPE Historical Section files).
40. NATO/SHAPE Civilian Personnel Regulations, Article 13.1.
41. Earlier, SACEURs had briefed NATO European Parliamentarians in the Western Union Assembly in Paris. On 21 December 1985 the Associated Press reported that Gen. B.W. Rogers had agreed to brief a group of Dutch lawmakers on Allied decision-making procedures for nuclear weapons use, according to one of the parliamentarians. The briefing, scheduled for January 1986, was to occur after Rogers had declined to appear at a Dutch parliamentary hearing earlier in December on the proposed U.S.–Dutch treaty governing the 1988 deployment of cruise-type missiles in the Netherlands.
42. Associated Press report, Washington, 26 Nov. 1974 (SHAPE PIO press cuttings). In Gen. Alexander Haig's case, as early as November 1974, when he already had been designated to become SACEUR but had assumed command only of U.S. forces in Europe (on 1 November 1974), the Senate Armed Services Committee rejected a motion to summon him for questioning in connection with earlier, Watergate-related events in the administration. The committee rejected the move on the grounds that such a review would be on a subject that had already been explored thoroughly in Congress and the courts and decided, instead, to call Haig for testimony after Congress reconvened in January 1975, when other matters might more properly be discussed.
43. Eisenhower, *At Ease*, 373.

44. Eisenhower to Lodge, 4 April 1952; to Woodruff, 27 Aug. 1951, and to McConnell, 29 June 1951; memo of briefing for Senate Foreign Relations Committee, 9 July 1951, all in 1652, EL.
45. Eisenhower to Lovett, 25 Sept. 1951, 1652, EL.
46. Eisenhower to Bermingham, 28 Feb. 1951, 1652, EL.
47. Andrew Goodpaster interview, EL.
48. DDE Diary, 10 Oct. 1951, EL.
49. Eisenhower to Bradley, 30 March 1951, 1652, EL.
50. Eisenhower address text, 6 June 1951, 1652, EL.
51. DDE Diary, 17 March 1951, EL.
52. Eisenhower to Paley, 29 March 1952, EL.
53. Quoted in Poole, *History of the JCS*, 99: 195.
54. Eisenhower to Marshall, 3 Aug. 1951, 1652, EL.
55. Ibid.
56. Eisenhower to Harriman, 30 June 1951, 1652, EL; DDE Diary, 11 June 1951, EL.
57. Eisenhower to Pleven, 24 Dec. 1951, 1652, EL.
58. Eisenhower to Gruenther, 23 March 1951 and 26 Sept. 1951; Eisenhower to Clark, 8 Oct. 1951, all in 1652, EL.
59. Eisenhower to Truman, 23 Jan. 1952, 1652, EL.
60. Osgood, *Entangling Alliance*, pp. 87-88; Eisenhower to George Whitney, 26 March 1952, 1652, EL.
61. Eisenhower to Lovett, Truman, and Ely, 2 April 1952, 1652, EL.
62. Eisenhower, *Report* (1952).
63. Montgomery to Gruenther, 12 March 1952, 1652, EL.

2. RIDGWAY

The bulk of this chapter, with some minor revisions, is taken from George Eugene Pelletier, "The Ridgway Regime at SHAPE: A Preliminary History," master's thesis, Georgetown University, March 1955, especially chapter 2.

1. Eisenhower, *Report* (1952), 26.
2. Ibid., 22ff.
3. Ibid., 26.
4. Document G009, NATO-620-SHAPE, files of chief of military history, Department of the Army, Washington.
5. Ibid.
6. Eisenhower, *Report* (1952), 37.
7. Ridgway, speech delivered at command turnover ceremony, 30 May 1952 (Paris: Public Information Division, SHAPE), 1.
8. Ibid.
9. Ibid., 2.
10. Ismay, *First Five Years*, 191. (Italics supplied.)
11. Ibid.
12. The public so little knew the meaning of NATO at that time that when John A. Hughes, U.S. permanent representative to NATO, told a woman on

shipboard that he was on his way to Europe as United States ambassador to NATO, she inquired, "And, tell me, Mr. Ambassador, what kind of climate do they have in NATO?" The story was told to friends, including an acquaintance of the writer, by the ambassador himself.
13. John Giles, *Washington Star*, 4 May 1952.
14. White House press release, 28 April 1952.
15. *United States Department of State Bulletin* 26, 5 May 1952, 743.
16. Andre Visson, *Washington Post*, 4 May 1952.
17. *Cleveland Plain Dealer*, 30 April 1952.
18. *Atlanta Constitution*, 30 April 1952. This editorial reflected concern in many quarters that hostilities were likely in Europe. Cf. comment by Col. Bruce Bidwell, United States Army (Personal interview, Feb. 1955).
19. Drew Middleton, *The Defense of Western Europe* (New York: Appleton-Century-Crofts, 1952), *passim*.
20. *Atlantic Alliance: NATO's Role in the Free World*, report by a study group of the Royal Institute of International Affairs (London: Chatham House, 1952), 58.
21. Ridgway, command turnover speech, 7, 21. (Italics supplied.)
22. *Milwaukee Journal*, 29 April 1952. The truce negotiations in Korea, begun under Ridgway, were still in progress and were to result in an armistice in July 1953.
23. *Minneapolis Tribune*, 1 May 1952.
24. Ismay, *First Five Years*, 58. (Italics supplied.)
25. Recounted in Jordan, *Political Leadership*, 44.
26. Jordan, *Political Leadership*, 44ff.
27. Ismay, *First Five Years*, 186.
28. Eisenhower to Lt. Gen. Paul Ely, chairman of the Standing Group, 2 April 1952. In this letter Eisenhower stated, "I have this date requested the United States government to *initiate* action looking to my relief as Supreme Commander" (Paris: SHAPE press release, 11 April 1952). (Italics supplied.)
29. James Michener, "Tough Man for a Tough Job," *Life*, 12 May 1952, 103.
30. Giles, *Washington Star*, 4 May 1952.
31. Ibid. This view certainly implies that there had been some discussion of this point; hence consultation with at least some of the other NATO nations.
32. It was essential that the chief-of-staff be an American because the supreme commander had to be kept aware of atomic developments, and such information, by United States law, could not pass into or through the hands of other nationals.
33. *Minneapolis Tribune*, 1 May 1952.
34. As recounted later, one of Ridgway's first acts after reaching France to become SACEUR was to take part in the celebration of the Normandy landings and to assure the French that "we seek by every honorable means to avoid the ultimate horror, war, which proves nothing, which settles nothing" (SHAPE press release, 6 June 1952).
35. Mr. Harper [pseud], "The General's Grenade," *Harper's Magazine* 203, no. 1216, (Sept. 1951): 101. General MacArthur's corncob pipe and

General Eisenhower's hip-short battle jacket were mentioned as other trademarks of noted military personalities.

36. *Reporter Magazine,* 25 Dec. 1951. While this story antedates Ridgway's arrival, it reflects French sentiment, which persisted after he got there.

37. Literally, "Ridgway, to the door!" (i.e., "Get out!").

38. Ridgway, address to joint session, U.S. Congress, 22 May 1952 (Washington: Department of Defense press release, 134-52S).

39. On the very day of his arrival, the European Defense Community Treaty was signed at Paris between France, Italy, West Germany, Belgium, the Netherlands, and Luxembourg.

40. Duclos was indicted for plotting against the security of the state. It was the first decisive action against a major Communist leader in France since the end of the war.

41. Theodore H. White, *Fire in the Ashes* (New York: Wm. Sloan Associates, 1953), 347-48.

42. International News Service dispatch, 13 May 1952.

43. Personal interview with Col. Bruce Bidwell, Feb. 1955.

44. Members of the counterintelligence unit told the writer of these incidents at the time.

45. *Kansas City Star,* 1 May 1952.

46. Personal interview with Lloyd Lehrbas, special assistant to Ridgway as SACEUR, Washington, Jan. 1955.

47. *New York Herald-Tribune,* 17 May 1952. Gruenther often said of those early days that "it took a genuine act of faith to call one of those divisions a division."

48. Michener, "Tough Man," 112.

49. *Time,* 20 Oct. 1952, 35.

50. Eisenhower to Marshal Juin (unclassified), Paris, SHAPE files. The implication is plain in this letter that the original Central Command organization was not intended to be permanent and that Juin would ultimately be made commander-in-chief.

51. Ismay, *First Five Years,* 74. It should be noted that U.S. forces in Europe, while organizationally under the Central Command, are operationally under the commander-in-chief, U.S. Forces Europe (CINCEUR).

52. Ibid. Besides, the Greek and Turkish governments declined to put their forces under an Italian commander (Benjamin Welles, *New York Times,* 16 July 1952).

53. The handshaking incident was related to the author by Brig. Gen. Anthony J.D. Biddle, U.S. Army, who accompanied Ridgway on this trip.

54. *NATO—Its Development and Significance,* United States Department of State Publication No. 4630, General Foreign Policy Series, (Washington, Aug. 1952), 20.

55. North Atlantic Council communiqué, Paris, 17 Dec. 1952.

56. Ismay, *First Five Years,* 73. Meanwhile, the United States Sixth Fleet had been redesignated, for NATO purposes, as Naval Striking and Support Forces Southern Europe and had elements of French and Italian naval strength attached to it for NATO training purposes.

57. The author was present at this conference. The expressions of mutual confidence did not cover up emotions deeply felt.

58. During one of the conferences, a high-placed British officer reportedly said, "In the event of war, there are only two directions in which the Sixth Fleet can go—out of the Mediterranean, or down!" Reported to the author by William Frye, former director of information, Department of Defense.

59. Welles, *New York Times*, 7 June 1952.

60. Ridgway, speech at Ste. Mere Eglise, France, 6 June 1952 (Paris: SHAPE press release (mimeographed).

61. Welles, *New York Times*, 7 June 1952.

62. Personal interview with General Biddle shortly after the visit. Pleven visited SHAPE several times during the Ridgway regime.

63. *U.S. News and World Report*, 29 Jan. 1954. Also previous issues, 1950 through 1953, for other interviews.

64. Montgomery, address to International Press Institute, London, May 1953, NATO Speech Series, No. 38, (Paris: NATO, May 1953); also address before Royal United Service Organization, London, 24 Oct. 1954, reprinted in U.S. Air Force "Information Services Letter," supplement 67 (Washington: Department of the Air Force, 1 Jan. 1955).

65. These incidents were related by staff officers at SHAPE or observed personally by the author.

66. Personal observation by the author, at that time special assistant to the secretary of the navy. Assistant Secretary Smith's comments were made in U.S. Navy press release. (Washington: Office of Information, Navy Department, 7 Dec. 1954).

67. Montgomery, International Press Institute address, 99.

68. *Army Information Digest*, Sept. 1954.

69. Ridgway, Ste. Mere Eglise speech, 13.

70. Ibid., 23.

71. Omar N. Bradley and Clay Blair, *A General's Life* (New York: Simon and Schuster, 1983), 659-60.

3. GRUENTHER

1. Col. Robert J. Wood, "The First Year at SHAPE," *International Organization* 6, no. 2 (May 1952): 181. Wood also recalled, "In December 1950, at one of my first meetings with General Eisenhower, he wrote out in pencil on a piece of Pentagon 'buck slip' paper a little note which he said I should use as guidance. This memorandum read: 'I shall reluctantly accept command responsibility if 1) German agreement secured, 2) All countries make fixed commitments, 3) Maximum authority and opportunity to SHAPE' [.] To which he added by way of explanation of the last point, 'No limitation as to area except in most general way—same as to functions'" (177.)

2. Pelletier, in chap. 2 above, says that the European members of NATO would have preferred Gruenther over Ridgway because they knew Gruen-

ther better (reported by John Giles, *Washington Star,* 4 May 1952). Gen. Omar Bradley, the chairman of the JCS at the time, commented: "The question of who would replace Ike at SHAPE was not easy to answer. Ike and Monty wanted Al Gruenther, Ike's chief of staff, to move up. But the British Chiefs of Staff were opposed to Gruenther because he had always been a staff officer and had never held a major command. The JCS felt the same way. Accordingly, the decision was made to name Ridgway to the post" (Bradley and Blair, *General's Life,* 655).

3. Eisenhower to Gruenther, 19 June 1952, Gruenther Papers, EL.
4. Ibid.
5. Gruenther to Eisenhower, 14 May 1953, Gruenther Papers, EL.
6. Robert Coughlan, "The Thinking machine Who Bosses NATO," *Life Magazine,* 1 June 1953, 88.
7. Ibid.
8. *U.S. News and World Report,* 4 April 1952, 52.
9. Ibid., and Coughlan, "Thinking Machine," 86, 88.
10. Collins to Gruenther, 4 Jan. 1955, Gruenther Papers, EL.
11. For background see James L. Richardson, *Germany and the Atlantic Alliance* (Cambridge, Mass.: Harvard Univ. Press, 1966), esp. chap. 1. As early as autumn 1949, the U.S. Army general staff had drafted a plan for the creation of German divisions that was endorsed by the JCS in April 1950 but was not adopted as official policy because the State Department claimed that European objections would be too strong (ibid., 18).
12. Ibid.
13. Quoted in Stephen E. Ambrose, *Eisenhower,* 1 (New York: Simon and Schuster, 1983): 506.
14. Eisenhower to Gruenther, 27 Oct. 1954, Gruenther Papers, EL.
15. Ibid.
16. Testimony given 26 March 1955, U.S. Senate, Committee on Foreign Relations (Washington: GPO, 1955), 6.
17. For a full discussion of this situation, see Francis A. Beer, *Integration and Disintegration in NATO* (Columbus: Ohio State Univ. Press, 1969), chap. 2, from which some of these paragraphs are drawn.
18. "Gen. Gruenther's Support for Atomic Weapons," *London Times,* 9 June 1954, 6.
19. Beer, *Integration and Disintegration,* 98.
20. For background on the relationship of the SACEUR with the secretary-general, see Jordan, *Political Leadership,* esp. chap. 1. For a thorough discussion of the origins and implications of the "New Look," see E. Raymond Platig, "The 'New Look' Raises Old Problems," *Review of Politics,* Jan. 1955, 111-35.
21. Gruenther to Eisenhower, 20 Dec. 1953, Gruenther Papers, EL.
22. Ibid.
23. Alfred Gruenther, "The Defense of Europe: A Progress Report" (reprint of an address before the National Security Industrial Association, New York City, 29 Sept. 1954, as printed in *Department of State Bulletin,* 18 Oct. 1954, 562-64).

24. Ibid., 563.
25. Ibid., 564.
26. Alfred Gruenther, "The Defense of Europe" (Reprint of an address at the Alfred E. Smith Memorial Foundation Dinner, New York City, 8 Oct. 1953, reprinted in the *Department of State Bulletin*, 9 Nov. 1953, 633-34).
27. Ibid., 634.
28. Ibid.
29. For more information on NATO's infrastructure program during this period, see Beer, *Integration and Disintegration*, esp. chap. 5, and Jordan, *International Staff/Secretariat*, esp. chap. 12.
30. Gruenther, Memorial Foundation Dinner speech. In this speech he commented: "One official with a cynical turn of mind, when asked 13 years ago, 'what do the Soviets need to march to the English Channel?' answered 'Only shoes!' " (p. 633). Gruenther himself has been cited as giving variations on this anecdote—i.e., Adm. Angus Nicholl stated in the *Listener* of 14 April 1954, "When NATO was first formed the allied defences were so weak that, as General Gruenther put it, all the Russians needed for a walk to the Atlantic coast of Europe was boots."
31. Gruenther to Eisenhower, 25 April 1954, Gruenther Papers, EL.
32. Eisenhower to Gruenther, 8 June 1954, Gruenther Papers, EL.
33. Ibid.
34. Quoted in Jordan, *International Staff/Secretariat*, 64.
35. Rear-Adm. Angus Nicholl, "Gaps in the Nato Defense Line," *Listener*, 14 April 1954.
36. The three paragraphs that follow are drawn from Jordan, *International Staff/Secretariat*, 64-78. Also *Manchester Guardian*, 9 Oct. 1952.
37. *Times* (London), 20 Feb. 1953.
38. See Marianna P. Sullivan, *France's Vietnam Policy: A Study in French-American Relations* (Westport, Conn.: Greenwood Press, 1978).
39. Quoted in Ismay, *First Five Years*, 68.
40. Bradley and Blair, *General's Life*, 646.
41. North Atlantic Council communiqué, 26 Sept. 1950 (Paris: NATO Information Service), 1.
42. Gruenther to Taylor, 3 July 1955, Gruenther Papers, EL.
43. Ibid.
44. Taylor to Gruenther, 4 July 1955, Gruenther Papers, EL.
45. Stevens to Gruenther, 16 March 1955, Gruenther Papers, EL.
46. Gruenther to Eisenhower, 2 Aug. 1953, Gruenther Papers, EL.
47. Eisenhower to Gruenther, 5 Aug. 1953, Gruenther Papers, EL.
48. Ibid.
49. Gruenther to Eisenhower, 9 Aug. 1953, Gruenther Papers, EL.
50. Gruenther to Eisenhower, 29 Nov. 1955, Gruenther Papers, EL.
51. Ibid.
52. Eisenhower to Gruenther, 2 Dec. 1955, Gruenther Papers, EL.
53. Gruenther to Valluy, 9 April 1956, Gruenther Papers, EL.

4. NORSTAD

Portions of this chapter were drawn from Robert S. Jordan, "The Supreme Commander in the Early Years: Some Thoughts on the Norstad Experience," a paper presented at a conference on "Leadership in NATO," 14-15 Oct. 1982, Dwight D. Eisenhower Library.

1. An adaptation of a speech delivered in November 1983 marking the fiftieth anniversary of the establishment of diplomatic relations between the United States and the Soviet Union (1 November 1933), as contained in an article in *Harper's*, April 1984, 9-11, at p. 9.
2. See Ambrose, *Eisenhower*, 521.
3. For a full discussion of the events leading up to, and the decisions taken at, the Lisbon conference, see Jordan, *International Staff/Secretariat*, esp. 26ff.
4. Quoted from *Washington Post*, 15 April 1956, in ibid., 177.
5. Portions of the following paragraphs are drawn from Jordan, *Political Leadership*, 47-49.
6. *Manchester Guardian*, 30 Jan. 1957.
7. Ibid., 11 Feb. 1957.
8. *Times* (London), 15 Feb. 1957.
9. Paul-Henri Spaak, *The Continuing Battle: Memoirs of a European* (Boston: Little, Brown and Co., 1971), 262. Spaak was not reticent in appraising the SACEURs. "By the time I had arrived in Paris, Lauris Norstad had succeeded Generals Eisenhower, Ridgway and Gruenther—the first and last of whom carried out their tasks with great distinction—as NATO's Supreme Commander. Norstad, as it turned out, was one of the best" (pp. 262-63).
10. Quoted in Jordan, *Political Leadership*, 63. A recent general formulation of Alliance aims and purposes was made at the meeting of NATO foreign ministers at the thirty-fifth anniversary of the Alliance, held in Washington, D.C., in June 1984 (see *New York Times*, 1 June 1984).
11. Spaak, *Continuing Battle*, 263.
12. Ibid.
13. Ibid., 351. Spaak was indeed out of harmony with the political attitudes of the Alliance at the time of his resignation in February 1961, although he was correct in his assessment of the continuing impact that events outside the NATO area would have on Alliance cohesion. Asia and the Middle East–Gulf are areas that subsequent to his tenure have given rise to tensions within NATO; during his period of office, it was Africa, and in particular the Congo, which is why he made a special point of this in his farewell letter to President Kennedy. "For my part, firmly convinced as I am that the battle against Communism will in the immediate future be fought in the economic rather than in the military sphere and that it will take place in Africa rather then [sic] Europe, I believe that NATO is doomed to fail in its efforts if it is denied the right to deal with these issues in a comprehensive way" (351).
14. See Jordan, *Political Leadership*, 126-27, for a discussion of the contrasting personal styles of Spaak and Stikker.
15. Ibid. Stikker found favor with the military staff, who saw in him a secretary-general who genuinely understood their needs, but also resented

what they saw as the secretary-general's intrusion into their domain. This probably represented both a bureaucratic protective reaction and a multinational manifestation of the familiar civil-military tension within governments (ibid., 139-40).

16. Ibid., 83. André de Staercke, the Belgian permanent representative to NATO and the doyen of the NATO diplomatic corps, played an important role in NATO diplomacy during this period. For example, he served to smooth over tensions between Spaak and Norstad, and during Stikker's tenure he helped to keep lines of communication open between the secretary-general and the NATO Council (see Spaak, *Continuing Battle*, 263, and Jordan, *Political Leadership*, 127).

17. Spaak, *Continuing Battle*, 341. Strauss and Norstad did not always agree on Alliance policy, although their personal relationship was friendly.

18. Doris Fleeson, "Norstad, Man of Many Talents," *Washington Evening Star*, 25 March 1959. That there are perceived limits—or liabilities—to this multifaceted role can be seen, for example, from the comment to Norstad made by his friend and colleague Gen. Nathan Twining, former chairman of the Joint Chiefs of Staff: "You have done a temendous job as the Supreme Allied Commander, and everyone knows it and, of course, would like to have you stay there forever. My worry is, Laurie, that the politicos—and this is with all due respect—sometimes get a little irked with us military folks, because they feel that maybe we are getting too strong a position as military people, which many of them resent. I know you appreciate that and fully understand why I have had some worries about your case because you have been very strong on numerous occasions" (Twining to Norstad, 9 Jan. 1961, EL). The following nine paragraphs are drawn in part from Francis A. Beer, *Integration and Disintegration in NATO* (Columbus: Ohio State Univ. Press, 1969), chap. 3.

19. Eisenhower to Sen. Henry M. Jackson, 17 May 1966, Senate Committee on Government Operations, *Hearings, The Atlantic Alliance*, 224-25.

20. Norstad's testimony, U.S. Congress, Joint Committee on Atomic Energy, Subcommittee on Agreements for Cooperation, *Amending the Atomic Energy Act of 1954, Hearings*, 85th Cong. 2d sess., 1958, 519.

21. Elizabeth Stabler, "The MLF: Background and Analysis of Pros and Cons," *Congressional Record, U.S. House of Representatives*, 5 Jan. 1965, 81.

22. Associated Press, 18 Dec. 1959. Norstad, address to the NATO Parliamentarians' Conference, *Addresses by Speakers*, 1960, 36 (NATO Information Service).

23. Senate Committee on Government Operations, *Hearings, The Atlantic Alliance*, 82-84. Norstad also commented emphatically: "The critical and immediate problem was not with some new longer-range strategic force of yet undetermined purpose and pattern, not with the deployment of weapons which do not bear directly on the NATO task, not with an MLF, for instance.... Rather the problem was 'how do we answer the European questions as to the availability and the control of weapons already deployed and, in a way, engaged'" (ibid., 70, 86).

24. Ibid., 82, 84. There were variations on the notion, as Norstad maneu-

vered among various national sensitivities to find a broadly acceptable formula.

25. Paul-Henri Spaak, address to the Imperial Defense College, 21 Oct. 1960 (mimeographed) (NATO Information Service).
26. North Atlantic Council, final communiqué, press release M2 (57) 2, 16-19 Dec. 1957 (NATO Information Service).
27. See Hanson Baldwin, *New York Times*, 25 July 1962.
28. Senate Committee on Government Operations, *Hearings, The Atlantic Alliance*, 206. The smaller member-states were not anxious to see the U.S. share its veto, either.
29. This entire question is discussed fully in Richardson, *Atlantic Alliance*, esp. chap. 3.
30. Quoted in ibid., 50-51.
31. Ambrose, *Eisenhower*, 508.
32. Richardson, *Atlantic Alliance*.
33. "Defending Europe without France," interview with Gen. Lauris Norstad, reprinted from *Der Spiegel*, 18 April 1966, in *Atlantic Community Quarterly* 4, no. 2 (Summer 1966): 183.
34. Quoted in Ernst H. Van Der Beuguel, *From Marshall Aid to Atlantic Partnership: European Integration as a Concern of American Foreign Policy* (New York: Elsevier Publishing Co., 1966), 405. The author spelled Norstad's name "Norstadt," which doubtless would not have pleased the general.
35. A complete discussion of types of alliances can be found in Julian Freedman et al., *Alliance in International Politics* (Boston: Allyn and Bacon, 1970). See esp. K.J. Holsti, "Diplomatic Coalitions and Military Alliances," 93-103.
36. Norstad, comment at a conference on "Leadership in NATO: Past and Present," Dwight D. Eisenhower Presidential Library, 15 Oct. 1982. For a good discussion of the French view, see Gen. Pierre Gallois, *The Balance of Terror: Strategy for the Missile Age* (Boston: Houghton-Mifflin, 1961).
37. Holsti, "Coalitions and Alliances," 103. (Author's emphasis.)
38. Norstad says that de Gaulle passed to him privately a copy of the memorandum of 17 September 1958, although it was addressed only to President Eisenhower and to Prime Minister Harold Macmillan (ibid.). Secretary-General Spaak in his memoirs also claims to have had in his possession a copy, passed to him in his capacity as secretary-general, but that this copy subsequently disappeared mysteriously from his files (Spaak, *Continuing Battle*, 312).
39. Norstad, Eisenhower Library conference.
40. For a complete discussion of this situation, see Jordan, *Political Leadership*, 86ff.
41. We should recall that in order to facilitate NATO's adoption of the strategy of tactical nuclear response, the United States had revised the restrictive Atomic Energy Act of 1946 (the McMahon Act), enabling atomic weapons to be supplied to NATO Allies provided the warheads remained under American control.
42. Quoted in Norstad, Eisenhower Library conference.

43. Taken from Richardson, *Atlantic Alliance*, 73-74. See also Lauris Norstad, "NATO: Strength and Spirit," *NATO Letter*, Jan. 1960, 7-11.
44. Norstad felt compelled to pursue a policy of forward strategy because not to do so would have sacrificed West Germany almost in advance of hostilities. But some of his policies that hinted at forms of disengagement met strong West German opposition.
45. See David N. Schwartz, *NATO's Nuclear Dilemmas* (Washington, D.C.: Brookings Institution, 1983), 82ff; Robert E. Osgood, *The Case for the MLF: A Critical Evaluation* (Washington, D.C.: Washington Center for Foreign Policy Research, 1964). Lemnitzer was particularly scornful of plans of the mixed-manned crews for the Polaris submarines. He claimed "he could not see it for dust," primarily because the close quarters of a submarine required a closely knit, integrated crew. (see interview of LTC Bickston with Lemnitzer at the Pentagon on 4 May 1972, Oral History Collection, Army War College, Carlisle Barracks, 38). Norstad had publicly opposed both MLF and the British ANF proposals as he said, "We should not for almost a thousand reasons think of creating a new strategic force, becaue you just cause more trouble than it is worth" (quoted in Beer, *Integration and Disintegration*, 111).
46. For an extended study of the Skybolt crisis, see Richard Neustadt, *Presidential Power: The Politics of Leadership* (New York: Wiley, 1960). The British had resisted Norstad's idea of a NATO nuclear force, preferring to retain for as long as possible the Anglo-American special relationship in nuclear affairs.
47. Lemnitzer, remarks at change-of-command ceremonies, 2 Jan. 1963, Lemnitzer Papers, National War College (NWC).
48. Frans A.M. Alting von Geusau, *Allies in a Turbulent World: Challenges to U.S. and Western European Cooperation* (Lexington, Mass: Lexington Books, 1982), 163.
49. Philip Ziegler, *Mountbatten* (New York: Alfred A. Knopf, 1985), 600-601. Ziegler went on to report that Norstad reciprocated the admiration and at one stage maintained that Mountbatten ought to succeed him as SACEUR. He would have been the first non-American to fill the post, but Norstad believed that he would have been acceptable in Washington if only the Europeans, in particular the French, had been more receptive to the idea (600).
50. Charles de Gaulle, transcript of luncheon address, 20 Dec. 1962, NATO Public Information Division.

5. LEMNITZER

1. *New York Times*, 25 July 1962; *Public Papers of the President, John F. Kennedy, 1962* (Washington, D.C.: GPO, 1963), 574.
2. *New York Times*, 26 July 1962.
3. Ibid.
4. *Times* (London), 21 July 1962; *Le Monde*, 22-23 July 1962.

5. Arthur M. Schlesinger, Jr., *A Thousand Days: John F. Kennedy in the White House* (Boston: Houghton Mifflin Co., 1965), 200; Jack Raymond, *Power at the Pentagan* (New York: Harper and Row, 1964), 287; Douglas Kinnard, *The Secretary of Defense* (Lexington: Univ. Press of Kentucky, 1980), 79.

6. *New York Times*, 5 June 1961; Lemnitzer testimony, *Hearings*, Executive Sessions of the Senate Foreign Relations Committee (Historical Series), 13, part 1, 87th Cong., 1st sess. (Washington, D.C.: GPO, 1984), 571ff.

7. *New York Times*, 27 May 1961.

8. Quoted in Henry C. Trewitt, *McNamara* (New York: Harper and Row, 1971), 22-23.

9. Ibid., 83-84.

10. See Lemnitzer, remarks at a dinner of the National Security Industrial Association, 27 Sept. 1962, Box no. 80, John F. Kennedy Library, Boston, Mass.

11. *New York Times*, 3 March 1961.

12. *Times* (London), 23 July 1962; *New York Times*, 26 July 1962.

13. SACEUR briefing notes, Box 63, Lemnitzer Papers, National War College (NWC).

14. Lemnitzer interview with Tom Margerison, *Sunday Times* (London), 6 Oct. 1963.

15. See Edward L. Rowny, "The Decision-Making Process in NATO" (Ph.D. diss., American University, 1976), 178-90, cited in Schwartz, *Nuclear Dilemmas*, 140-41.

16. Ibid., 32-33.

17. Margerison interview, 6 Oct. 1963.

18. Schwartz, *Nuclear Dilemmas*, 184.

19. Paul Edward Buteux, "The Politics of Nuclear Consultation in NATO, 1965-1974: The Experience of the Nuclear Planning Group" (Ph.D. diss., UCLA, 1972), 78, cited in ibid.

20. *New York Times*, 17 March 1965.

21. Ibid.

22. Statements by General de Gaulle taken from Jean-Raymond Tournoux, *La Tragedie du General* (Paris: Librairie Plon-Paris-Match), 306. See also Robert Kleiman, *Atlantic Crisis: American Diplomacy Confronts a Resurgent Europe* (New York: W.W. Norton and Co., 1964).

23. Tournoux, *La Tragedie*, 167.

24. Ibid., 267.

25. Michael M. Harrison, *The Reluctant Ally: France and Atlantic Security* (Baltimore: Johns Hopkins Univ. Press, 1981), 135. See also Simon Serfaty, *France, de Gaulle, and Europe* (Baltimore: Johns Hopkins Univ. Press, 1968), esp. chap. 6.

26. Harrison, *Reluctant Ally*.

27. Ibid.

28. Lemnitzer to Adm. Harry W. Hill, 22 June 1965, Box 42, 1-228-71, Lemnitzer Papers, NWC; Lemnitzer to Wilber M. Brucker, 3 Aug. 1965, Box 41, ibid.

29. Lemnitzer to Gen. Lauris Norstad, 12 May 1965, Lemnitzer Papers, NWC.
30. *New York Times*, 28 July 1965.
31. *Scrantonian*, 4 Aug. 1963.
32. De Gaulle to Lemnitzer, 7 Feb. 1967, Box 48, L-355-71, Lemnitzer Papers, NWC.
33. Lemnitzer, to Lydia and Bill (Lemnitzer), 20 March 1967, Box 66, Family, Ibid.
34. See *NATO Letter* 14 (May 1966): 22-23.
35. Harlan Cleveland, *NATO: The Transatlantic Bargain* (New York: Harper & Row, 1970), 102; George Ball, *The Past Has Another Pattern: Memoirs* (New York: W.W. Norton & Co., 1982), 333-34; Charles E. Bohlen, *Witness to History* (New York: W.W. Norton, 1973), 506. Bohlen, then U.S. ambassador to France, admitted to being "fooled by de Gaulle," after being told in January that France would do nothing precipitate.
36. *New York Times*, 10 March 1966.
37. 29 March memorandum, *NATO Letter* 14 (May 1966): 24. Harrison, *Reluctant Ally*, 144-45.
38. *New York Times*, 13 March 1966.
39. *New York Times*, 18 March 1966; Cleveland, *Transatlantic Bargain*, 106-7.
40. *New York Times*, 15 March 1966.
41. Harrison, *Reluctant Ally*, 146; Don Cook, *Charles de Gaulle: A Biography* (New York: G.P. Putnam's Sons, 1983), 383.
42. Ball, *Another Pattern*, 334.
43. Cleveland, *Transatlantic Bargain*, 106; John M. Leddy, oral interview, 12 March 1969, Oral History Collection, Lyndon B. Johnson Library, Austin; Gen. Andrew J. Goodpaster interview, 21 June 1971, Oral History Collection, ibid.
44. *New York Times*, 19 March 1966.
45. Cleveland, *Transatlantic Bargain*, 105-6.
46. Bohlen, *Witness*, 507-8. See also Jordan, *Political Leadership*, esp. chap. 4.
47. *New York Times*, 31 July 1966; Elliot R. Goodman, "de Gaulle's NATO Policy in Perspective," *Orbis* 10 (Fall 1966): 716-17.
48. *Aviation Week and Space Technology*, 29 May 1967, 315.
49. Harrison, *Reluctant Ally*, 155-56.
50. Ibid., 157.
51. Lemnitzer to Margaret and Ernest (Lemnitzer), 19 March 1966, Box 66, Family, Lemnitzer Papers, NWC. As Lemnitzer pondered his problems, he noted in a letter to his brother and sister-in-law that the miserable weather at the onset of spring 1966 worsened a "stubborn cold" that had hung on over late winter.
52. Ibid., 1 July 1966.
53. Lemnitzer to Maj. H.E. Simpson, Jr., 26 Sept. 1966, ibid. Lemnitzer later commented that the problems stemming from the physical separation of SHAPE from EUCOM, i.e. from Mons to Stuttgart, impelled him to extend his service as SACEUR for two years after the withdrawal. In France a twenty-

minute drive separated the two headquarters (Col. Richard A. Hatch interview with General Lemnitzer, 13 Nov. 1972, p. 3, Oral History Collection, Army War College, Carlisle Barracks, Pa).

54. These recommendations were largely the product of Working Group "D" on Relocation (see undated memorandum for the secretary of defense, subject: evaluations of relocation alternatives; also Lemnitzer to Secretary-General Brosio, 3 May, 1966, Box 164, L-1502-7H, Lemnitzer Papers, NWC.

55. Air Marshall MacBrien's memo to Lord Coleridge, 26 July 1966, "Broad outline of the SHAPE requirement when relocated in Belgium," ibid.

56. De Kerchove to Lemnitzer, 12 Aug. 1966, Box L-1502, Lemnitzer Papers, NWC.

57. Lemnitzer to Norstad, 8 July 1966, Box 44, L-316-7,; ibid. *New York Times*, 22 Aug. 1966; *Pourquoi Pas* comment listed in continental press summary, 11 Aug. 1966, Box 163, L-1495-71, Lemnitzer Papers, NWC.

58. Lemnitzer to Brig. Gen. Orwin C. Talbott, 28 Aug. 1967, Box 45, L-327-71, ibid.

59. Ibid.

60. Lemnitzer to General Ridgway, 20 March 1966, Box 50, L-373-71, ibid.

61. News release no. 67-22, SHAPE, Belgium, 20 Nov. 1967. Lemnitzer, remarks at the Thirteenth Annual Session of the North Atlantic Assembly, Brussels, Box 109, L-1000-71, Lemnitzer Papers, NW; *New York Times*, 21 Nov. 1967. These were reproduced under the title "Collective Defense—the Basis of Military Security," *NATO Letter*, (Jan. 1968): 6.

62. Lemnitzer to Brig. Randolph T. Pendelton, 17 May 1968, Box 50, L-372-71, Lemnitzer Papers, NWC.

63. "The Crisis in NATO," *Hearings* before the Subcommittee on Europe of the Committee on Foreign Affairs, H.R., 89th Cong., 2d sess., 1966, 37.

64. News release, OSD (Public Affairs), statement by secretary of defense on relocation of U.S. Forces from Europe, 3 April 1967.

65. *New York Times*, 3 May 1967.

66. "The North Atlantic Alliance," *Hearings* before the Subcommittee on National Security and International Operations of the Committee on Government Operations, U.S. Senate, 89th Cong., 2d sess., part 6, 21 June 1966, 187. McNamara's statement.

67. Quoted by Cyrus L. Sulzberger, *New York Times*, 8 June 1966.

68. See McNamara statement, "North Atlantic Alliance," 187.

69. *New York Times*, 31 July 1967.

70. *House Report no. 85*, 10381.

71. "The Atlantic Alliance: Unfinished Business," A study submitted by Subcommittee on National Security and International Operations to the Committee on Government Operations, U.S. Senate, 90th Cong., 1st sess., 1 March 1967, 2, 5, 7.

72. *NATO Letter* (16 January 1968): 4.

73. Lemnitzer, speech, 14th General Assembly of Atlantic Treaty Association, in *Atlantic Community Quarterly* 6 (Winter 1968-69): 501.

6. GOODPASTER

1. See, for example, the oral history transcript of Ambassador Robert Murphy at the Eisenhower Library and, for an example of a compatible view presented by one who was then much younger and less experienced in government, the oral history of Timothy Stanley, also at the Eisenhower Library. Stanley, who was then working for Paul Nitze in the Office of International Security Affairs at the Defense Department, describes Goodpaster as a "remarkable model of objectivity," quite "the calmest man under pressure" he had ever seen, and "one of the most remarkable men...of our time."

2. Goodpaster interview, Washington, 3 Dec. 1985. Hereafter cited as Goodpaster interview.

3. Ibid.

4. This was a theme he hammered away at consistently throughout his tenure, beginning as early as his first address to the North Atlantic Assembly only a few weeks after assuming his post (See Box 22, Goodpaster Papers, National Defense University Library, Washington: Remarks, North Atlantic Assembly, 18 Oct. 1969. Hereafter cited as GP 22, and the like.

5. Richard Nixon, *RN: The Memoirs of Richard Nixon* (New York: Grosset & Dunlap, 1978), 343.

6. GP 9: Lemnitzer, address to Association of the United States Army Memorial Dinner, Washington, 14 Oct. 1970. For Henry Kissinger's comments see his *White House Years* (Boston: Little, Brown, 1979), 394.

7. *NATO's Fifteen Nations* (Oct.-Nov. 1969): 15.

8. GP 30; Goodpaster, remarks at USAREUR and Seventh Army Commanders' Conference, Heidelberg, 11 Dec. 1969.

9. *NATO's Fifteen Nations* (Feb.-March 1970): 81.

10. Maj. E. Hinterhoff, "NATO and Spain," *NATO's Fifteen Nations* (April-May 1970): 67.

11. *Washington Post*, 17 Aug. 1970, as quoted in Kissinger, *White House Years*, 537.

12. Kissinger, *White House Years*, 81.

13. GP 27: Goodpaster, remarks at CLOUD COVER '72 Conference, SHAPE, 29 Nov. 1972.

14. GP 24: Goodpaster, remarks at Royal United Services Institute, 16 Dec. 1970.

15. Goodpaster interview.

16. Ibid.

17. Ibid.

18. GP 31: Goodpaster, remarks at National War College/Industrial College of the Armed Forces, Washington, 27 Oct. 1969.

19. Gen. Andrew J. Goodpaster, "On the Service of Peace," *NATO's Fifteen Nations* (April-May 1971): 20-21.

20. Goodpaster interview.

21. See GP 24: Goodpaster, remarks at Royal United Services Institute, for a comprehensive description of the focus and outcome of AD-70.

22. Ibid.
23. GP 25: Goodpaster, remarks to Council on Foreign Relations, New York, 22 April 1971.
24. GP 27: Goodpaster, remarks at CLOUD COVER '72 Conference.
25. GP 26: Goodpaster, remarks at SHAPE Alumni Banquet, Fort Myer, Va., 16 Nov. 1972.
26. Ibid.
27. GP 2: Goodpaster to Gen. Pierre M. Gallois, 9 May 1967.
28. GP 24: Goodpaster, remarks at Royal United Services Institute. The early date of these remarks, in a sweeping tour de horizon presented by Goodpaster in a fifty-four page speech to RUSI members, illustrates that détente, and dealing with it so as to maintain the viability of the Alliance, was a concern that occupied him virtually throughout his tenure as SACEUR.
29. Ibid.
30. GP 30: Goodpaster, address to American Institute of Aeronautics and Astronautics, Orlando, Fla., 25 Feb. 1974.
31. GP 24: Goodpaster, remarks at Royal United Services Institute.
32. See, for example, Jordan, *Political Leadership*, chap. 4.
33. Goodpaster described the impact of these events on the outlook in Western Europe at the SHAPE Alumni Banquet. See GP 26.
34. GP 30: Goodpaster, remarks at USAREUR and Seventh Army Commander's Conference.
35. Goodpaster interview.
36. Kissinger, *White House Years*, 941.
37. See, for just one of the many formulations of this fundamental conviction on Goodpaster's part, GP 25: Goodpaster, remarks at Distinguished Visitors' Dinner, Exercise REFORGER 3, Garmisch, Germany, 10 Oct. 1971.
38. Goodpaster interview.
39. Dr. Stanley L. Harrison, "Congress and Presidential Conflict: Foreign Policy and NATO," *NATO's Fifteen Nations* (June-July 1972): 84.
40. GP 27: Goodpaster, keynote address at Georgetown University Center for Strategic and International Studies, Washington, 28 June 1973.
41. GP 28: Goodpaster, remarks to Council on Foreign Relations, New York, 14 Nov. 1973.
42. Ibid.
43. GP 30: Goodpaster, address to American Institute of Aeronautics and Astronautics.
44. Goodpaster interview.
45. GP 28: Goodpaster, remarks to Council on Foreign Relations.
46. GP 19: Goodpaster to Gen. C.H. Bonesteel III, 18 March 1974.
47. See note 1 re: the Stanley oral history.
48. Confronted with that suggestion, Goodpaster observed that "he'd better be standing on some pretty solid military ground. He would be a flop otherwise." Goodpaster interview.
49. Richard M. Nixon, *U.S. Foreign Policy for the 1970's: A New Strategy for Peace* (Washington: White House, 18 Feb. 1970), 33.
50. Goodpaster interview.
51. Ibid.

52. As quoted in Stanley R. Sloan, *NATO's Future: Toward a New Transatlantic Bargain* (Washington, D.C.: National Defense Univ. Press, 1985).
53. Kissinger, *White House Years*, 218.
54. Robert E. Osgood, *Alliances and American Foreign Policy* (Baltimore: Johns Hopkins Press, 1968), 3.
55. Goodpaster interview.
56. Ibid.
57. GP 28: Goodpaster, statement to Randall Subcommittee of the House Armed Services Committee, Brussels, 4 March 1974.
58. GP 28: Goodpaster, remarks to Council on Foreign Relations.
59. Ibid.
60. Ibid.
61. Goodpaster interview.
62. See, for example, GP 9: Goodpaster to Lemnitzer, 7 Dec. 1970.
63. This point, too, Goodpaster stressed at every opportunity. See, for example, one of his frequent addresses at the various war and command and staff colleges, GP 31: Goodpaster, remarks at National War College/Industrial College of the Armed Forces.
64. GP 24: Goodpaster, remarks at Royal United Services Institute.
65. For a recent assessment of the improvements brought about during the period, by one who was a principal decisionmaker at the time, see Melvin R. Laird, "A Strong Start in a Difficult Decade: Defense Policy in the Nixon-Ford Years," *International Security* (Fall 1985): 5-26, 15-21.

7. HAIG

1. Inclement weather conditions and the time of the year forced the observances indoors for the first time. However, the change actually permitted the attendance not only of the highest political and military authorities of the NATO nations, or their representatives, but also of a large number of members of the press and public.
2. Research does not reveal a rationale for the choice of medley, which consisted of themes from "Smoke Gets in Your Eyes," "Why Do I Love You," "Who," "All The Things You Are," and "Amour, Amour, Amour," followed by "The Stars and Stripes Forever."
3. As a Lieutenant Colonel in 1950, General Goodpaster had served as a member of the original SHAPE Advance Planning Group, which arrived in Paris in December 1950. (See the introduction above.)
4. Goodpaster specifically referred to the misunderstanding which he hoped had been removed "regarding the reasons for my absence at General Haig's [change-of-command] ceremony at Stuttgart [Headquarters, U.S. European Command], six weeks earlier, and the fact that [my] absence was occasioned by personal considerations on my own part."
5. Gerd Schmuckle, *Ohne Pauken und Trompen: Erinnerungen au Krieg a Frieden* (Stuttgart: Deutsch Verlags-Antalt, 1982). I am grateful to the SHAPE Linguistic Section for an unofficial translation.
6. In agreeing to the release of Goodpaster, the committee had par-

ticularly noted that he had "fully discharged the trust reposed in him" since his designation on 12 March 1969. (NB: Goodpaster had officially assumed command of ACE on 1 July 1969, by SHAPE General Order Number 11, 1969.)

7. Haig was the second youngest officer ever to be approinted to the post of SACEUR. Gen. Lauris Norstad, the fourth SACEUR at forty-nine years, eight months—only four months Haig's junior at the time of his own appointment—had been the youngest. The proximity of age at assumption of command and the events that characterized the tenures of both would lend themselves, subsequently, to frequent comparison. To one senior assistant of the new SACEUR, the temper, rhythm, and even the types of crises affecting both periods of command (e.g., Suez, Hungary, Cuba vs. Cyprus, Greece, Poland, etc.) would later appear to have been "cloned."

8. Haig's previous senior appointments at governmental level had begun with his assignment as senior military advisor to the assistant to the president for National Security Affairs in January 1969. In June 1970 he became deputy assistant to the president for National Security Affairs. During his four years as a deputy to Dr. Henry Kissinger, later the U.S. secretary of state, Haig made fourteen assessment trips to Southeast Asia as the personal emissary of the president. His last four diplomatic trips contributed to the successful negotiation of the cease-fire agreement between North and South Vietnam and the return of U.S. prisoners of war. In addition, Haig was selected by the president to coordinate the advance preparations and substantive details of the president's historic trip to the People's Republic of China.

9. Interview with Col. R. Sinnreich, U.S.A., former assistant to SACEUR for Analysis, Research, and Coordination (ARC), and later director, School for Advanced Studies, U.S. Command and General Staff School, Ft. Leavenworth, Kan., 18 April 1986.

10. See, for example, "Détente with the Soviet Union: The Reality of Competition and the Imperative of Cooperation," in Lester A. Sobel, ed., *Kissinger and Détente* (New York: "Facts on File," 1975).

11. In the sometimes lighter vein with which Haig introduced such matters—often colored by slightly self-deprecating humor—he would later recall an earlier experience in Washington as Henry Kissinger's aide. "I rushed into his office one day," said Haig, "and reminded him that he was due at the Washington Press Club to give a speech on détente. He was very upset because he felt that I had not managed his time properly and had not given him sufficient preparation time. So he went into one of those classic Kissinger tantrums. In an effort to restore peace, I said, 'Henry, I reckon you can go over there and tell these gentlemen all you know on the subject of détente in 15 minutes.' His eyes narrowed. He looked at me and said, 'I can go over there and tell those gentlemen all we both know, and it will not take a second longer'" (Haig, address to the Assembly of the Western European Union [WEU] 23rd Ordinary Session, part 2, Paris, 29 Nov. 1977).

12. Sobel, *Kissinger and Détente*, 9, 10. In the 1970s, commented one analyst of the events of that period, "the most powerful unifying force in NATO was the constraining influence imposed by the absence of alternatives. This

unwilling interdependence led NATO into a reevaluation of détente in the mid-1970s. Although originally the inspiration of European critics who deplored the unthinking bellicosity of American behavior toward the Soviet Union and its putative insensitivity to changes within the Eastern bloc in the late 1960s and 1970s, it had become in the first Nixon administration part of Kissinger's apparatus for constructing complicated linkages with the Soviets. Detente as a relaxation of tension derived from the delicate balance of terror" ("NATO: The Second Generation... Limits of Detente," in Lawrence S. Kaplan and Robert W. Clawson, eds., *NATO after Thirty Years* (Wilmington, Del.: Scholarly Resources, 1981).

13. Haig, remarks at the 21st Ordinary Session, part 1, third sitting, of the WEU, 27 May 1975.

14. Haig, 1975 WEU address.

15. "Congress and Foreign Policy, 1974," Committee on International Relations, U.S. House of Representatives, 94th Cong. 1st sess., report by Library of Congress, 18 March 1975.

16. For example, in October 1969 Ambassador Robert Ellsworth, U.S. permanent representative to NATO, informed the NATO secretary-general that he was issuing the U.S. reply to the Defense Planning Questionnaire (DPQ) for 1969, already delayed pending a presidential review and assessment of the impact upon NATO commitments of a $3 billion U.S. defense budget cut. President Nixon instructed Ambassador Ellsworth to stress that the changes (reductions) which the U.S. proposed to make in its forces did not affect the chief executive's commitment to maintain substantial forces in Europe.

17. See Robert W. Komer, "NATO's Long Term Defense Programme: The Origins and Objectives," *NATO Review*, no. 3, June 1978, pp. 9-12.

18. See also, below, *Declaration on Atlantic Relations (Extracts)*. The Declaration was signed by NATO heads of government (President Nixon for the United States), in Brussels on 26 June 1974, in which the United States stated its resolve to "maintain forces in Europe at the level required to sustain the credibility of the strategy of deterrence and to maintain the capacity to defend—with its Allies—the North Atlantic area should deterrence fail" (press release, 26 June 1974, NATO Information Service).

19. Haig, remarks at the Annual Meeting of the Association of the United States Army, Sheraton Park Hotel, Washington, D.C., 12 Oct. 1976.

20. See Komer, "NATO's Long Term Defense Programme."

21. The EUROGROUP officials were in the United States to inform American and Canadian defense policy experts on European contributions to the common defense of NATO. The delegation was headed by Henry Wijnaedents of the Netherlands. (The EUROGROUP had been born in 1968, soon after the Soviet invasion of Czechoslovakia.) (Report by William H. Durham, USICA staff correspondent, in USICA Wireless File, U.S. Embassy, Brussels, 17 Oct. 1978).

22. Gen. Gerd Schmuckle, interview with the author, SHAPE, 17 March 1980.

23. On Hill-Norton's view of Haig's appointment, Schmuckle recalled

that "rivalry developed between them. Formally speaking, Hill-Norton was the 'senior-most' officer of the Alliance. Although lacking power his nature spurred him into action. [But] the real power was vested in Haig" (Schmuckle, *Ohne Pauken*).

24. Another DSACEUR's view of senior appointments in NATO was contained in an article by Gen. Gunter Kiessling who served in that capacity from 1982 to 1984 (see "The German Representation in NATO," by General Kiessling, which appeared in "Europaische Wehrkinde," in Nov. 1982). In his rationale for "equivalent" German representation, Kiessling proposed that the SACEUR's chief-of-staff also should be a German officer.

25. Ibid.

26. See Gen. A.M. Haig, Jr., "NATO—An Agenda for the Future," *NATO Review* 27, no. 3 NATO Information Service, Brussels, June 1979.

27. Haig, 1975 WEU address.

28. Haig, "Agenda for Future."

29. Arthur L. Gavshon, AP diplomatic correspondent, Brussels, 4 Dec. 1978, as cited in SHAPE Public Information Division report, "SACEUR Interview."

30. Haig would jest, for example, that when he considered his earlier political background and the change that had occurred in Washington in January 1977, he was "glad to be anywhere in an official capacity." When he tore cartilages in his knee while playing tennis, he recounted, the Joint Chiefs of Staff had debated that issue for a considerable period—after which he received a get-well-quick card that had been approved by a vote of 3-2. More pointedly, Haig observed with tongue in cheek that he had left Washington quite confused because when he had had political responsibilities, pundits in the press insisted that he was far "too military to bear those responsibilities," but that no sooner had he been assigned to Europe than the same fellows insisted that he was "too political to bear his military responsibilities." (Haig, remarks to the International Relations Council, Kansas City, Mo., 16 Aug. 1977.)

CONCLUSIONS

1. Quoted in William R. Swarm, "Impact of the Proconsular Experience on Civil Affairs Organization and Doctrine," in Robert Wolfe, ed., *Americans and Proconsuls: United States Military Government in Germany and Japan, 1944-1952* (Carbondale: Southern Illinois Univ. Press, 1984), 400.

2. As far as the location of SHAPE was concerned, France rather than Germany was viewed as a necessary cornerstone. As Gruenther's chief-of-staff, Gen. Cortlandt van R. Schuyler, put it: "When, in 1951, General Eisenhower was appointed NATO's first Supreme Commander Europe, almost any one of the member nations would have been happy to play host to his new command. But with the Soviet's main threat pointed at the West German border, a headquarters site somewhere in Central Europe was obviously a necessity. Since NATO's weak covering forces, if attacked, would have had to

withdraw quickly to the line of the Rhine River, any command post location for SACEUR in West Germany or Holland had to be ruled out at once. Belgium and Luxembourg likewise appeared too exposed. Portugal, isolated, was too far to the rear. Realistically then, France alone met the geographical requirement." (letter printed in *Atlantic Community Quarterly* (Winter 1966): 531). (General Schuyler was commenting in his letter, dated 15 Nov. 1965, on the prospect of de Gaulle's inviting NATO and in particular SHAPE to leave France.)

3. Quoted in Olav Riste, ed., *Western Security: The Formative Years* (New York: Columbia Univ. Press, 1985), 153.

4. Richardson, *Atlantic Alliance*, 22.

5. Ibid., 70.

6. John Ehrman, *Grand Strategy* (London: HMSO, 1956), 6: 322.

7. Dwight D. Eisenhower, *Crusade in Europe* (Garden City, N.Y.: Doubleday, 1948), 487.

8. Riste, *Western Security*, introduction, 13. For a recounting of how long the Combined Chiefs-of-Staff arrangement should continue after the war, see Elisabeth Barker, *The British Between the Superpowers, 1946-55* (Toronto: Univ. of Toronto Press, 1983).

9. For a comparative assessment of the secretaries-general, see Jordan, *Political Leadership*, esp. conclusions.

10. See Bradley and Blair, *General's Life*, 655-57. As Bradley commented: "With Ike's tacit approval, the Old Guard and Ike's running mate Richard M. Nixon, conducted a reprehensible smear campaign, one of the worst I'd seen. Ike himself, holding to a loftier level, used our foreign and military policy as political footballs, hypocritically calling into question policies that he himself had helped formulate or approved or had carried out. ... Politics was further widening our close personal relationship" (Ibid.).

11. James W. Riddleberger, "Impact of the Proconsular Experience on American Foreign Policy," in Wolfe, *Proconsuls*, 396.

12. For a discussion of Brosio's views toward détente and its relation to deterrence, see Jordan, *Political Leadership*, 214ff.

13. Gerald R. Ford, *A Time to Heal* (New York: Harper and Row, 1979), 285.

14. Gruenther to Lt. Gen. Sir Nevil Brownjohn, 15 April 1954, Gruenther Papers, EL.

15. Gruenther to Montgomery, 7 June 1955, Gruenther Papers, EL.

16. Gruenther to Eisenhower, 12 June 1955, Gruenther Papers, EL. Montgomery had said to Gruenther: "I had seen the clipping from Table Talk in the Observer. It is a definite 'foul' for reports to be made of private interviews at SHAPE and I have written to David Astor and told him what I think of his action in no uncertain voice.... As regards the NATO Defense College. Darvall asked me to open up on the German problem. I asked if the same rules applied as at the National War College or I.D.C.—and he said they did, and nothing went outside.... But what makes me really sorry is the thought that I may have caused you some embarrassment. My great object in life is so to speak and act that no embarrassment is caused you. I shall most

certainly not air any views on that matter again." (Montgomery to Gruenther, 9 June 1955, Gruenther Papers, EL).

17. Gruenther to Eisenhower, 3 April 1954, Gruenther Papers, EL. Eisenhower replied, "Of course I applaud your decision to have no part of Juin's quarrel and your insistence that this is a matter for the French Government alone to handle" Eisenhower to Gruenther, 5 April 1954, Gruenther Papers, EL.

18. Ibid.

19. Col. Robert J. Wood, "The First Year at SHAPE," *International Organization* 6, no. 2 (May 1952): 183.

20. Riste, *Western Security*, introduction, 16.

21. For an elaboration, see Wood, "First Year," 185-86.

22. John Gunther, *Procession* (London: Hamish Hamilton, 1965), 309. (Gunther's emphasis.)

23. Ibid. See also Pelletier, "Ridgway Regime," esp. 33-35.

24. For a profile of Ismay, see Jordan, *International Staff/Secretariat*, esp. chap. 4.

25. Norstad was fortunate in having as his secretaries-general persons who were not particularly interested in the social aspects of diplomacy. Spaak was limited in this respect because of his misassessment of the proper role of his office in relation to the Council, Stikker because at least in part he suffered from ill-health which kept him away from Brussels and for some time at Walter Reed Hospital in Washington, D.C.

26. Spaak, *The Continuing Battle*, 335. Belgian Permanent Representative André de Staercke was considered a very valuable asset in NATO diplomacy. Gruenther, for example, commented in a letter to Eisenhower dated 17 May 1955: "He is of great help to me. Whenever I am in trouble with the Belgian Government...I go to de Staercke and he carries the ball—usually with great success" (Gruenther Papers, EL). For a more generalized commentary of de Staercke's usefulness as doyen of the NATO permanent representatives, see Jordan, *Political Leadership*. De Staercke's own comments—almost a valedictory—on NATO are contained in André de Staercke, *NATO's Anxious Birth: The Prophetic Vision of the 1940s* (New York: St. Martin's Press, 1985).

27. Ismay, *First Five Years*, 61. General Rogers, speaking in March 1987 of his announced relief as SACEUR, to take effect in mid-1987, made the point that the U.S. president's intention to replace him as CINCEUR necessitated also his release as SACEUR. Although technically perhaps correct, this gives the impression that the SACEUR's national U.S. command assignment takes priority over his NATO multinational command assignment. I doubt this has been the case in practice for any of the SACEURs.

28. Gruenther to Eisenhower, 8 May 1956, Gruenther Correspondence, EL.

THE CONTRIBUTORS

Stephen E. Ambrose is Alumni Distinguished Professor of History, University of New Orleans, and author of *Eisenhower: Soldier, General of the Army, President-Elect, 1890-1952.*

Morris Honick is Command Historian and Chief of the Historical Section of SHAPE. His thirty-two years of NATO-international service extend through the tenures of five of the seven SACEURs described in these pages.

Robert S. Jordan has been Distinguished Visiting Professor, Naval War College, as well as Professor of Political Science, University of New Orleans. He is author of several books, including *Political Leadership in NATO: A Study in Multinational Diplomacy.*

Lawrence S. Kaplan is University Professor of History Emeritus and former Director of the Lyman L. Lemnitzer Center for NATO Studies, Kent State University. His books include *The United States and NATO: The Formative Years.*

Kathleen A. Kellner is a doctoral student in American diplomatic History at Kent State University, where she is writing a biography of Gen. Lyman L. Lemnitzer.

George Eugene Pelletier was a journalist whose career included serving on active duty in the U.S. Navy in the Office of Public Information, Department of Defense.

Lewis Sorley is a public policy consultant and a former officer in the U.S. Army. He is author of *Arms Transfers under Nixon: A Policy Analysis.*

INDEX

Abrams, Gen. Creigton, 123, 149
Adenauer, Chancellor Konrad, 26, 79, 100
AD-70, 130-33
Ailleret, Gen., 112, 113
Alexander, Lord: and Mediterranean Command, 47-48
Allied Command Europe (ACE), xiv, xvii, 22, 117, 136, 153, 168; and Mobile Force, 101-02; and deterrence, xiv, xx-xxi; and naval command, 157-58; purpose of, xiv, 9
Anglo-American Combined Chiefs-of-Staff, 66-68, 179-80, 192, 194. *See also* Ismay, Lord; World War II
Auriol, French President Vincent, 32, 48, 189

Ball, Undersecretary of State George, 109
Beaufré, Gen. André, 144
Belgium, 21; and NATO headquarters, 115-16; and SHAPE, 115-17
Berlin crisis, 120
Biddle, Brig. Gen. Anthony, 3
Bidwell, Col. Bruce, 42
Bohlen, Ambassador Charles F., 109

Bonesteel, Maj. Gen. Charles T., 97
Bradley, Gen. Omar, 25; and Eisenhower, 101; relationship to SHAPE, 67; and Ridgway, 38, 51
Brandt, West German Foreign Minister Willy, 112
Brind, Adm. Sir Patrick: as Commander Allied Forces Northern Europe, 18, 44
Britain. *See* United Kingdom
Brosio, Secretary-General Manlio, 130, 182
Brownjohn, Lt. Gen. Sir Neville, 185
Brussels Treaty Organization (BTO). *See* Western Union Defense Organization
Buchan, Alastair, 8

Canada, 127-29
Carney, Adm. Robert, 71; as Commander-in-Chief Allied Forces Southern Europe, 45; and Mediterranean, 3, 19-20; and Mediterranean Command, 47-48
Carter, President Jimmy, 166
Churchill, Winston, 10; and Deputy SACEUR, 169; and Lord Ismay, 179; and Mediterranean Command, 47-48

INDEX

Clark, Gen. Mark, 55
Cleveland, Ambassador Harlan, 106, 109, 110, 182
Cold War, 10, 18, 107, 177, 183
Collins, Gen. J. Lawton, 51; and Gruenther, 56
Commander-in-Chief, U.S. European Command (U.S. CINCEUR), xvii
Congress, U.S.: and defense expenditures, 125; and Eisenhower speech, 13; and Jackson-Nunn Amendment, 139; and Mansfield Amendment, 138-39; and troop force levels in Europe, 159-60
Conventional Defense Improvement Initiative (CDI), NATO, xxii, 133, 165
conventional forces, NATO, xx-xxi, 60-62
Cook, Don, 43
Council of Ministers, NATO. *See* North Atlantic Council
Council on Foreign Relations, 140
Couve de Murville, Foreign Minister Maurice, 112
Cyprus, 141-42

De Castiglioni, Gen. Maurizio L.: as Commander Allied Land Forces Southern Europe, 19
de Gaulle, French President Charles, 79; and Directorate proposal, 87-88, 103; and Lemnitzer, 90, 105-06; and Norstad, 92; and nuclear sharing, 88-91; and U.S., 102-03
de Kerchove, Count Charles, 115
de Salazar, Prime Minister Antonio, 13
détente, 137-40, 156-57
deterrence, NATO, xiv, xix, xxi, 145
Draper, William H., 37
Duclos, Jacques, 40
Dulles, Secretary of State John Foster, 90

Eden, Anthony, 186
Eisenhower, Dwight D.: appointed SACEUR, xiv; assessment of, as SACEUR, 175-76; and European unification, 27, 30; and Gruenther, 51, 52-56, 69-70; and Indochina, 64-65; and Marshal Juin, 45; and military leadership, 175; nomination by Republican party, 11, 27-28; organizes SHAPE, 2-7, 8-30, 73-74, 122-23; personality of, 35, 189-90; and Pleven Plan, 26-27, 32, 64-65; as president, 9-10, 58-59, 69; rallies West, 12-14, 23, 31, 189; resignation, 29-30; and Ridgway, 51; and Standing Group, 17, 20, 29; and supercarriers, 28; as symbol for NATO, 10-12, 180, 189; and U.S. troop withdrawals, 58; and West German rearmament, 11, 14, 25, 57-58
Ely, Gen. Paul, 29
Embry, Air Chief Marshall Sir Basil: as Commander Allied Air Forces Central Europe, 45
European Defense Community (EDC), 26-27, 30, 32, 35, 41, 44, 60-62, 74-75, 91, 176. *See also* Gruenther, Gen. Alfred M.

Fechteler, Adm. William M., 20; and Mediterranean Command, 47-48
Finletter, Ambassador Thomas, 182
Fitzalan-Howard, Maj. Gen. Michael, 102
flexible response, NATO strategy of, 20-21, 83-84, 99-100, 130-31, 133-43
Ford, President Gerald, 152, 159, 183
Forrestal, Secretary of Defense James, 93
France: and ACE Mobile Force, 102; and Algeria, 75; and Directorate proposal, 87-88; and

223

EDC, 26-27, 30, 62-64; and *force de frappe*, 83; and Indochina, 26, 64; and MLF, 102; and NATO forces, 26, 103-04, 160; and Norstad Plan(s), 79-85; and Pleven Plan, 26-27, 32; and West German military relationship, 112-13; and West German rearmament, 13, 25-26, 32; withdrawal from NATO military structure, 103-21, 143, 146-47
Fulbright, Senator William, 125

Germany, Federal Republic of: and Contractual Agreement, 40; and conventional war, 101; and Deputy SACEUR, 168-71; and Eisenhower, 11-14; and forward strategy, 61-62, 74-75, 83, 176; and French military relationship, 113-14; and MLF, 177; and NATO membership, 32; and nuclear weapons, 82-85, 100; and Offset Agreement, 159-60; and rearmament, 11-12, 14, 25-27, 35, 58-59, 83-85, 176; and relocation of U.S. EUCOM, 107, 113-14; and reunification, 183
Giles, John, 38
Girosi, Vice Adm. Massimo: and Allied Forces Southern Europe, 20
Goodpaster, Gen. Andrew J.: and AD-70, 131-33, 143; appointment as SACEUR, 122-25; assessment of, as SACEUR, 175-96; attitude toward France, 146-47; and creation of SHAPE, 1-7, 122, 128; and détente, 137-40, 149; and Eisenhower, 25, 122-23, 128, 145; and "hit list," 132; and Mansfield Amendment, 137-39; and MBFR, 136-37; and MC14/3, 130-31; and Middle East War (1973), 140-41; and NATO commonality and standardization, 147-48; and NATO readiness, 124-26; personality of, 122-23, 142, 184, 195; and President Johnson, 109; retirement, 149, 151-53; views on strategy, 144-47
Gortz, Lt. Gen. Ebbe: as Commander Allied Land Forces Norway, 18
Grantham, Adm. Sir Guy: and Mediterranean Command, 47-48
Greece, 3, 28, 33, 43, 125, 141-42, 154, 173, 188; and Allied Forces Southern Europe, 45-46
Gruenther, Gen. Alfred M.: appointment as SACEUR, 51, 53-54; assessment of, as SACEUR, 175-96; and Eisenhower, 51, 52-56, 70-71; and forward strategy, 61-62; and France, 64; and Ismay, 74; and Juin, 186-87; and MC-48, 60; and Montgomery, 186; and NATO Advanced Planning Group, 1-3; and NATO readiness, 5, 7, 19, 65-66; and NSC-68, 57-58; and nuclear weapons, 58-60, 83; personality of, 35, 56, 60, 190; retirement of, 68-72; and Ridgway, 37-39, 51, 53-54; and SHAPE chief-of-staff, 13, 15, 21, 34, 36-39, 54-56; and U.S. command role, 67-69; and West German rearmament/EDC, 57-64, 186-87

Haig, Gen. Alexander M.: appointment of SACEUR, 151-53; assessment of, as SACEUR, 175-96; and conventional forces, 165; and détente, 153, 156-57; and geostrategic outlook, 161-66, 172-74; and Long-Term Defense Program (LTDF), 166-67, 171; and nuclear forces, 165; personality of, 153, 184, 189, 195; and rapid reinforcement, 169-70; retirement of, 174; and second Deputy SACEUR, 168-71; speech

INDEX   225

to WEU, 155-59; and three "R's," 159, 166, 171; and White House, 153
Handy, Gen. Thomas T., 50, 143
Hansteen, Lt. Gen. Wilhelm: as Commander Allied Land Forces Norway, 18
Healey, Defense Minister Denis, 101
Helsinki Accords, 183
Herter, Secretary of State Christian: and Herter Plan, 89-90
Hill-Norton, Adm. Peter, 168
Hittle, Lt. Col. J.D., 16
Howard, Michael, 188

Ismay, Lord, secretary-general of NATO: and Gruenther, 60-61; and NATO consultation, 66; and Norstad, 74, 76-77; and organization of SHAPE, 16, 20, 191; as secretary-general, 74, 76-77, 190; and selection of Ridgway, 36-37; World War II career, 179-80

Jaujard, Vice Adm. Robert, 18, 44-45; as Commander Allied Forces Central Europe, 45
Johnson, President Lyndon B., 182: and de Gaulle, 106, 109; and MLF, 100
Joint Chiefs of Staff (JCS), U.S., 38, 54, 89, 93, 96, 191; and Bradley, 38; and Lemnitzer, 93-96; and Maxwell Taylor, 96-97; and Earle Wheeler, 128
Juin, Marshal Alphonse: and Central Command, 4, 18, 44-45; and EDC, 44; and Gruenther, 186-87; and Ridgway, 33, 44

Kennan, George F., 73, 91-92
Kennedy, President John F.: and administration, 89-90; and Lemnitzer, 94-98; and MLF, 98, 100; and Norstad, 90-91, 94-96;

and Skybolt, 90-91, 94; and Western security, 148
Kennedy, Senator Ted, 125
Kissinger, Henry, 124, 125-26, 137, 145, 154
Komer, Robert W., 166
Korean War, 1, 14, 28, 38, 40-42, 85, 181; and creation of SHAPE, 57; and Lemnitzer, 94; and Ridgway, 39-41
Kruls, Gen. H.J., 17-18

Laniel, Premier Joseph, 186
Leber, Defense Minister Georg, 169
Leddy, Assistant Secretary of State John M., 109
Lemnitzer, Gen. Lyman L.: appointment as SACEUR, 89, 91, 94-98; assessment of, as SACEUR, 175-96; and conventional forces, 101; and de Gaulle, 105-06; and flexible response, 99-100; and forward defense, 119; and French withdrawal from NATO military structure, 104-21, 124, 196; and international staff, 21-22; and MC-70, 99-100; and McNamara, 96-98; military career of, 93-94; and MLF, 100; personality of, 97, 181-82; and relocation of U.S. EUCOM, 107, 113-14; retirement of, 121
Lincoln, Lt. Gen. George "Abe," 143
Lisbon goals. *See* North Atlantic Council
Lovett, Secretary of Defense Robert A., 29: and Mediterranean Command, 47-48; and U.S. EUCOM, 50
Luns, Secretary-General Joseph, 155, 182-84

McCarthy, Senator Joseph, 181
McCormick, Adm. Lynde D.: and creation of SACLANT, 46-47

Macmillan, Prime Minister Harold, 91
McNamara, Secretary of Defense Robert S.: and conventional forces, 101, 119, 144; and French withdrawal from NATO military structure, 108-09, 117-19; and Norstad Plan(s), 83, 96-97; and "whiz kids," 195
McNaughton, Assistant Secretary of Defense John T., 117
Mansfield, Senator Mike, 108, 118, 119, 124, 125, 137; and Mansfield Amendment/ Resolution, 136-39, 184
Marshall, Secretary of Defense George C., 26, 143, 175, 181
massive retaliation, NATO strategy of, 57-59, 83, 99
MC14/3, 130-31
MC-48, 60
MC-70, 99-100
Michener, James, 38, 43
Middleton, Drew, 35
Military Assistance Advisory Group (MAAG), 6, 51
Military Committee, NATO, 17, 47, 51, 66-67, 111, 168; and Integrated Military Staff (IMS), 111
Moller, Lt. Gen. Erik: as Allied Commander Land Forces Denmark, 18
Montgomery, Field Marshal Lord Bernard: as deputy SACEUR, 9, 49-50, 180; and Eisenhower, 30, 49; and Ridgway, 33, 49-50
Mountbatten, Adm. Lord Louis: and Mediterranean Command, 3, 20, 47-48; and Norstad, 92
multilateral force (MLF), 89-90, 98, 100, 102, 177
Mutual Balanced Force Reductions (MBFR), 136-37, 140
Mutual Defense Assistance Program (MDAP), 6, 15, 28, 31

National War College (NWC), 1, 143
Nixon, President Richard M., 125-27, 143, 153
Norstad, Gen. Lauris: as air deputy to SACEUR, 45, 86, 88; appointed SACEUR, 70-71; assessment of, as SACEUR, 175-96; as Commander Allied Air Forces Central Europe, 44-45; and forward strategy, 74-75, 83, 89; and France, 86-88, 104; and Ismay, 74; and Kennedy administration, 90-91; and MLF, 89-90; and Norstad Plan(s), 79-85; and nuclear sharing, 79-87, 90; personality of, 181, 189-90; and public diplomacy, 78-79; and retirement, 90-92; and Spaak, 77-78, 180-81, 190; and Stikker, 78, 95, 181; and troop withdrawals, 75-76; and West Germany, 74-75, 82-85
North Atlantic Assembly, 116-17, 120
North Atlantic Council, NATO: and AD-70, 132-33; and appointment of SACEUR, 11; Athens meeting, 100; chain of command, 17, 31, 33-34, 76-78, 98-99, 191, 193-94; and consultation, 77; and Defense Planning Committee, 110, 152; and French withdrawal from NATO military structure, 109-10; and Lisbon goals, 5, 28-29, 32, 34, 60, 73-74, 99-100, 176; and Mediterranean Command, 47; and NATO secretary-general, 77, 181; and Nuclear Defense Affairs Committee (NDAC), 101; and Nuclear Planning Group (NPG), 101, 110; and "out of area" responsibilities, 65-66, 78, 173; and selection of Haig, 152-53; and selection of Lemnitzer,

94-95; and selection of Ridgway, 36-37; and use of nuclear weapons, 59, 60, 98-99, 103; and West German rearmament, 57, 62
North Atlantic Treaty Organization (NATO): and de-coupling, xxii-xxiii, 118; and forces-in-being, 4-5, 19, 61-62, 119, 149; and forward strategy, 61-62, 74-75, 83, 119; and NATO territory, 17, 65, 74-75; and no first-use, xxiii; and northern flank, 156-57, 170, 188; and nuclear sharing, 79-88; and U.S., xxii-xxiii; and Western European Allies, xxii; and withdrawal of members, 106
Nuclear Defense Affairs Committee (NDAC), 101
Nuclear Planning Group (NPG), 101, 110
nuclear weapons, NATO, xxi, 21, 58-60

Osgood, Robert, 146

Parliamentarians, NATO, 125
Philippe, Mayor, 48
Pleven, René: and EDC, 49, 65, 186; and Eisenhower, 13, 32; and Indochina, 64-65; and Pleven Plan, 26; and Ridgway, 49
Portugal, 142
Poswick, Belgian Defense Minister, 115

Ridgway, Gen. Matthew B.: appointment as Army Chief-of-Staff, 51; appointment as SACEUR, 3, 29, 33-37; assessment of, as SACEUR, 175-96; and Bradley, 38, 51; and Central Command, 4, 43-44, 48-49; and CINCEUR/U.S. EUCOM, 50-51; and communist opposition, 40-42; and conception of SACEUR, 36,

42-43; and Eisenhower, 53-55; and Greece and Turkey, 46; and Juin, 44-45; and Mediterranean Command, 47; and NATO readiness, 5-7, 32-33; personality of, 33, 35, 39-40, 51, 53, 60, 71, 189-90; and Pleven, 49; and St. Mere Eglise, 48
Rogers, Gen. Bernard W., 59, 170, 174, 176, 187
Rusk, Secretary of State Dean, 109

SACEUR. *See* Supreme Allied Commander, Europe
Sala, Vice Adm. Leon: and Allied Forces Southern Europe, 20
Saunders, Air Chief Marshal Sir Harold: as deputy to SACEUR, 45
Schlatter, Maj. Gen. David M.: as Commander Allied Air Forces Southern Europe, 19
Schmuckle, Gen. Gerd, 168-71
Schoenbrun, David, 39
Schuyler, Gen. Courtlandt van R., 39, 70; Gruenther's opinion of, 71
Secretary-General, NATO: and Conventional Defense Improvement Initiative (CDI), xxii; and Ismay, 16, 191; and Norstad Plan(s), 85; office of, ix, 31-32, 51-52, 73-74, 76-78, 91-92, 129, 180; and Spaak, 76-78, 180-81. *See also* Brosio, Manlio; Luns, Joseph; Stikker, Dirk U.
Sixth Fleet, U.S., 20, 47-48
Smith, Lt. Col. Alexander, 44
Smith, Assistant Secretary of the Navy James H.: and Montgomery, 50
Snyder, Maj. Gen. Howard: and Gruenther-Eisenhower relationship, 55
Spaak, Secretary-General Paul-Henri, 76; and Adenauer, 79; conception of office, 77-78,

180-81; and Norstad, 77-78, 82, 190
Standing Group, NATO, 17, 20, 29, 51, 66-67, 71, 110
Stevens, Secretary of the Army Robert, 69
Stikker, Secretary-General Dirk U.: and Norstad, 78, 95, 98
Stoneman, William H., 36
Strategic Defense Initiative (SDI), xx
Strauss, Franz-Joseph, 79
Suez crisis, 77, 177
Sulzberger, C.L., 111
Supreme Allied Commander Atlantic (SACLANT), 46-47, 155
Supreme Allied Commander, Europe (SACEUR): and international staff, 22-23, 185, 188; and leadership role, x, xvi-xviii, 35-36, 51-52, 74, 91-92, 142, 175-96; and Military Committee, 67; nature of command, xv, 2-4, 31-32, 34, 67, 77, 100, 175; office of, ix, 31-32, 73-74, 76, 94, 123, 128, 175, 191, 192-96; and Parliaments, 23, 192-93; and public diplomacy, 78-79, 193; relations with European Allies, 176-79, 194-95; relations with NATO Secretary-General, 179-84, 190-91; relations with U.S., 175-79, 190-91, 194-95. *See also* SACEURs *by name*
Supreme Headquarters, Allied Powers Europe (SHAPE): and AD-70, 131-33; and air defense, 63-64; command structure, 18, 32, 100; creation of, ix, xv, 1-4, 15-17, 122; and liaison with U.S., 6; and National Military Representatives (NMRs), 3, 21, 22; relocation to Belgium, 114-17, 124

Taft, Sen. Robert A., 11, 12, 14-15

Taylor, Henry J., 105
Taylor, Gen. Maxwell, 68-69, 89, 96-97
Taylor, Maj. Gen. Robert: as Commander Allied Forces Northern Europe, 18
Trudeau, Prime Minister Pierre, 127
Truman, President Harry, 10, 11, 28, 29, 34, 37, 38, 181; and Mediterranean Command, 47-48; and NSC-68, 57
Truman, Margaret, 189
Turkey, 3, 28, 33, 43, 102, 141-42, 173; and Allied Forces Southern Europe, 45-46

Union of Soviet Socialist Republics (USSR): and comparison with U.S., xxiii, 156-57, 162-64; and global military expansion, 173-74; and naval forces, 157; negotiations with NATO, xxiv; and nuclear deterrence, 11, 61, 83; Red Army, 9, 17, 27; relationship with U.S., 73
United Kingdom: Labour Party, 24; and Mediterranean Command, 20, 33, 43-44, 47-49; and NATO forces, 21, 75-76, 101, 160; and Norstad Plan(s), 79-83; and Skybolt, 90-91, 94
United States: and defense of Europe, 24, 61-62, 100; and Indochina, 64-65; and NATO forces, 21, 118, 126-27, 159-60; relationship with France, 87, 102-03; relationship with Soviet Union, 73, 162-64; Sixth Fleet, 20, 47-48; and Skybolt, 90-91; and troop reductions, 118, 125, 139, 160
U.S. CINCEUR. *See* Commander-in-Chief, U.S. European Command

Valluy, Gen. Jean E., 71

Index

229

Vietnam, 123, 125, 126, 138, 182-83

Walters, Maj. Gen. Vernon, 147
Warsaw Pact, xix, 119, 124, 129-33, 162, 171
Washington, George, 188
Western European Union (WEU): and Haig speech, 155-59, 172; and West German rearmament, 76
Western Union Defense Organization (WUDO), 16, 21, 176; and Lemnitzer, 93
West Point, 13, 152
Wheeler, Gen. Earle, 128
White, Theodore H., 41
Wilson, Secretary of Defense Charles, 99

Wood, Col. R.J.: and creation of SHAPE, 1, 53
Worden, Col. R.F., 1
World War II, 10, 12, 36, 74, 94, 101, 127, 139, 143, 157, 161, 180; and Anglo-American Combined Chiefs-of-Staff, 66-68, 179-80, 192, 194; and French attitude toward NATO, 102; and Overlord, 25
Wust, Gen. Harald, 169
Wyman, Lt. Gen. Willard G.: as Commander Allied Land Forces Southeastern Europe, 46

Yugoslavia, 27

Zimmerman, Adm., 169

RAYMOND H. FOGLER LIBRARY
DATE DUE

BOOKS ARE SUBJECT TO
RECALL AFTER TWO WEEKS

NOV 1 9 1987